Bassin'
with the Pros

MARK ROMANACK

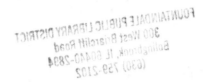

Published by

krause
publications

700 E. State Street • Iola, WI 54990-0001
Telephone: 715/445-2214

www.krause.com

Please, call or write us for our free catalog of sporting publications.
To place an order or receive our free catalog, call 800-258-0929.

Library of Congress Catalog Number: 2001086512
ISBN: 0-87349-217-X

Printed in the United States of America

TABLE OF CONTENTS

FOREWORD

Imagine having the collective knowledge of the nation's top bass fishing professionals at your finger tips. *Bassin' with the Pros*, is just such a resource. You'll find yourself hanging on every word as author Mark Romanack takes the favorite angling tactics of leading bass pros and converts the information into a language anyone can understand.

Inside you'll find solid fishing information from legendary bass anglers including Bill Dance, Woo Daves, Penny Berryman, Tommy Martin and many others. Each chapter stresses the fundamentals of bass fishing along with fine tuning tips that help anglers catch more bass no matter where you live or how you fish.

Grab a cup of coffee, sit back and start your journey into the world of bass fishing. *Bassin' with the Pros* will not only open your eyes to new fishing methods and little known tricks of the trade, each chapter puts you in the boat with those who know the most about catching bass. Enjoy the ride.

Best regards,
Kevin VanDam
Three-time B.A.S.S. Angler-of-the-Year

ACKNOWLEDGMENTS

Everyone is good at something. My gift is the ability to write and communicate information with others. I'm also a pretty good fisherman, but the individuals who really deserve credit for this book are the many tournament pros, guides and others who shared their knowledge of bass fishing and made this book possible.

Thanks to these exceptional anglers Bassin' with the Pros contains a wealth of information on how to better understand and catch bass. The anglers quoted throughout this book represent a who's who list of top bass anglers, duplicated nowhere else.

I also want to pay special thanks to a couple insiders in the fishing/marine industry who helped make this project possible. Mike Fine' of Tracker Marine was instrumental in making his extensive pro staff available for interviews, photo sessions and brainstorming sessions. Also, Jim Sprague of K&E Tackle was a constant source of enthusiasm, helping not only with "how-to" information, but also providing tons of valuable contacts, help with the chapter outline and helping to set up a number of important photo opportunities.

Louie Stout, an accomplished bass writer and noted book author himself, also helped by providing some key photographs.

Numerous tackle and marine manufacturers provided either product samples or photos used throughout the book. This list includes, but isn't limited to Normark/Rapala, Storm Lures, PRADCO, Assassin Lures, Uncle Josh Pork Rind, Culprit/Riptide Lures, Gamakatsu Hooks, Mustad Hooks, Bait Rigs Tackle, Lindy Little Joe Tackle, Luhr Jensen, Mann's Bait Company, Plano Molding Company, Pure Fishing, Snag Proof Manufacturing, Bullet Weights, Wright & McGill Company, Zebco and many others.

It's also important to provide praise to the staff at Krause Publications that take a raw manuscript and photos and convert it into a finished book everyone involved in can be proud of. The amount of work that takes place after a book manuscript leaves the author's desk is staggering. Kevin Michalowski was the chief editor on this project and is one of the easiest editors in the business to work with.

And finally, I must thank my creator for giving me the talent, dedication and drive to complete yet another book project.

Best fishes,
Mark Romanack

DEDICATION

PASSING ON THE PASSION

I feel as if I'm the most fortunate man on Earth. I get to fish for a living and in return all I have to do is share what I've learned with others. To my way of thinking, writing books, magazine features and conducting seminars isn't work. Work has a broad definition, but what I do for a living feels more like fun.

I've been fortunate to have shared a fishing boat with some of the most talented anglers in America. To these men and women who have helped shape my knowledge of fishing I will forever be indebted. Not only have these individuals helped me become a better fisherman, they have helped me develop a more important skill. Thanks to the many anglers I have fished with, I enjoy a burning passion for sportfishing that has made my life rich and rewarding.

I strongly believe that everyone should be passionate about something; anything. Too many people go through life without experiencing a burning drive to excel. Passion is the emotion that motivates people. In my opinion, those who are not passionate about something are accepting their willingness to be average. I can think of nothing more sobering.

For me and almost 50 million other Americans, the passion is about sportfishing. The desire to learn more about fishing and refine my angling skills hasn't wavered in the past 30 years. The same can be said for my desire to share fishing information with others.

Currently, I'm working on a project that's even more important to me than books, articles and seminars. I'm tackling the task of passing on my passion for fishing to those who mean the most to me.

My boys Zackery (7) and Jacob (5) are old enough to have experienced and developed an interest in fishing. Unfortunately, bass aren't a big part of their lives at this point. Instead they are more interested in less finicky species such as bluegills, drum, catfish, bullheads, perch and crappie. Any fish that bites without hesitation is tops on their hit parade.

I spend a lot of time praying that my boys will develop the same passion for fishing I've enjoyed. My wife, Mari, helps this process along by insuring I don't overwhelm the boys with too much of a good thing. Every father wants his sons to share his interests. The question is how to achieve the necessary balance?

Fortunately, I'm not carrying this burden alone. Mari is just as dedicated as I am to fishing. Few activities are as fun and exciting or as effective at bringing families closer together. At this point, our primary focus is to make fishing as fun as possible for our boys. Down the road we pray this fun will blossom into a full-fledged passion for the sport. I can think of no greater gift.

It's with the greatest love and caring that I dedicate this book to my wife, Mari, and my sons, Zackery and Jacob. It's their enthusiasm for fishing and all I do that makes my life complete.

  Bassin' with the Pros

BASS

&

BASS

FISHIN'

Bassin' with the Pros

CHAPTER 1

BASS FISHING
IN THE NEW MILLENNIUM

Bass fishing can best be described as a work in progress. During the past 40 years, interest in fishing for largemouth, smallmouth and spotted bass has grown and matured into one of the most popular pastimes in the United States, Canada, Mexico and even Japan where these fish have been widely introduced. Second only to gardening, sportfishing continues to rank near the top in the number of participants and the dollars spent.

According to a 1997 survey conducted by the U.S. Fish and Wildlife Service, some 40 million Americans spend an estimated 626 million days per year enjoying sportfishing! That's a lot of days off work!

Some $38 billion dollars per year are spent by anglers and an amazing 43 percent of these anglers consider themselves bass fishermen. Just the money spent on fishing equipment and related accessories alone totals $44 million per year!

Of those who fish for bass, nearly 80 percent are male. Among anglers 16 to 65 years of age, 27 percent are in the 35 to 44 age bracket, 20 percent in the 45 to 54 age category and another 20 percent in the 25 to 34 age bracket. Working men make up 67 percent of the anglers in America.

The average bass angler fishes 12 or more days per year and takes home an income exceeding $30,000 per year. As you might expect, the majority of American bass anglers reside in the south and eastern regions of the nation. The western and northwestern parts of the nation have fewer fishing opportunities and smaller numbers of anglers. Interest in bass fishing is growing in the Midwest and northern parts of the country.

Despite growing interest in bass fishing in many areas, the South continues to dominate the bass fishing scene. Some popular bass fishing states such as Florida, Oklahoma and Maryland say that a whopping 60 percent of their licensed anglers fish for bass.

Compared to other hobbies, anglers are big spenders. While traveling to enjoy fishing, American anglers spend more than $6 billion on food and lodging and another $3.7

While traveling to enjoy fishing, American anglers spend more than $6 billion on food and lodging and another $3.7 billion on fuel and other transportation costs.

billion on fuel and other transportation costs.

That's not all the money anglers spend. Other fees such as licenses, club memberships and magazines total another $1 billion annually. In case you're wondering what else these people enjoy spending their money on, outdoorsmen are responsible for 57 percent of all the jeans sold in America, 52 percent of automobile tires and 49 percent of all new cars.

In the past 40 years bass fishing has matured into one of the most popular pastimes in America; second only to gardening. Some 40 million individuals participate in sportfishing annually.

Bass are widely distributed throughout the United States, yet the roots of the sport are firmly set in the South. Some states such as Florida claim that as much as 60 percent of their licensed anglers target bass.

Among the nation's army of anglers a whopping 43 percent consider themselves bass anglers.

With this kind of money up for grabs, it's no wonder that bass fishing has continued to grow for over the past four decades. Manufacturers have discovered that developing new and better equipment is the way to sustain this growth. Most of the equipment is created for those anglers who are always striving to learn more about bass fishing and become more successful on the water.

Professional anglers also do their part to keep bass fishing on the cutting edge. With tournament payouts reaching six figures, the anglers who participate in these events do everything in their power to develop new and better ways to catch bass. Not only are the monetary rewards of winning a tournament a motivation for these anglers, the product endorsements and royalty checks that come as a result of tournament success can be even more lucrative.

This may all sound like big business, but compared to other American businesses, the marine and sportfishing industries

aren't powerhouses. Huge corporations spend more each year in advertising than the total net worth of the fishing and marine industries combined. Ironically these same big corporations frequently market their products directly to bass fishermen. Bass anglers are the target audience of major corporations because research shows men from 24 to 54 purchase their products. No surprises there!

Television commercials and national print advertisements from these companies are frequently targeted at the bass fishing market. When was the last time you saw a national TV commercial or advertisement targeted at anglers seeking another species? It almost never happens, because no other group of anglers outside of bass fishing represents the audience size advertisers are interested in attracting.

The stereotypes depict bass anglers as portly rednecks who have trouble speaking in complete sentences. Not true. Ironically, the U.S. Fish and Wildlife survey concluded that those who fish for bass are more apt to be urban dwellers, college-educated and employed at a some form of technical, professional or skilled labor position.

As far as fish go, bass lend themselves perfectly to this crazy business we call sportfishing. Unlike other species that are most often caught using live bait or a modest number of lures and angling techniques, bass are routinely taken with dozens of popular lure types and countless fishing presentations.

Let's use walleyes as an example because these popular fish are another species that support a growing number of regional and national tournaments and a significant number of professional anglers. Even among those who fish walleyes professionally, the techniques used to catch fish revolve around a handful of live-bait techniques. Jigs tipped with live bait and live-bait rigs are the most commonly used methods to catch walleyes. A modest number of artificial lures are also used to catch walleyes. Primarily minnow- and shad-shaped crankbaits and spoons are the hard baits used for walleye fishing.

Anglers typically need less gear to catch walleyes than they do to catch bass. The list of gear needed by the walleye angler includes fewer hard baits, fewer soft baits, fewer hook types and sizes, fewer line sizes, fewer rods and fewer reel types.

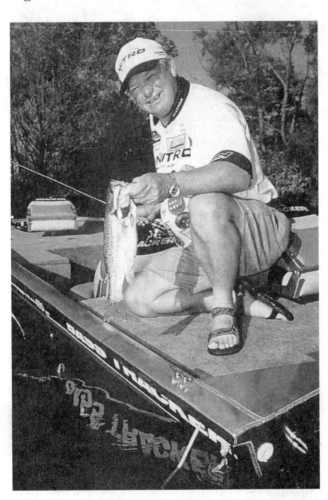

Professional anglers such as Woo Daves, the 2000 Bass Masters Classic champion, play a major role in the evolution of bass fishing both as a sport and as a business.

Bass lend themselves perfectly to the sportfishing business. These fish are readily caught on a wide variety of artificial lures.

As a whole, bass fishing is a complex sport that by its very design requires anglers to own more equipment than just about any other form of sportfishing. The fact is, bass fishing has grown to the point that learning anything more than the basics can take years of experience. Capturing all there is to know about bass and bass fishing in a single book isn't possible. It would take a library to do justice to this chore.

Also, bass fishing never stands still. By the time this book is written, edited, published and distributed there will already be new products and fishing techniques on the horizon. The way technology continues to march forward, who knows what new products will soon be available to make bass fishing more fun and productive?

Just take a look at the recent past. Not that long ago fiberglass rods were the norm. Today graphite fishing rods are lighter, stronger and more sensitive than any fishing rods every built and marketed. What about braided super lines? High-tech fishing lines have generated an amazing burst of revenue for the sport-fishing industry. In the electronics department, global positioning systems are almost as common on bass boats as fish-finders. A few years ago GPS units were only available in permanent-mount units that cost thousands of dollars. Today there are hand-held products that retail for a little over $100.

And that's not all. There are flotation vests that inflate upon contact with water; outboards that burn less fuel and give off fewer emissions; boats built from 100 percent com-posite materials; clothing that's waterproof yet breathable; hooks that are sharper and stronger than ever before, and on and on.

Many of the fishing luxuries we enjoy and often take for granted have been developed as a direct result of bass fishing. The market is so large, most manufacturers tailor their product designs to meet the needs of bass anglers.

Bass fishermen tend to purchase and use much more fishing gear than other groups of anglers. Even professional anglers such as these walleye tournament professionals consume far less fishing tackle than comparable bass anglers.

To a large degree, bass fishing is also media-driven. Because tournaments and tournament anglers have become high-profile figures in the United States, feature articles and television programs based on these individuals and the fishing techniques they have perfected or popularized are common. National outdoor magazines and outdoor television programs spend more time focusing on bass fishing than any other single outdoor topic.

All this exposure is good for the industry and good for those who want to learn more about fishing. A ton of good, solid fishing information is made available to millions of anglers.

> *Professional anglers are, for the most part, dedicated to the sport of bass fishing and to helping others better enjoy their time on the water.*

Unfortunately, the system isn't perfect. Professional anglers are often pressured by sponsors to spend more time promoting specific products than simply promoting bass fishing. Much of the magazine copy published today reads more like a product endorsement than a "how-to" story. Instead of offering the information-packed features anglers crave, some magazine articles are nothing but printed fluff that talk more about products than how to use them.

Obviously, for magazines to survive they must attract advertisers and lots of them. Holding onto these critical advertising dollars forces publishers to appease their clients with mentions of their various

To a large degree bass fishing is media-driven. A wealth of monthly publications target bass anglers.

products. Mentioning products in fishing features is a necessary part of both the education process and the business of bass fishing. Some of this product-based literature is okay. However, an environment has been created where anglers are exposed to a growing amount of hype and "junk" products that do little to help anglers catch fish.

Magazines aren't the only branch of the media guilty of producing "product-biased" information. Many of the leading outdoor television programs are starting to look and sound a lot like commercials instead of educational and recreational programming.

What all this means is that anglers who are interested in learning more about bass fishing may have to be careful who they listen to and what they read or watch. Professional anglers are, for the most part, dedicated to the sport of bass fishing and to helping others better enjoy their time on the water. This book is a good example of how the experience of professional anglers can be converted into helpful information for those who want to become better anglers. A lot of good, solid fishing information is available to the public in seminars, magazine features, books, television programming and video products. We'll try to add to that pool of knowledge with this book.

In Chapter Two we'll take a long look at the most common species of bass and explore how these fish are alike and how they are different.

Bassin' with the Pros

CHAPTER 2

UNDERSTANDING BASS

Depending on where you live, anglers may have the opportunity to catch largemouth, smallmouth or spotted bass. The author lives in northern Michigan where smallmouth are the most common species of bass.

Bass fishing is like no other type of freshwater angling. Collectively the many different species and subspecies of bass are the most widespread group of gamefish in America. There's hardly a corner of this great nation that doesn't offer outstanding opportunities to catch one or more species of bass.

The group of fish we so affectionately refer to as 'bass' are actually part of a complex fish community biologists categorize as the Centrarchidae or the sunfish family. In addition to the popular and widespread largemouth and smallmouth bass, some 28 other species of fish also belong to this bulging family. Some of the most numerous members of the Centrarchidae are panfish such as bluegills, crappie, pumpkinseed sunfish and rock bass.

Many of the lesser known bass in this family are localized species. One of the most rare and least known bass species — the Guadalupe bass — is found only in the Colorado, San Antonio and Guadalupe river systems of Texas. Another rare species, the Redeye bass was first identified from tributaries of the Savannah River drainage in Georgia. This unique fish is similar to the smallmouth bass and can also be found in the Conasauga drainage system of Tennessee and the Chipola River system in Florida.

Another bass, native only to Florida, is the Suwannee bass that lives in the Santa Fe, Withlacoochee and Suwannee river systems. This stream bass is tolerant of both the high-acid and low fertility levels of these river systems.

Similar in appearance to the spotted or redeye bass, the Suwannee is a small fish that rarely exceeds 2 pounds. The most distinctive marking is the blue coloration located on the underside of the fish around the head, throat and pectoral fins.

The spotted or Kentucky bass is a widespread species when compared to distribution of the aforementioned Guadalupe, redeye and Suwannee bass. However the spotted bass is not as numerous as the largemouth or smallmouth bass. Amazingly, this species was not identified by fishery taxonomists until 1927. Prior to this it was falsely believed the spotted bass was a natural hybrid produced by crossing largemouth and smallmouth bass.

It's true the spotted bass has physical characteristics similar to both largemouth and smallmouth bass, but the spotted bass is a unique species within the Centrarchidae family. This attractive fish is olive green on the dorsal surface with dark blotches along the sides. The lateral band is made up of a series of dark diamond-shaped blotches. The dorsal fins are connected, helping to distinguish this species from the largemouth. It differs from the smallmouth by having spotting below the lateral line and no vertical bars on the sides.

Smaller than either the largemouth or smallmouth bass, the Kentucky bass rarely exceeds 5 pounds. Found mostly in the Ohio and Mississippi River drainage systems from

> **Found mostly in the Ohio and Mississippi River drainaage systems from Ohio south to the gulf states, spotted bass range as far west as Oklahoma, Kansas and Texas and as far east as Florida.**

Ohio south to the gulf states, spotted bass range as far west as Oklahoma, Kansas and Texas and as far east as Florida.

Generally speaking, the spotted bass prefers deeper water than either the largemouth or smallmouth bass. This species has been documented to live in water up to 100 feet deep. Clear gravel-bottom rivers and cool spring-fed lakes are the most likely haunts for spotted bass.

Spotted bass are not as widespread as largemouth or smallmouth bass. Photo courtesy of Keith Sutton.

Smallmouth bass are in many ways the king of the North, despite the fact that largemouth inhabit a wealth of waters throughout the region. Originally indigenous to Lake Ontario and the Ohio River drainage system, smallmouth distribution benefited from casual stocking efforts. Beginning around 1869, smallmouth bass populations started to spread with an ever-expanding railroad system. As the wood-burning engines rolled farther south and west, smallmouth traveling in buckets ended up in countless waterways along the route. Eventually this unlikely commuter was introduced as far west as California.

Today the primary range of the smallmouth is from Minnesota to Ontario and east to Quebec. Strong populations exist throughout New England and south to Alabama, then west to Kansas and Oklahoma.

Outside of this core area, pockets of smallmouth bass have been introduced throughout the country. In recent years the reservoirs of North Dakota, South Dakota and Nebraska have produced noteworthy fishing for this species.

The smallmouth is easily recognized. It's jaw bone does not extend past the line of the eye as with largemouth bass. The stout body is normally bronze or brown in color with obvious dark vertical bars.

Although smallmouth and largemouth bass often exist in the same body of water, the habitat requirements of the smallmouth are different enough that this fish is usually associated with its own unique niche. More tolerant of moving water than largemouth, smallies thrive in large and small river systems, deep natural lakes, the Great Lakes and reservoir systems.

As a general rule of thumb smallmouth favor waters that range in temperature from 60 to 80 degrees in summer. The largest populations of fish are often found in clear, cool and rocky waters, but smallmouth are also very adaptable fish. This amazing species also thrives in waters with abundant weed cover, submerged brush or timber.

Smallmouth bass rarely exceed 10 pounds in size, yet this

Smallmouth were originally native to Lake Ontario and the Ohio River system. Today this species is found throughout most of the nation with the exception of the Southwest and Deep South.

modest-sized bass is without doubt one of the hardest fighting fish around. Impressive leaps, line-breaking runs and stubborn determination are hallmarks of a fight with a smallmouth bass.

Mr. Popularity

The granddaddy of all bass is the largemouth. This fish enjoys not only the widest distribution and largest overall population, but also the most popularity among anglers. This popularity rating

The largemouth bass is both the most widely distributed and the largest member of the bass family.

Despite the possibility of catching much larger fish, a largemouth in the 10-pound class is considered a rare and coveted trophy just about everywhere bass live.

can be explained by the types of waters and habitat largemouth favor. As a species that's strongly associated with cover and shallow water, largemouth bass are often easier to locate and catch than the other members of this family.

Originally the largemouth — or what anglers often refer to as black bass — were indigenous to southeastern Canada through the Great Lakes and south into the Mississippi Valley, east to Florida and north up the Atlantic coast to Maryland. By 1887 largemouth had been planted west of the Rocky Mountains and east into New England. Today, largemouth are the most widely distributed bass in the Centrarchidae family, commonly found almost anywhere suitable habitat exists.

Largemouth thrive best in shallow lakes with plenty of aquatic weed growth and sluggish river backwaters. This environment provides not only a constant supply of forage, but also a significant amount of cover where bass can lay in ambush.

This species is rarely found in water deeper than 20 feet, preferring instead to take advantage of shallow-water cover and structure.

The ever-growing distribution of the largemouth is surpassed only by the impressive size and legendary fight this species delivers. Monsters approaching 20 pounds are sometimes caught in the deep South, in Western reservoirs and in Mexico, but the average fish taken throughout its range is closer to 3 pounds. The world record is 22 pounds, 4 ounces and was taken in Montgomery Lake, Georgia. Despite the possibility of catching much larger fish, a largemouth in the 10-pound class is considered a rare and coveted trophy just about everywhere bass live.

The Florida largemouth bass is the only subspecies of the largemouth. The two fish are essentially identical except for scale counts, however the Florida bass grows considerably larger. Biologists are not sure if heredity or environment are responsible for creating this race of "super bass."

Widespread plantings of Florida bass have taken place in Florida, Georgia, California, Nevada, Mexico and many other locations.

Only one subspecies of the smallmouth bass is known to exist. The Neosho smallmouth bass is a river fish located in the Neosho River and tributaries of the Arkansas River in Oklahoma, Arkansas and Missouri.

More slender than the northern race, the Neosho smallmouth is easily recognized by its protruding lower jaw which juts out past the snout far enough that the teeth can be seen from above, it can be described as a bass with an overbite. The habitat of the Neosho bass has been seriously diminished as large impoundments have been created along its native rivers. Also, it's believed that this subspecies has crossed with northern smallmouth, further diluting the original bloodline.

Two subspecies of spotted bass are recognized by fish taxonomists. The Alabama spotted bass is found in the Alabama River system in Mississippi, Alabama and Georgia. Fish up to 8 pounds are occasionally taken.

The Wichita spotted bass is isolated to the Wichita Mountains of Oklahoma.

With the exception of the Florida largemouth bass, none of these subspecies or lesser-known species of bass are important sport fish. The largemouth, smallmouth and spotted bass are the most numerous and important members of this family.

DIFFERENCES AND SIMILARITIES

Each of the three major bass species have their own unique differences and similarities. Largemouth bass spawn in shallow water usually less than 4 feet deep. The male bass cleans out a nest approximately 20 inches in diameter from the sand or gravel bottom. If hard bottom areas aren't available, largemouth will spawn on silt or clay bottoms. The nests are spaced out usually 20 or more feet apart.

When the water temperature reaches 62 to 65 degrees the female bass are ready to deposit eggs. Female bass are attracted to the nest site by the male, who fertilizes the sticky eggs immediately after the female deposits them. Normally the female lays only a few hundred eggs in the nest at one time. Amazingly, the same female often returns to lay eggs in the same nests, or nests in the same area, several times. It's also common for several different females to lay their eggs in the same nest.

The male guards the nest until the eggs hatch. In water 65 degrees it takes 10 days

The male largemouth is an excellent parent, providing care for both the eggs and young fingerlings.

for the eggs to hatch. In water 80 degrees the eggs hatch in just five days. After hatching the bass fry stay in the nest for a few days until the yoke sac has been absorbed. Once the nutrition of the yoke sac has been exhausted, the bass school up and hunt for plankton in shallow water until they reach about 1 inch in length.

Smallmouth spawn in much deeper water than do largemouth. Depending on water clarity, smallmouth will select spawning sites in water from 3 to 20 feet deep. The clearer the water, the deeper this species prefers to spawn.

Like largemouth bass, the male smallmouth builds a nest by fanning away bottom sand, gravel and debris into a depression 14 to 30 inches in diameter. Hard bottom areas are favored.

When the water temperature reaches 60 to 70 degrees, the male bass seeks out a ripe female and drives her to the nest. After the female deposits the eggs, the male fertilizes them and drives the female away. Up to three different females are attracted by the male smallmouth. A nest may contain 200 to several thousand eggs. The average smallmouth nest contains about 2,000 eggs.

Incubation is very short. Depending on water temperature, the eggs hatch in two to nine days while the male provides a constant vigil. After the eggs hatch into fry, the young bass disperse quickly. Little parental care is given to the young fry.

Growth of the young bass varies depending on latitude and available forage. In the far north where waters are often cold and infertile, smallmouth grow painstakingly slow. In many of these waters it takes small-

> *The primary difference is that spotted bass usually migrate upstream in the rivers or reservoirs where they live before building a modest nest of 12 to 15 inches in diameter.*

mouth four years to reach 9 inches in length! In more fertile waters, 9 inches is usually reached during the second summer. To reach an adult size of 18 to 20 inches takes seven to 10 years in most bodies of water.

The spawning habits of the spotted bass are similar to those of the largemouth bass. The primary difference is that spotted bass usually migrate upstream in the rivers or reser-

Smallmouth bass grow painfully slowly in northern latitudes. This 3-pound fish from a Michigan lake could easily be 10 years old.

building a
ameter.
er quickly,
er. Sexual
hes.
feeding on
w, the size
arvae and
foods for
eir diet is
ows, young
has been
times feed

yet some of the best largemouth fishing takes place in northern waters where these fish are often overlooked by anglers targeting other species.

on snakes, mice, baby blackbirds, young ducks and muskrat kits. Although these animals may occasionally end up in the stomach of a large bass, in the big picture, none are considered important forage types.

Despite a reputation of being a southern species, largemouth bass thrive in a wealth of northern waters. Some of the most untapped fishing opportunities for largemouth exist in southern Ontario, the Great Lakes and the Midwest, where largemouth are often overlooked by anglers targeting other species.

Largemouth bass are so widely dispersed that they are commonly found in waters containing smallmouth or spotted bass. A few waters harbor all three of the primary bass species.

This widespread and popular group of fish attracts more attention from anglers than any other group of fish in America. Some 40 million Americans fish and an estimated 43% of these anglers consider themselves bass fishermen.

In the next chapter we'll explore the types of water where bass are most often found, including an in-depth look at rivers, natural lakes, reservoirs, ponds and the Great Lakes.

...THE INFAMOUS "SLUG-GO" PROVOKES ANOTHER REACTION STRIKE...

Bassin' with the Pros

CHAPTER 3

BASS WATER

Categorizing bass water is no easy task. The many species of bass inhabit so many different types of water, just about any puddle big enough to support fish can be prime bassin' real estate.

Part of what makes bass fishing so popular boils down to the adaptable nature of these fish. The many species of bass found throughout America are able to survive and thrive in a wide variety of water types including, but not limited to, reservoirs, natural lakes, rivers, river backwaters, the Great Lakes and even modest stock ponds.

THE GREAT LAKES

The Great Lakes are believed by many to be the ultimate bass fishing environment. While smallmouth are the primary fish targeted by Great Lakes bass anglers, many areas also provide outstanding largemouth fishing.

When talk turns to bass fishing in the Great Lakes, Lake Erie's world-famous smallmouth action often dominates the conversation. It's easy to see why Lake Erie gets all the hype.

The vast waters of the Great Lakes are home to outstanding smallmouth and overlooked largemouth bass fishing opportunities.

This fertile body of water is the fourth in a chain of five Great Lakes waterways. Lake Erie is shallow compared to the other Great Lakes, and has more surface area that's suitable for bass than any other Great Lake. In addition to being shallow, Lake Erie is more fertile than the other lakes and supports an enormous biomass of potential bass forages. Just some of the forage species bass can choose from include gizzard shad, alewives, smelt, emerald shiners, spottail shiners, goby and millions upon millions of crayfish. For newly hatched bass, the lake is full of insect larvae and other invertebrates that are the ideal food source for these young predators.

In addition to nearly perfect living and hunting grounds, Lake Erie offers bass hun-

The Bass Islands area of Lake Erie is famous for smallmouth. This bass factory produces both numbers of fish and, as this picture shows, brutes worth bragging about.

dreds of miles of prime spawning real estate. Rocky shorelines, numerous islands and countless hard-bottom reefs provide spawning smallmouth with everything they could hope for.

Taken as a whole, Lake Erie can't be topped for available habitat or the numbers of bass produced annually. The center of the prime bass water is located in Ohio waters, but good smallmouth fishing is also found in Michigan, Ontario, Pennsylvania and New York waters.

The area known as the Bass Islands is located between Toledo and Cleveland on Lake Erie's south shore. Anglers from all around the country converge on this beautiful and bass-rich region to enjoy not only numbers of fish, but quality size as well. The best fishing runs from May to October.

The Ohio state record smallmouth caught by Randy VanDam — the brother of professional bass angler Kevin VanDam — was taken near the Bass Islands. At more than 9 pounds, this monster smallmouth is the product of a nearly perfect environment. Tournaments held in this region regularly produce 6-pound bass and a 20-pound, five-fish basket is considered only average.

Lake Erie is such an outstanding smallmouth bass fishery, it overshadows some excellent largemouth fishing also found here. Most of the largemouth fishing is limited to bays, marinas, sloughs, cuts and the mouths of river areas where the water is shallow and weed growth more extensive.

Compared to Lake Erie, the other Great Lakes don't shine as brightly in the bass habitat department. This isn't to say there aren't pockets of great bass fishing action.

In Lake Huron, most of the better bass fishing takes place in protected bays that offer the ideal combination of cover, forage and shallow water. Saginaw Bay is one of Lake Huron's most famous bass destinations. Historically this fishery has been a largemouth factory, but in recent years some environmental changes have given smallmouths a strong foothold.

Low water levels throughout the Great Lakes and including Saginaw Bay have left some of the prime marsh habitat where largemouth live and spawn high and dry. In addition, the widespread introduction of the zebra mussel has had a dramatic impact on improving the water clarity throughout the entire area. Weeds that were once limited to very shallow water, now grow in much deeper water.

These changing environmental conditions favor smallmouth bass. Not surprisingly, this species has expanded quickly, while largemouth struggle to maintain their numbers in the remaining habitat. Both species of bass are still readily available in Saginaw Bay, but the handwriting appears to be on the wall as to which species will ultimately dominate.

Other prime smallmouth fisheries in Lake Huron include the protected waters of Thunder Bay and the many islands located near the Straits of Mackinaw. On the Canadian side of the lake, Georgian Bay and the Manitoulin Islands are exceptional bass destinations.

The bass fishing opportunities on Lake Michigan are similar to those of Lake Huron. Bass, primarily smallmouth, are abundant in isolated areas that provide ideal habitat.

Some spectacular bass fishing is found in Little Grand Traverse Bay and both the east and west arms of Grand Traverse Bay. Smallmouth are also plentiful in and among a series of islands located in the northern region of the lake including Beaver, Fox and South Fox Islands.

Both Big Bay de Noc and Little Bay de Noc, located along Lake Michigan's north shore, are spectacular smallmouth destinations. Fishing pressure in this remote area is exceptionally light and bass thrive in these shallow bays teaming with reefs and endless weed edges.

Following Lake Michigan south along the western edge of Michigan, smallmouth are found living on virtually every pierhead from Grand Traverse Bay to Benton Harbor.

> *Some spectacular bass fishing is found in Little Grand Traverse Bay and both the east and west arms of Grand Traverse Bay.*

Adjacent to Lake Michigan are a number of drowned river mouth lakes that also provide exceptional bass action.

The Wisconsin waters of Lake Michigan are also known for producing first-class smallmouth fishing. Green Bay is similar to Saginaw Bay in that this large and sprawling body of water offers both smallmouth and largemouth bass. Sturgeon Bay is located along a peninsula that juts into Lake Michigan. Smallmouth bass in this area are seemingly hiding behind every rock.

Lake Superior offers little in the way of smallmouth habitat. Even during the summer the waters of Superior are too cold to support significant smallmouth populations.

Lake Ontario, like lakes Michigan and Huron, offers isolated pockets of smallmouth fishing. The Bay of Quinte located on the north shore near Belleville, Ontario is Lake Ontario's strongest smallmouth fishery.

GREAT LAKES' CONNECTING WATERS

In addition to the Great Lakes, bass thrive in a number of lakes and rivers known as Connecting Waterways. Lake St. Clair is a Connecting Waterway between Lake Huron and Lake Erie.

Next to Lake Erie, Lake St. Clair is the richest bass fishery in the north. The entire lake is shallow enough to provide ideal bass habitat. The lake is so shallow, a shipping channel had to be dug so Great Lakes freighters could travel from Lake Huron to Lake Erie and eventually to the Welland Canal that connects Lake Erie to Lake Ontario.

Lake St. Clair is feeling many of the same environmental changes occurring in Saginaw Bay. Improving water clarity due to the invasion of the zebra mussel is the primary factor that is impacting on smallmouth. Clearer water allows weed growth to become established in deeper waters favored by the smallmouth. In addition, smallmouth find this clearer water more conducive to finding and catching their favorite foods.

Other connecting waterways that harbor exceptional numbers of bass include the Detroit, St. Clair and St. Mary's rivers.

The Great Lakes and their Connecting Waterways are viewed by many as the richest bass fishing waters in America. The sheer vastness of these waters helps to insure that angling pressure has little impact on the fish.

A fleet of charter boats target smallmouth bass in Lake Erie every day during the prime fishing months. These boats often produce limit catches of bass that are kept! Despite this intensive harvest of fish, the population of smallmouth appears to be stable or growing in the region.

Biologists believe that the biggest threat to smallmouth isn't angling pressure or harvest, but rather weather conditions that can potentially destroy nesting success. Rough weather while the fish are spawning and tending the nest destroys the eggs. The results are obvious holes in the year class or recruitment of bass from year to year.

Unfortunately, smallmouth living in the north do not spawn a second time if their nesting efforts are destroyed. Bad weather that strikes at the brief time bass are spawning can wipe out an entire year class of fish.

NORTHERN RESERVOIRS

Next to the Great Lakes, reservoir systems are the largest water systems that provide suitable bass habitat. Most of the major reservoir systems of the North are located in the western states of North Dakota, South Dakota, Wyoming and Montana. The Missouri and Platte River systems support a number of major reservoirs that are home to a growing number of bass.

Some of the major reservoirs in this region include Fort Peck in Montana, Sakakawea in North Dakota and Lake Oahe, Lake Sharpe and Lake Lewis and Clark in South Dakota. Collectively these reservoirs provide as much shoreline habitat as the Great Lakes and only a fraction of the fishing pressure.

Primarily known as walleye fisheries, these lakes have ample smallmouth bass habitat and the fish are abundant in many areas. The population of smallmouth bass in these areas appears to be on the rise.

SOUTHWESTERN RESERVOIRS

Two huge reservoir systems have become bass fishing staples in the southwest. Lake Powell and Lake Mead stretch from the southeastern corner of Utah,

Lake St. Clair isn't one of the Great Lakes, but rather a great lake connecting water that links Lake Erie and the St. Clair River. In the past decade the bass fishery here has exploded, making this one of the hottest fishing destinations in the nation.

across a portion of Arizona, to the southeastern corner of Nevada. A number of major waterways, including the Colorado, Green, San Juan and Virgin rivers feed this sprawling chain of reservoirs.

SOUTHERN RESERVOIRS

Throughout the American South there are more reservoir systems that harbor bass than can be mentioned in the space provided. Just a few of the most famous and popular reservoirs include Toledo Bend, Lake Sam Rayburn, Eufaula Lake, Lake of the Ozarks, Stockton Lake, Bull Shoals Lake, Table Rock, Geers Ferry, Lake Lanier, Lake Cumberland, Pickwick Lake and many others.

These waters have made states such as Oklahoma, Texas, Nebraska, Arkansas, Kansas, Missouri, Tennessee, Kentucky, Alabama, Georgia, West Virginia, North Carolina and South Carolina the heart of American bass fishing.

Many of these reservoirs are Tennessee Valley Authority projects while others were built by the U.S. Army Corps of Engineers.

In all cases, bass fishing was one of the last things on the engineers' minds when these expansive reservoir systems were built. Stockpiling water for agricultural irrigation or to support industry and cities with a constant supply of fresh water was the primary motivation.

Sport fishing for bass and a wealth of other species has become a major byproduct of these reservoirs. In fact, the recreational use of some waters has become more of a positive economic impact than agriculture or industry. Billions of dollars are spent each year on fishing, boating, camping and other outdoor pursuits made possible by these numerous reservoirs.

Throughout the South largemouth bass are the primary species to benefit from these reservoir systems. Spotted bass have also expanded their range and become the dominate species on many waters. Pockets of smallmouth also exist, especially on the clear-water reservoirs in Missouri, Arkansas, Kentucky and Tennessee.

What about Florida, Louisiana and Mississippi? These states also have their share of reservoir systems, but they also have a significant number of natural lakes teaming with bass. Something many other areas of the South can not claim.

AMERICA'S TOP BASS RIVERS

Bass fishing isn't limited to the Great Lakes or large reservoirs. A wealth of river systems also produce smallmouth and largemouth fishing.

The Mighty Mississippi divides the nation in two. Nearly every inch of its course from Minnesota to Louisiana can be classified as prime bass water. Largemouth thrive

Reservoirs account for the majority of bass water in the Southern and Southwestern states.

in the countless backwaters, sloughs and marshy ecosystems. In the main river, smallmouth find suitable habitat along the shoreline, channel edges and especially on the countless wing dams built to control water flow and sedimentation.

Wing dams are finger-like rock piles placed perpendicular to the shoreline. Current striking these dams is forced to the center of the river, helping to increase current speed and keep the main shipping channel free from silt and sedimentation.

The front face of wing dams are perfect places for bass to wait in ambush for prey washed down with the current. Wing dams are a little tricky to fish, but they attract impressive numbers of river bass.

In addition to the Mississippi, other major rivers that are famous for bass fishing include the Tennessee, Ohio, Illinois, Rock, Missouri, Wabash, Cumberland, Green, Arkansas and Red rivers.

NATURAL LAKES

Natural lakes suitable for bass fishing range in size from a few acres to those measured in square miles. Many of the nation's best natural lakes are located in the far North, Deep South and Eastern states. The states of Michigan, Wisconsin and Minnesota undoubtedly have more natural lakes than the rest of the nation combined.

Bass in this part of the nation are often overlooked by anglers specializing in walleye, muskie and northern pike. The natural lake bass fishing in this region rivals or exceeds that found anywhere in the bass heartland.

Both largemouth and smallmouth bass thrive in the natural lakes of this region. In the northern reaches of these states, smallmouth bass dominate the deep, clear-water basins. In the southern farm belts of the same states, countless small and fertile natural lakes provide largemouth bass the per-

> *The front face of wing dams are perfect places for bass to wait in ambush for prey washed down with the current.*

fect habitat. A great number of lakes have suitable habitat to support good populations of both species.

In the Deep South it's natural lakes that offer up some of the nation's top trophy bass. Lakes Kissimmee and Okeechobee are famous for producing big Florida strain largemouth bass. Lake Pontchartrain in Louisiana is another famous destination for trophy bass.

In general, however, natural lakes are not as fertile as reservoir systems nor as able to support large harvests of bass such as on the Great Lakes. Even the most

In the Deep South a number of natural lakes produce monster largemouth.

lightly-fished natural lakes can quickly suffer from angling pressure if catch-and-release practices aren't followed.

PONDS & STOCK DAMS

The ability to survive and thrive in even small bodies of water is one of the most beloved attributes of the largemouth bass. Farm ponds and stock ponds located just about anywhere in the nation support amazing numbers of largemouth bass.

One of the most overlooked sources of bass water is the many ponds that were built along our nation's expanding highway systems. The need for fill dirt at these road

construction sites was satisfied in many areas by digging small to medium-sized ponds.

Many of these ponds were later stocked with bass and opened to public fishing. Anglers can enjoy good fishing from shore or by dragging small boats or canoes to the water's edge. A belly boat can be one of the best ways to explore these bass fisheries that are modest in size, but often big producers of fishing action.

Often these small bodies of water are stocked and managed specifically for the pleasure of catching bruiser-sized bucketmouths. Largemouth bass are amazingly easy to raise in small ponds. As long as the lake has some cover to provide hiding places and enough bluegills or other small fish to feed on, largemouth are likely to thrive.

Unfortunately, smallmouth and spotted bass don't do as well in small-water environments.

The many types of water where bass can survive and thrive is one of the major reasons these species continue to expand their range. While each bass species has a preferred niche, the adaptability of these fish is absolutely amazing.

In the next chapter we'll look at the rods and reels most commonly used to catch bass.

Even small bodies of water can provide bass fishing excitement. Ponds, stock dams and small natural lakes are another excellent bass fishing resource.

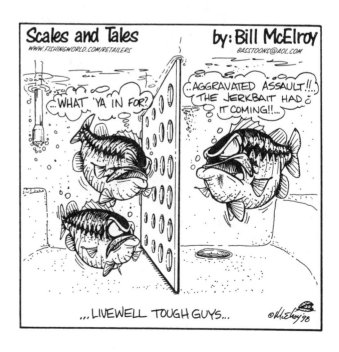

Bassin' with the Pros

CHAPTER 4

RODS & REELS FOR BASS FISHING

Compared to those who target crappie, walleye, catfish or other freshwater species, bass anglers are likely to own a much wider assortment of rod and reel combinations. To the casual observer, the number of combos a bass fisherman feels necessary ranks right up there with golfers who insist on carrying every club type made.

Like golf clubs, fishing rods are tools. Anglers use these tools to achieve success in a wide range of fishing situations. In the same way a golfer wouldn't dream of using a putter to drive off the tee, a serious bass angler wouldn't dream of using a spinning rod and light line to fish jigs in heavy cover.

Matching the rod and reel to the presentation at hand is a skill at which the most successful bass anglers excel. One look at the front casting deck of a typical "bass boat" says it all. Neatly organized on the casting deck you're likely to find half a dozen or more rod and reel types rigged and ready for action. Some typical combinations include a spinning outfit for throwing grubs and other light lures, a pistol-grip baitcaster for fishing spinnerbaits, a triggerstick baitcasting combination for pitching jigs, a fiberglass baitcasting rod for crankbaits and a heavy-weight baitcasting combination for flippin' heavy jigs or Texas-rigged worms into heavy cover.

Bass anglers use lots of different types of rods and reels because they fish a wide variety of presentations. Presentation-specific rod and reel combinations are a direct result of feedback from tournament anglers. These elite anglers are looking for any edge that helps them catch more fish. Selecting a rod and reel combination that's ideally suited for a specific type of fishing is one way bass anglers refine their sport. Think of bass fishing rods like golf clubs. You can tee off on a long par five with your seven iron, but wouldn't a driver get you closer to the hole?

SPINNING COMBINATIONS

Bass fishermen are fond of lumping fishing techniques into neat little categories. One such category that has become amazingly popular and productive in recent years is "finesse" fishing.

Collectively just about any fishing method that incorporates light line and light lures falls within the finesse fishing category. Some of the most popular finesse fishing methods include casting grubs or tube baits, working jerkbaits, fishing a split shot rig on a grub or worm and wacky rigging a worm or plastic jerkbait.

Spinning tackle is an essential element of these and other finesse fishing methods. Ideally suited to casting modest lures on line from 6- to 12-pound test, it's important to note that finesse fishing isn't conducted using light or ultra-light gear. Rods in the 6- to 7-foot range featuring medium to medium-heavy actions are best suited for most finesse tactics.

A finesse fishing rod must be capable of throwing lures in the 1/16- to 1/4-ounce range, but also have enough backbone to control stubborn bass. High quality graphite rods provide the ideal combination of lightness, sensitivity and power.

Three different grades of graphite are commonly used in making spinning rods. Lower grade rods are the least expensive and can be best described as entry-level products. Rods in this group usually range in price from $40 to $60 each. Stepping up a notch, the most popular grade of graphite rods range in price from $75 to $100 each. Rods in this category feature light and sensitive graphite blanks, quality cork handles and premium guides. The most expensive

The deck of a bass boat doubles as a fishing platform and as a place to store the many rod types a bass fisherman uses. Photo courtesy of Berkley.

Spinning tackle, such as used by this angler, is most often used in a variety of "finesse" fishing presentations.

graphite rods can cost upwards of $200 to $300 each! As you might expect these rods feature the highest quality graphite blanks and rod building technology. These are the lightest and most sensitive rods available and their sales are limited mostly to professional anglers and serious amateurs.

The reels best suited to these spinning rods range in features and price as much as the rods themselves. Spinning reels are classified by size (usually a number rating) and by the number of ball bearings featured in their construction. A No. 1 size reel is designed for light freshwater use. A No. 2 is designed for medium freshwater use and a No. 3 is classified as a light saltwater reel. For finesse bass fishing, reels in the No. 2 and 3 sizes are ideal. All these reels are capable of handling the line sizes most commonly used with finesse fishing tactics.

The cost of a spinning reel depends not so much on size, but rather on how many ball bearings and special features are offered. The more ball bearings that are used, the smoother the reel feels when line is retrieved.

Selecting a spinning reel that's smooth is important, but don't overlook the importance of a dependable drag system and a feature known as continuous anti-reverse feature. Most quality spinning reels use front-mounted drag systems. Over time, this drag system has surfaced as the most functional and dependable choice.

A good spinning reel should also include a continuous anti-reverse feature. The continuous anti-reverse on a reel enables the reel handle and bail to rotate smoothly without any play or slop in the system. Because the line is in direct contact with the bail all the time, the entire rod and reel combination becomes more sensitive and better able to telegraph light strikes. Also, since the angler has a more direct connection to the fish, a more powerful and positive hookset is possible with reels featuring a continuous anti-reverse.

> *The more ball bearings that are used, the smoother the reel feels when line is retrieved.*

Most bass anglers settle on spinning reels that retail for less than $100. An angler can spend much more on a spinning reel, but mid-priced equipment offers the best combination of features, quality and value.

An avid bass angler will want at least two different spinning combinations from which to choose. One of the combinations should be a 6- to 6-1/2-rod suitable for casting small jigs and tube baits. A slightly longer 7-foot spinning rod is handy for getting maximum casting distances from small jerkbaits, split-shot rigs and for wacky-rigged worms and soft plastic jerkbaits.

PISTOL-GRIP BAITCASTERS

A pistol-grip style baitcasting rod is one of the most useful, versatile and comfortable to use rods a bass angler owns. As with spinning gear, a quality graphite rod is essential. Generally these rods are from 5-1/2 to 6 feet long and feature a medium or medium-heavy action.

The ideal reel to match with a pistol-grip rod is a baitcasting reel capable of handling 125 yards of 12- to 17-pound test line. Depending on which reel type an angler is more comfortable with, both round-frame and low-profile style reels can be used. When casting, the reel is held in the palm of the hand with the little finger supported on the rod's trigger.

Ideally suited for tossing spinnerbaits, small crankbaits, worms, jigs and top-water plugs, this style of rod is most often used for short, but precise casting situations. A pistol-grip style baitcasting outfit is perfect for casting to obvious targets such as flooded brush, sunken logs, rock piles, blow downs and other visual cover typically found along shorelines. It should be considered a "must-have" bass rod. The angler's best strategy is to position the boat perpendicular to and a short cast away from cover. Using an electric motor, move the boat along the shoreline rather quickly while making short and accurate casts to likely bass haunts.

The short length and comfortable grip make for a rod that works like an extension of your arm. From a standing position, an angler using a pistol-grip style baitcasting outfit makes an underarm style cast using the wrist to flick lures at desired targets. Meanwhile the thumb is used to feather the spool so just the perfect amount of line plays out.

The result is an accurate cast that presents the lure with the least amount of splash possible. A skilled angler can fish this way for hours, covering huge amounts of cover and suffering little from casting fatigue.

Every bass angler should own at least one pistol-grip style baitcasting combination. This workhorse will undoubtedly become a favorite for fishing fast-moving lures such as spinnerbaits, buzzbaits, crankbaits and jerkbaits.

TRIGGERSTICKS

Triggersticks are straight-handle baitcasting rods. Most rods in this category are 6 to 7-1/2 feet long with actions that range from medium-light to heavy. Either a low-profile or round-frame style baitcasting reel can be used on these rods.

The extra rod and handle length of triggersticks is essential for making longer casts and also for casting heavier lures. Triggersticks can be used for a wealth of bass fishing presentations including Texas rigging plastic worms, tossing medium-sized weedless jigs, casting jerkbaits and larger-sized spinnerbaits, working jigging spoons and Carolina rigging.

A pistol-grip style baitcasting rod is favored by many anglers who use this style of rod for a wealth of presentations including top-water, worm fishing, spoons and pitching jigs.

The most common style of bass rod is a triggerstick like the one used here by Tommy Martin. The workhorse of bass rods, these rods can be used to cast just about everything from spinnerbaits to soft plastics.

A standard baitcasting reel capable of handling 125 yards of 12- to 17-pound test line is a good match for a triggerstick. Because these rods are used frequently, it's important to select a quality graphite model that's both light and sensitive. It's not uncommon for a serious bass angler to own several triggersticks in different lengths and actions.

It could be considered essential to own at least two different actions of triggersticks. The lighter action rods can be used for working small spinnerbaits, worms, grubs and smallish weedless jigs, while the heavier action rod is best suited to casting beefy spinnerbaits or Carolina rigs.

FIBERGLASS CASTING RODS

Owning and using a quality graphite rod is an advantage in most bass fishing situations. The light and responsive nature of these rods enables the angler to detect sub-

tle bites and drive the hook home with authority.

Ironically, when fishing crankbaits and surface lures, a fast-action graphite rod can actually make it tougher to get a good hook-set. Graphite rods are so responsive that an angler can literally set the hook and pull the bait away from the fish. Selecting a slower (softer) action fiberglass rod for certain presentations such as casting crankbaits or working top-water plugs helps to slow up the angler's response time. Using the fiberglass rod essentially builds in a few extra milliseconds between the strike and hookset that insures a better hooking ratio.

Many anglers think of fiberglass rods as being of lower quality when compared to graphite. The truth is, a quality fiberglass

A baitcasting reel that's capable of handling 125 yards of 12- to 17-pound test line is ideal for most baitcasting outfits.

Designed especially for casting crankbaits, this soft-action baitcasting rod can help anglers hook and land more bass.

rod costs about the same as a mid-range graphite rod. Fiberglass rods are not only slower actions, but they also deliver a shock-absorbing feature that makes it tough for fish to shake the lure after being hooked. Another advantage of fiberglass rods is the durability they offer. They are far less brittle and fragile than graphite. A good quality fiberglass rod will last for years of hard use.

The biggest disadvantages associated with fiberglass rods are the added weight and loss of sensitivity. These trade-offs are worth accepting when fishing crankbaits or top-water plugs.

Both fiberglass triggersticks and spinning rods are offered for bass fishing. When casting larger crankbaits, jerkbaits and top-water plugs, the triggerstick is the best choice. Smaller crankbaits, jerkbaits and pint-sized top-water lures require the casting features of a spinning rod.

FLIPPIN' STICKS

Flippin' is to bass fishing what magnum rifles are to hunting. Fippin' is the farthest you can get from finesse fishing, and designed to present weedless jigs or Texas rigged worms and other soft plastic baits into dense cover — a.k.a. the slop. Good places to flip include dense patches of coontail, cattails, submerged brush, lily pads, arrowhead and hydrilla.

This style of fishing is done with short underarm casts that literally flips the lure into position. The cast begins with the lure in the angler's hand and about 6 feet of slack line played out. The rod is held in the other hand and positioned at about a 45-degree angle to the water. When the lure is dropped it begins to pendulum forward. At this instant the angler raises the rod tip with a flick of the wrist catapulting the lure towards the target. As the lure nears the target the angler uses his thumb to slow up line playing off the reel. At the same time the rod tip is lowered to allow the lure to enter the water without so much as a ripple.

It takes practice to master the art of flippin'. A skilled angler can flip a jig 40 feet and hit a target the size of a coffee cup time after time. The smoother the lure enters the water, the better this technique works at triggering strikes.

The casting accuracy possible with flippin' is a major reason why this angling technique is so deadly. Also, flippin' allows anglers to fish cover that would be impossible to work with traditional bass fishing gear.

It is a unique and productive method, but flippin' requires a specially designed fishing rod. In addition to being a little longer than most bass fishing rods, a flippin' stick features an extra-heavy action from the butt to the tip. Flippin' rods are usually

These anglers are using heavy action flippin' sticks to work jigs in flooded brush. Normally this combination is equipped with 20- to 30-pound test line.

telescopic models with 7-1/2 feet being the most common length.

Graphite is the most common material used for building flippin' sticks. Graphite is selected to achieve the necessary stiffness without adding unnecessary weight to the rod.

This extra stiff and powerful action is used to literally jerk bass out of dense cover. When a bass bites a lure presented on a flippin' stick the angler sets the hook with a powerful swing of the rod that often ejects the bass from cover as if it were shot from a cannon. The fish is then quickly swung into the boat before it can regain its composure and dive down into the dense cover.

A bass landed on a flippin' stick has to ask itself, what bus hit me? Obviously this style of fishing requires heavy line. Anglers who favor monofilament spool up with 25- to 30-pound test. Braided super lines are also popular among anglers who flip because 30- to 40-pound test braided is only the diameter of 14-pound test monofilament. The thin diameter of braided lines allow anglers to flip their lures farther and with more accuracy.

The baitcasting reels used on flippin' rods are a little larger to better handle the large line sizes recommended for this style of fishing. Also, a baitcasting reel should also be equipped with a flippin' feature. When engaged, the flippin' feature allows the angler to press the bail release and allow line to play off the reel. As long as the bail release is depressed, line can play out. When the angler removes his thumb from the bail release, the reel automatically engages into gear.

This feature allows the angler to set the hook without having to turn the reel handle to engage the line pick up. When flippin', bites often occur the instant the lure touches down. Without a reel equipped with a flippin' feature the angler's response time on the hookset would be slowed considerably.

Flippin' sticks are a little more expensive than other types of bass fishing rods. Despite the extra expense, a good flippin'

stick ranks is also a must-have item of bass fishing.

SUMMARY

The five types of rod/reel combinations outlined here are the primary tools required to master the major bass fishing presentations. The beginner who wants to keep expenses on the modest side can get by with a three-rod arsenal including a 7-foot medium action spinning combo, a 6- to 7-foot medium action triggerstick/baitcasting combo and a flippin' stick. Other rod and reel combinations can be added as the angler's interest grows and skills increase.

The bass angler who sticks with the sport, will undoubtedly end up owning two or three times as many rods. Many of the top sticks in the bass game carry a dozen or more rods with them every time they go fishing. Someone has to keep the tackle companies in business.

Now, the topic turns to fishing lines and how to get the best from these critical products.

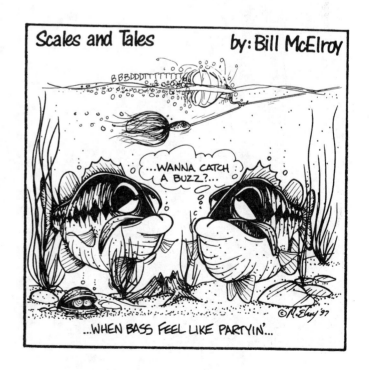

Scales and Tales   by: Bill McElroy

...WANNA CATCH A BUZZ?...

...WHEN BASS FEEL LIKE PARTYIN'...

Bassin' with the Pros

CHAPTER 5

A LINE ON BASS

Not so many years ago, fishing line was one of the least complex issues of bass fishing. Nylon fishing lines dominated the scene and anglers had few choices to consider. Outside of some brand considerations, monofilaments were largely limited to two types including limp versions designed for maximum castability and stiffer lines that offered more abrasion resistance.

Today, anglers can choose from a wide variety of fishing lines including monofilament, hard nylon monofilament, co-polymer lines, fluorocarbon products and high-performance braided lines. Just about every manufacturer of fishing lines offers several choices in each category. To further complicate matters, a flood of new manufacturers has popped up in the last few years, each touting the latest and greatest in fishing line technology. What once was a simple decision, is now one of the most complex issues facing the modern bass angler.

Making the right choices when it comes to fishing lines requires a basic understanding of the advantages and disadvantages of each line type. Like most things, selecting a fishing line is a series of compromises.

NYLON MONOFILAMENT

Despite some impressive advancements in fishing line technology, good, old-fashioned nylon monofilament is the overwhelming choice of most bass anglers. The reason monofilament continues to dominate the fishing world can be explained in two ways. First off, monofilament fishing lines offer a unique combination of castability, strength, thin diameter, knot strength, controlled stretch and durability that has stood the test of time. While some of the newer high-tech lines may excel at one or more of these important characteristics, none of them surpass monofilament in all areas.

Secondly, monofilament represents an exceptional value in the market place. Premium quality monofilament line is relatively inexpensive compared to the new high-tech lines on the market. Costing only pennies per foot, an angler can fill his or her favorite reels with monofilament for a fraction of the cost of co-polymers and super braids.

Monofilament line is manufactured in two basic flavors designed to meet the needs of a wide variety of angling situations. Flavor one is best described as spinning line. Formulated to be limp and soft, spinning line has an unique characteristic known as low memory. Lines with too much memory tend to take on a coil when the line has been on the reel spool for some time. When casting this coiling effect cuts casting distance and can even make it more difficult to detect subtle strikes.

A low memory line flows off the reel smoothly, increasing both casting distance and accuracy. Berkley's famous Trilene XL (the XL stands for extra limp) is a good

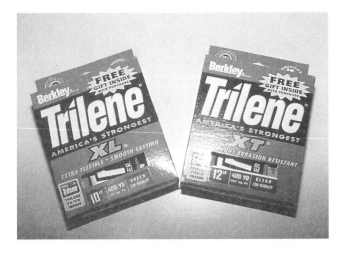

Trilene and other major line manufacturers offer two types of monofilament including limp lines designed for spinning tackle and more abrasion-resistant lines best suited for baitcasting gear.

Fishing line is one of the least expensive, yet most important, elements of fishing. Despite the introduction of high-tech lines, ordinary monofilament continues to dominate the sale of fishing lines.

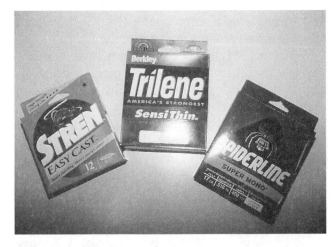

Co-polymer lines offer thinner diameter, less stretch and more abrasion resistance than most monofilaments.

example of a line designed for spin fishing situations.

In order to make a line limp and castable, some other important properties must be sacrificed. Spinning line isn't overly abrasion resistant, a characteristic that's important in many types of bass fishing. Also, spinning line's ability to withstand sudden shock isn't as good as a second type of monofilament we'll call casting line.

Casting line features a stiffer and more abrasion resistant make-up. Stiffer line also has more memory making it a poor choice for using with spinning tackle. Instead, casting line is most often used on baitcasting reels.

The increase in abrasion resistance makes casting line the obvious choice for fishing among heavy cover. Berkley's Trilene XT (the XT stands for extra tough) is an example of a popular casting line. All the major line manufacturers produce monofilament products similar to Trilene XL and XT.

Spinning style monofilament lines perform best in finesse fishing situations, while casting style lines are the workhorse in the bass fishing world. Casting lines perform well for just about any presentation where a baitcasting reel is favored.

CO-POLYMERS

The differences between nylon monofilaments and the new co-polymer style fishing lines is subtle, at best. However, if any type of fishing line comes closest to matching and exceeding the properties of monofilament, it's co-polymer line.

The primary advantages of co-polymer lines include the limpness and castability of spinning style monofilament with the abrasion resistance and strength of casting line. This type of line is also noted for being among the thinnest available and also for having a little less stretch than nylon

> *Because the line has less stretch and tends to be thinner than monofilament, any imperfection in the line may increase the chances of the line breaking.*

monofilament. This marriage may appear to produce the perfect fishing line, but in practice co-polymers don't always live up to their advertised claims.

For finesse fishing and other spinning situations, co-polymer lines are an outstanding choice. These high quality lines combine limpness, castability, strength and thin diameter into a very promising fishing line.

When it comes to abrasion resistance, co-polymers don't shine as brightly. Many co-polymer lines nick and abrade rather easily. Because the line has less stretch and tends to be thinner than monofilament, any imperfection in the line may increase the chances of the line breaking.

In the larger line sizes, co-polymers can be used for heavy cover fishing situations such as flippin', but the line must be checked often for abrasion and the lure must be retied frequently.

As you probably have guessed, co-polymer lines are more expensive than nylon monofilament. Depending on the brand and pound test, some co-polymer lines cost twice as much as monofilament.

Co-polymers have become most popular among finesse fishermen who spend a considerable amount of time using spinning tackle.

HARD MONOFILAMENT

Hard monofilament has been around for years, but only recently has this fishing line found a more popular niche. The nylon used in this monofilament is tougher and much stiffer than that used in ordinary monofilament. The result is a very stiff line that's amazingly tough.

Hard monofilament is too stiff to be a practical spinning or casting line. Instead this line has become popular as a super durable leader material for fishing techniques such as Carolina rigging.

FLUOROCARBON

Fluorocarbon line is another new entry into the fishing line market, and it offers some unique properties. Fluorocarbon-based fishing line looks like monofilament, but because its reflex index is near that of water this line is virtually invisible in water. First touted as a leader material for fishing ultra-clear waters, a number of manufacturers are now producing fluorocarbon products designed to be used as main lines.

Compared to monofilament and co-polymers, fluorocarbon line is stiffer and more abrasion resistant. While these lines are advertised as being suitable on both spinning or casting reels, most anglers used to using monofilament will be frustrated by the handling characteristics of fluorocarbon.

Fluorocarbon lines have enough memory to make them most desirable as a casting line or as a leader material. The cost of fluorocarbon lines is considerable, further suggesting that this line may best be used as super-strong and ultra-clear leader material.

Fluorocarbon lines first appeared as leader material, but now are available as filler spools. Fluorocarbon lines are nearly invisible in water and they are more abrasion-resistant that monofilament or co-polymers. Because these lines are rather stiff, they are best suited to baitcasting reels.

SUPER BRAIDS

When the braided super lines first hit the market a few years ago, the hype was enough to attract the attention of just about anyone who owned a fishing reel. Fishing line manufacturers spent huge chunks of their advertising budget promoting what many believed would be the ultimate fishing line.

The first super braids were made with a strong and thin fiber known as Spectra. Before the fishing tackle industry started using Spectra fibers for fishing line, this product was most commonly used as kite string. When these fibers are braided tightly, the result is a very strong, ultra limp and super-thin fishing line.

In addition to these important characteristics, super braids have very little stretch, making them the most sensitive of all fishing lines. Early on it appeared that the new generation of super braids had it all. Limp enough for both spinning and casting reels, super-thin diameter for maximum casting distance, toughness for fishing among cover and ultra low stretch for the maximum in sensitivity.

Unfortunately, reality started to set in. One of the first problems discovered was the knot strength. Spectra is a super slick fiber that doesn't bind well on itself. The ordinary fishing knots used by most anglers wouldn't hold in the new super braid lines. Special knots were developed, but another problem soon became evident.

The knot strength of super braids was only half that of monofilament. In other words, a line rated for 10 pound test would break at the knot when exposed to only 5 pounds of pressure.

Anglers who spooled up with these new lines quickly discovered some other problems. The lack of line stretch provided a degree of sensitivity never before experienced, but this same lack of line stretch also made it easy to over-fight hooked fish. Although it's hard to imagine, many anglers were literally tearing the hooks free of otherwise solidly hooked fish. To combat this problem, some anglers started using softer action rods and light drag settings to build a shock absorber into the system.

As if these problems weren't enough, the early Spectra lines also suffered from abrasion rather quickly. After only a modest amount of use the line would start to fuzz up and because of the lack of stretch, it could break suddenly. Cutting the line also posed a problem. Line clippers normally used to cut fishing line were almost useless. Instead it takes a sharp pair of scissors to cut braided super lines.

Since these early and often unpleasant experiences with braided lines, the manufacturers of these products have made some

> *Flippin' in heavy cover is one such situation where braided lines have proven to be outstanding.*

major strides towards improving their products. Not only are Spectra fibers braided into tighter and more durable lines, some lines feature fibers that are fused together to create a line with more body.

To add a little stretch some manufacturers have developed lines that feature Spectra fibers braided with Dacron. New fibers such as Micro Dyneema that feature better knot strength have also found their way into the marketplace.

In defense of the braided lines, the current products available are many times superior to the early introductions. However, some of the characteristics of these lines still pose anglers some problems. It's safe to say

Berkley Fireline has quickly become the most popular super braid on the market. Available in small sizes suitable for spinning gear or larger sizes suitable for baitcasting and flipping, this line is also offered in a low-visibility smoke or high-visibility flame color.

that super braids have not become the ultimate fishing line, but rather a specialty product that can work exceptionally well in a number of fishing situations.

Flippin' in heavy cover is one such situation where braided lines have proven to be outstanding. The ultra-thin line diameter allows anglers to cast farther, use smaller lures and to maintain contact with the lure better than with other fishing lines. The toughness of these lines also excels when fishing in flooded brush, sharp rocks and other cover that can abrade ordinary lines in no time.

The low stretch makes braided lines a great choice for jigging or fishing spoons in deep water. The increase in sensitivity achieved by using these lines adds up in more detected strikes and landed fish.

The manufacturers of braided lines have overcome many of the early problems associated with these new fishing lines. Price however is one area where a major problem still exists. The most common brands of super braids are two or three times as expensive as monofilament per filler spool.

SUMMARY

Sometimes the more you learn about new technology and products, the more you come to appreciate old and trusted fishing tools. While countless new fishing lines have hit the market in the last decade, nylon monofilament continues to outsell them all. Anglers shouldn't, however, blind themselves to the advancements being made in fishing line. For certain fishing situations specialty lines such as co-polymers, fluorocarbons and super braids can perform better than monofilament.

It's also important to note that no fishing line is perfect. Anglers must carefully weigh the properties of the various line types when using various fishing presentations.

One fact of fishing lines remains true: the more a line is used the more often it should be replaced. Limp spinning style lines should be replaced frequently, while tougher casting style lines can withstand considerable abuse.

Many tournament anglers replace their fishing line daily to

No matter what type of fishing line you use, the line must be replaced frequently. Commercial line winders like this are often the least expensive way to fill a reel with fresh line.

insure the ultimate performance from whatever line they choose to use. The average bass angler doesn't need to replace his or her line after each day on the water, but you should monitor the line closely for signs of wear.

The last three or four feet of the line receives the most abuse. Cut and retie your lures frequently to reduce line failures.

Many reels also hold more line than necessary. For example a typical bass-sized spinning reel will hold 150 yards of 8-pound test. Only 30 or 40 yards of this line is being used, while the rest of the line simply fills up the spool.

Cut and retie your lures frequently to reduce line failures.

To achieve maximum casting distance the spool needs to be full, but when it's time to replace the line there's no reason to strip off all the old line. Simply strip off half the used line and add fresh line. This simple tip allows anglers to enjoy a 50 percent savings on the line budget without sacrificing any performance.

Fishing line is the critical connection between angler and fish. Should this connection fail, time, money and energy spent on other aspects of bass fishing are wasted. The best possible advice? Choose your line types wisely, and change line often.

In Chapter Six the focus switches to the popular types of tackle used to catch bass.

Scales and Tales   by: Bill McElroy

"IT'S SILICONE, LEAD, & PORK FAT!...THEY SAY IT TASTES LIKE CHICKEN!"

Bassin' with the Pros

CHAPTER 6

THE WELL-STOCKED TACKLE BOX

In some ways bass fishing is simple and in other ways it is very complex. Most bass fishermen limit themselves to fishing exclusively with artificial lures. That's simple. No need to get confused with a wealth of live bait fishing methods or gear.

Unfortunately, no other type of freshwater fishing is plagued with so many different types and colors of artificial lures. Fishing lures designed to catch bass number in the tens of thousands and every year the market is flooded with a new batch of baits that promise to produce more and bigger bass.

If all the lure choices available are confusing and frustrating, don't despair. When choosing lures for bass fishing it helps if you can laugh a little at yourself and admit some common human failings. It's the slightly gullible and somewhat crazed nature of bass anglers that fuels the constant supply of "new and improved" products constantly being pumped into the marketplace. Anglers

(not just bass anglers) are constantly looking for that "magic" lure that turns an otherwise slow day on the water into bragging rights.

It's not hard to understand why anglers tend to take short cuts and look for the easy way out. No one likes to admit his angling "skills" could be sharper. Furthermore, most fishermen don't spend enough time on the water to refine even the most basic lure presentations.

Instead of spending our fishing time refining the basics, we look for shortcuts that promise more and better fishing success. Lures are the primary focal point that anglers turn to when looking for that "magic" that makes us better anglers than we really are!

Don't get me wrong. Artificial lures are important tools for bass fishing. In due time we'll get to the place in this chapter that outlines how to select the most important lure types. The point is, many anglers forget that no matter how good a lure may be, it can't catch fish if the angler doesn't throw it into the right spot at the right time. Too often we lose sight of the fact that the "magic" in bass fishing doesn't come in a lure package, but rather in the form of old-fashioned hard work, practice and dedication.

Memorable days on the water are usually credited to whatever lure was being used at the time. Unfortunately, anglers tend to glamorize a successful lure by giving it more credit than it deserves. The truth is, locating bass is the hard work. Once an angler has pinpointed a group of bass, any number of

> *Too often we lose sight of the fact that the "magic" in bass fishing doesn't come in a lure package, but rather in the form of old-fashioned hard work, practice and dedication.*

good lures are likely to produce the desired results.

Anglers also have a natural tendency to exaggerate when telling the story. A lure that produced half a dozen bass, can amazingly have taken twice that many by the time the story is told and retold!

Television commercials and endorsements by big-name bass fishermen fuel this whole mess into a bonfire that lures (no pun intended) more moths to the flame. Nothing I write here is likely to change the way the industry sells its products or the way bass anglers purchase fishing lures. Still, anglers must realize that the fishing lure business is just that, a business. To some of these companies sales are more important than teaching anglers how to become more skilled.

The marketplace is full of classic lures every bass angler should own, a wealth of new lures that are noteworthy and deadly fishing tools, plus far too many twitching, rotating, twirling, chirping and gurgling "junk" lures that are designed to stimulate corporate profits, not bass.

You can't blame the lure manufacturers for producing convincing commercials to sell their products. You can't blame bass pros for endorsing these products to make a living. And you can't blame anglers for wanting to catch more fish. When it's time to stock your tackle box you simply have to be able to wade through the hooey and have a knack for making every dollar you spend on fishing lures a dollar well-spent.

The thousands of lures designed to catch bass can all be lumped into one of half a dozen categories including crankbaits, top-water lures, jigs, rigs, spinnerbaits and soft plastics. Every bass angler should have a few lures from each of these categories in his or her tackle box. You'll find outlined in the coming pages recommendations for classics and a few of the up-and-coming baits that are well worth exploring.

Crankbaits are just one of many artificial lures that anglers will find valuable for catching bass.

CRANKBAITS

When it comes to artificial lures, crankbaits reign as the most expensive and also as the most extensive. An angler could spend his or her entire fishing budget just on crankbaits and still not have everything available.

Because these lures are expensive, anglers need to take special care in selecting baits that have proven themselves as consistent producers. The category of crankbaits can be further broken down into several subcategories including jerkbaits, diving minnows, lipless baits, shad baits and fat-body lures.

Jerkbaits are shallow-diving minnow lures that are most often fished at or near the surface. The term jerkbait comes from how these lures are worked. The rod tip is snapped in short twitches that cause the bait to dart back and forth like a wounded and dying minnow. Normally jerkbaits are used to fish over the top of cover in water less than 10 feet deep. However, in exceptionally clear water a jerkbait can often pull bass from much deeper water.

Not only are jerkbaits effective, this style of fishing is easy to master and productive on all species of bass. Some of the classics in this category include the Bomber

Crankbaits come in a wide variety of sizes, shapes and colors. Best suited for catching active bass, these lures are among the best for covering water quickly.

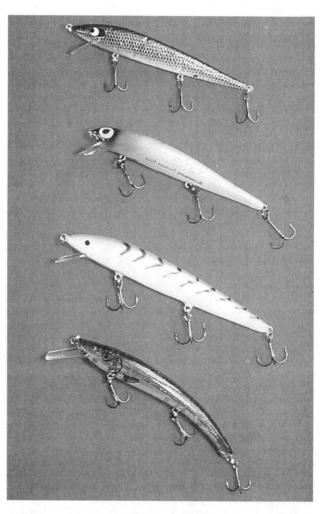

Jerkbaits — like these popular models — are a type of crankbait, but these lures are fished using a unique twitching and jerking motion that imitates a dying minnow.

Long A, Storm Thunder-Stick and Smithwick Rattlin' Rogue. In recent years a few newcomers have carved out a niche in the jerkbait market. These promising new lures include the Rapala Husky Jerk, Reef Runner Rip-Stick and Yo-Zuri Crystal Minnow.

In the diving minnow category, anglers will find a host of small, medium and large baits. All these lures feature a thin minnow profile with a larger diving lip than is found on a jerkbait. Medium-sized lures do the best job of matching the forage that bass are most likely to feed on. Some of the classics in this category include the Storm Deep Jr. ThunderStick, Bomber 24A and Rebel Spoonbill. Newcomers in this category that hit the water running include Rapala's Deep Diving Husky Jerk, Reef Runner's Deep Lit-

> *One of the best selling crankbaits of all time, the sales of this lure aren't attributed to advertising and hype, but rather to the countless bass this lure has produced.*

tle Ripper and Berkley's Deep Diving Frenzy Minnow.

Lipless crankbaits are so important to bass fishing, these lures almost deserve a category all their own. Easy to fish and amazingly effective, lipless baits are designed for fishing shallow water cover, especially where submerged aquatic growth (grass) holds bass.

Classics in this category have to start with the legendary Bill Lewis Rat-L-Trap. One of the best selling crankbaits of all time, the sales of this lure aren't attributed to advertising and hype, but rather to the countless bass this lure has produced. Other outstanding lipless cranks include the Rapala Rattlin' Rap, Excalibur Super Spot, Bass Pro Shops Extreme Rattle Shad and Berkley's Frenzy Rattler.

Shad-shaped crankbaits are another important crankbait category. The various species of shad are collectively among the most abundant and preferred forages of bass. A few crankbaits that resemble the distinctive "shad" shape can only be described as must-have items in any tackle box.

Classics in the shad body category include the Rapala Shad Rap, Bagley Balsa Shad, Rebel Shad-R, Bill Norman Little N, Mann's Legend and Bomber A series. Soon-to-be-classics in this category include the Rapala Suspending Shad Rap, Excalibur Fat Free Shad, Yo-Zuri 3D Shad and Storm Lightnin' Shad.

A group of crankbaits we'll call "fat-bodies" represent a family of high-action lures that deliver a pronounced side-to-side wobble. The short and fat profile of these baits does an excellent job of imitating another important bass forage, sunfish. Bluegills, punkinseed sunfish, crappie and a host of other young panfish make up the majority of a bass' diet in many waters. This category of cranks is available in shallow-, medium- and deep-diving versions.

Lipless cranks can be worked through cover impossible to fish with other crankbait styles.

Classic fat-body lures include the Mann's 1-Minus, Storm Wiggle Wart, Bagley Kill'r-B and Rebel Wee-R. Other great lures in this category include the Rapala Fat Rap, Worden's Timber Tiger, Luhr Jensen Brush Baby, Strike King's Series 3 and the Rebel Crank-R.

TOP-WATER BAITS

Top-water fishing is a bigger fishing category than many anglers realize. Fishing on the surface can involve a wealth of lures including jerkbaits, popper-style plugs, prop baits, buzzbaits and even soft plastic lures that imitate frogs, mice and a host of other critters bass sometimes feed on.

Top-water is such an exciting way to catch bass, everyone should stock up on a few of the lures commonly used to stimulate surface strikes. Jerkbaits such as the legendary Zara Spook are a good place to start the thrill of top-water fishing. This slender minnow-shaped bait is worked by twitching the rod tip to impart a darting stop-and-go style retrieve. This classic top-water presentation has proven itself and can be used to catch all species of bass.

Other jerkbaits similar to the Zara Spook include the Bass Pro Shops Extreme Shad Topwater, Excalibur Spit'n Image, Excalibur Super Spook and Bass Arms Walk'N Dog.

Top-water fishing ranks as one of the most exciting forms of bass fishing. Clear water situations like this are ideal for working a wide variety of surface baits.

The Zara Spook is undoubtedly the most popular surface bait of all time.

Popper-style plugs are second in popularity only to the spook-style baits. Designed with a concave face that gurgles and spits water when the rod tip is twitched, a host of lures in this class are available. The long time favorite in this category has to be the Rebel Pop-R. Similar baits that have hit the market in recent years include the Excalibur Pop'n Image, Rapala Skitter Pop, Bass Pro Shops Z-Pop and Storm Chug Bug.

Prop baits are another top-water classic that have stood the test of time. Similar to jerkbaits, these lures however are dressed with props on the front or back of the lure that spin and gurgle when the bait is retrieved. There is only a handful of lures to choose from in this category. The most popular ones include the Heddon Torpedo and Smithwick's Devil Horse.

Buzzbaits are one of those lure choices that could be counted as a top-water bait or as a member of the spinnerbait family. Because they are designed to be gurgled along the surface, we'll consider them a top-water choice.

> *No matter what species of fish anglers target, jigs are always an important lure.*

A buzzbait can feature either a metal or plastic blade that rotates in front of a rubber skirt or plume of bucktail. All the major manufacturers of spinnerbaits produce buzzbaits, plus there are about 1,000 smaller lure makers working to keep anglers supplied. Terminator has become one of the big names in buzzbaits made from Titanium wire. Titanium is much stronger and has better "spring" than other types of wire. Just a few of the buzzbaits anglers can choose from include the Lunker Lure Flash Tail, Bass Pro Shops Titan 375, Uncle Buck's Buzzer, Lazer Eye Buzz Master and Enticer Pro Series.

Some soft plastic lures are also popular choices for fishing on the surface. Normally these lures are used to walk right over the top of heavy cover such as lily pads, arrowhead, hydrilla, moss and other forms of aquatic plants that grow right up to the surface. In fact, these lures are often times the only way to fish this dense slop.

Classic choices in this category include the Snag-Proof Moss Mouse, Snag-Proof Frog and Mann's Legends Frog. Other good choices in this category include the Bass Pro Shops XPS Lazer Eye Tender Toad, Snag-Proof Frogzilla, Scum-Frog and Mustad's new Swamp Frog.

JIGS

No matter what species of fish anglers target, jigs are always an important lure. In bass fishing, the jigs used can be broken down into two distinctive groups including weedless jigs, which are most often used to fish heavy cover, and traditional leadheads that are teamed up with soft plastic grubs and tubes.

Weedless style jigs have become so popular there's hardly a lure manufacturer who doesn't produce several different versions of these baits. Generally, weedless jigs are rather heavy lures

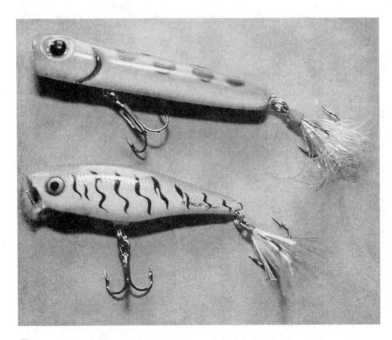

These top-water baits are typical of the lure types available.

designed to penetrate dense cover such as lily pads, cattails, coontail, arrowhead, hydrilla and submerged brush. The weedguard on most of these jigs is made from a nylon fiber that is stiff enough to allow the jig to work in among any potential snags without hanging up. When a fish strikes the weedguard folds down on the hookset.

Most of these jigs are dressed with either a living rubber skirt, feather or hair body that helps the jig sink a little more slowly and provides some added action. In addition, most anglers tip their weedless jigs with a chunk of pork rind or a soft plastic trailer.

Rattles are also a big thing on weedless jigs these days. Many manufacturers add a rattle chamber to generate a clicking sound similar to that produced by crayfish.

Some of the most popular weedless jigs include the Stanley Flat Eye, Strike King Rattlin' Pro Model, Pflueger Summit, Bass Pro Shops Enticer series, Zorro Booza Bug and Northland Weedless Rattlin' Jungle Jig. The most common sizes in this jig style are the 3/8- and 1/2-ounce models.

A few weedless jigs are designed not for heavy cover use, but rather for fishing grubs and other soft plastics in moderate cover. These leadheads normally feature a weedguard made from a piece of braided wire. The Hoot Ninny Head is a good example of this style of weedless jig.

Leadheads used for fishing grubs and tubes are more along the traditional side. The most popular styles of leadheads for grub fishing are darter or bullet shaped heads and round heads. These jigs should feature a rather large No. 1, 1/0 or 2/0 hook. Paint on these jigheads is optional. Many anglers simply rely on the grub to provide the necessary color. Anyone who fishes with grubs will need a good selection of 1/8- 1/4- and 3/8-ounce darter heads.

A somewhat different style of leadhead is used for tube bait fishing.

Since the head of the jig is positioned inside the hollow tube body, an elongated head style is best. The most common sizes used for fishing tubes include the 1/16-, 1/8-, 3/16- and 1/4-ounce. In some deep-water situations anglers may need an assortment of 3/8-and 1/2-ounce tube jigheads.

An even more unique style of leadhead for fishing tubes and grubs is produced by Bait Rigs. The Slo-Poke GrubMaster is an elongated leadhead that is designed to slip right inside a tube, grub or skirted grub. The eye tie comes out the nose of the grub making the lure amazingly snag resistant in

Jigs make up one of the largest categories of bass baits including weedless jigs, flippin' jigs, jigs designed for fishing grubs, and those for use in tube baits.

grass and weed cover. These jigheads are sold separately in 1/8- and 1/4- ounce sizes or in kits that contain an assortment of pre-rigged grubs.

RIGS

Technically rigs are not fishing lures. Rigs are the weights used to present various lures on or near bottom. However, the popularity of Carolina rigging has spawned a number of pre-assembled rigs that make it easier to fish and even easier to change weights.

The Bullet Weight company has been an innovator in this area with their Ultra Steel

Many anglers feel that spinnerbaits are the single most important lure a bass angler owns.

2000 weights. Steel weights are more environmental friendly and when steel weights click together they produce more fish-attracting sound than traditional lead weights.

The Carolina Quick-Rig is a pre-assembled rig that features two weights with a bead sandwiched between. The three-part rig is held together with a short length of wire that can easily be clipped to the main line. At the business end, another clip accepts a leader armed with a lizard, craw or other soft plastic bait.

It only takes seconds to change weight sizes. Simply clip on a different sized Quick-Rig and you're good to go. These handy rigs have helped to make Carolina rigging more popular than ever. Quick-Rigs are available in sizes ranging from 1/4 to 1 ounce.

Other ready-to-fish Carolina rig weights include the Kalin Carolina clacker, Bass Pro Shops Short Cut Rig Kit and the Top Brass Tackle Ready Rig.

SPINNERBAITS

The spinnerbait ranks supreme in bass fishing as the one lure every angler needs. No matter where you live or fish, spinnerbaits are going to be important bass fishing tools.

Part of what makes spinnerbaits so productive is the versatility of these lures. A spinnerbait can be retrieved just over the top of dense weed cover, buzzed over slop on the surface, slow rolled through patches of grass and weed cover, fluttered down a steep cliff or bumped along bottom in deep water.

Spinnerbaits are also easy to fish. The only hard part of fishing spinnerbaits is choosing from the hundreds of styles offered. The combinations of blade and skirt types are enough to keep even the top pros scratching their heads with indecision.

The biggest news in spinnerbaits is of course the new models produced using titanium wire. Titanium wire is used in the construction of spinnerbaits because this material is lighter, stronger and has better memory or spring than other wire types. A spinnerbait built from titanium is going to "snap back" into shape fish after fish. Steel wire spinnerbaits get bent out of shape after catching only a handful of fish. To insure the bait runs true in the water the wire must be bent back into its original shape. This process is known as tuning.

Of course titanium is expensive and spinnerbaits made from this material can be as much as twice the cost of ordinary spinnerbaits. In the big picture, titanium actually saves the angler money because they are more durable, need less tuning and last much longer.

Some top picks in titanium spinnerbaits include the Terminator T-1, Strike King Titanium Elite and Stanley's Taper Titanium. Other outstanding steel wire spinnerbaits include the Mann's Legend, Gambler Ninja Spin, Lunker Lure Triple Rattleback, Stanley Wedge and the Strike King Premier Pro-Model.

Good features to look for in any spinnerbait include ball bearing swivels that allow the blades to spin at the slightest movement. Also, blades that are genuine silver- and gold-plated, produce the maximum amount of fish-attracting flash.

Every bass angler needs a modest assortment of spinnerbaits including some models featuring willow and Colorado style blades. The most common sizes are 3/8 and 1/2 ounce, but a few smaller 1/4-ounce models are excellent for fishing smallmouth and spotted bass. Also, don't forget to pick up at least a couple 3/4- to 1-ounce spinnerbaits for fishing in deep water.

SOFT PLASTICS

Soft plastic lures are almost as essential to bass fishing as hooks. Soft plastic lures do such a good job of imitating just about

> *When shopping for plastics it helps to break the different types down according to how they are most commonly used.*

anything a bass might eat, there's no need for live bait!

Most fishing situations a bass angler encounters scream for soft plastic lures. The first soft plastics on the market were basic worms and action-tail grubs. Today the assortment of soft plastic lures is nothing short of mind boggling. Just a few of the soft plastic lures available include worms, finesse worms, rigged worms, grubs, skirted grubs, leeches, lizards, reepers, spinnerbait trailers, jig trailers, jerkbaits, shad bodies, tubes, caterpillars and many others.

When shopping for plastics it helps to break the different types down according to how they are most commonly used. For example, worms are most often used Texas rigged, while lizards and centipedes are usually fished on a Carolina rig.

When selecting an assortment of soft plastic worms plan on purchasing a couple different sizes and several worm styles. A 6- or 7-inch worm is the most popular size, but a few smaller worms are handy for finesse fishing situations. Ribbontail worms are among the most popular, but don't overlook a few paddle and ring-style worms. Rigged worms are also standard equipment when fishing for bass in small or weed-choked natural lakes.

In the grub category the basics include action tails such as the popular Kalin's Salty Lunker, Berkley Power Grub and Zoom's Salty Fat Albert. Twin-tail grubs and skirted grubs are also good choices. Shad bodies are yet another excellent grub body style.

When Carolina rigging, a wide variety of soft plastics will produce bass. Some of the most popular styles include lizards and centipedes, but craws, worms and even grubs are often used at the business end of a Carolina rig.

Soft plastics also see a lot of use as trailers for jigs and spinnerbaits. Usually those used on spinnerbaits are split tails like the Zoom Split Tail Trailer or Bass Pro

Shops Yum Cajun Trailer. When it comes to jig trailers the choices are almost without limit. Some of the popular trailers used on weedless style jigs include the Zoom Salty Pork Chunk, Uncle Josh J-Frog, Gambler's Guido's Original, Bass Pro Shops Yum Caterpillar Craw, Power Bait Craw and Gene Larew Salt Craw. Pork chunks and craws are the most popular jig trailers, but a wealth of other plastics can be used.

Jerkbaits are another category of soft plastics that have really taken off in recent years. The original Slug-O started a ball rolling that has ended up with dozens of other manufacturers following suit. These lures can be used without weights, weighted with a nail or piece of solder or used with a Carolina rig.

Some popular choices include the Berkley PowerBait Jerk Shad and Slug, Zoom Fluke, Lunker City Slug-O and Bass Pro Shops Squirmin' Jerk.

Tubes are often lumped into the grub category, but these unique soft plastic lures deserve special consideration. The most popular sizes are the 3-1/2- and 4-1/2-inch versions. Just a few of the popular tubes include the Strike King Kevin VanDam Pro Model, Stanley Tuba Tube, Gambler Hibdon Super Tube, Chompers Ultra Tube and Bass Pro Shops XPS Tube.

Crankbaits, jigs, rigs, topwater, spinnerbaits and soft plastics are the primary lure groups with which bass fishermen need to be concerned. A few other assorted lures also have a place in the bass fishing tackle box.

Jigging spoons are often overlooked baits that excel at deep-water bass fishing. Some of the classics in this category include the Bass'N Bait Rattle Snakie, Mann's Legends Rattling Spoon, Hopkins Shorty, Luhr Jensen Crippled Herring and Prism Image Minnow Jig. The most common sizes of these spoons include the 3/8-, 1/2-, 3/4- and 1-ounce versions.

Blade baits such as the classic Heddon Gay Blade also excel in deep water. These baits are created by combining a blade with a lead body. When jigged or retrieved quickly the lure sends out vibration like no other lure. Other good blade baits include the Reef Runner Cicada, Silver Buddy and Bass Pro Shops XPS Lazer Blade.

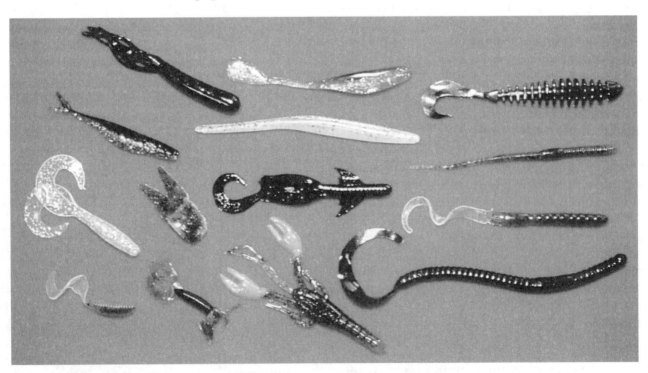

These are just some of the soft plastic lure types bass anglers use frequently.

TACKLE STORAGE

The list of tackle outlined here is enough to fill a pick-up truck, much less a tackle box. The vast amount of tackle a bass angler lugs onto the water has fueled a whole new wave of tackle storage systems. Traditional hard-side tackle boxes are simply too difficult to store in the limited dry storage available in most boats. The move these days is towards soft tackle storage systems that allow anglers to keep their gear organized while allowing an amazing amount of tackle to be stored in a small space.

Many of these soft tackle systems are nylon bags that are designed to hold a number of clear plastic utility boxes such as those produced by Plano and Woodstream. In addition, these bags have pockets and pouches suitable for storing a wealth of smaller binder-style bags and other essentials such as pliers, sharpening stones, line clippers, hand towels and miscellaneous gear. The major names in soft tackle storage systems include Tackle Logic, Flambeau, Pflueger, Bass Pro Shops and Cabela's.

Binder-style zipper bags are the best way to store soft plastics, pork rind and the accessories needed to fish these lures such as hooks, worm weights, lead-heads and Carolina rig weights.

Crankbaits are one of the most difficult items to store. The treble hooks on these lures makes it impractical to store more than a couple baits in the same tackle box compartment without creating a nightmare of twisted hooks. Zippered binders can be used to store a modest number of cranks. Usually the pages of the binder are separated by foam pieces that hold the treble hooks in place. Most anglers simply stuff as many cranks as possible in a plastic utility box and worry about getting the hooks untangled when the time comes to use them!

The angler who packs wisely can stuff everything needed for a complete day of bass fishing into one shoulder bag. Tournament anglers who never know who's boat they will be fishing in are masters at trimming their tackle needs down to the essentials.

Those anglers who own their own boat are more likely to fill every storage box and compartment with something designed to catch bass!

Choosing bass fishing tackle is one of the most intimidating aspects of learning this exciting sport. Newcomers and veteran anglers alike are best served with the common sense approach to tackle selection. It's important to start with a modest selection of the classics that, over time, have proven to be consistent fish producers. As time passes and your interest and angling skills grow, you'll no doubt feel obligated to purchase way more tackle than you'll ever use! Welcome to bass fishing.

I've intentionally avoided the question of color to keep this bulging chapter within reason. Color and how it relates to bass fishing will be handled in detail throughout many chapters of this book.

Next up, the focus switches from lures to electronics and the changing role these products have had on bass fishing.

Scales and Tales   by: Bill McElroy

"...SINCE WHEN DID CRAWFISH START BUNGEE JUMPING?!"

  Bassin' with the Pros

CHAPTER 7

THE ROLE OF ELECTRONICS IN BASS FISHING

Few elements of bass fishing have changed the sport as profoundly as sonar. Prior to the introduction of sonar, bass anglers spent their time fishing shorelines and visible cover. Sonar changed the face of fishing forever by providing anglers with a practical means of locating structure, cover and fish.

Despite some huge advancements in technology, the basic flasher type sonar units that first hit the market over 30 years ago are still in wide use today. Along the way paper graphs, video sonar and liquid crystal readout graphs and even underwater video have entered the picture.

HOW SONAR WORKS

Anglers can choose from a wide variety of sonar types. All the major brands and models of sonar units operate using the same principles of science. The major differences among sonar types is the way the information is displayed. Behind the viewing screen, sonar technology is based on the fact that sound travels through water at a constant speed of 4,800 feet per second.

All sonar units are made up of three basic parts including a transmitter, transducer and receiver. The transmitter sends an electrical pulse to the transducer, which in turn converts the electrical signals to sound energy. This transmission of sound is directed into the water. Sound waves traveling through the water strike and bounce off objects more dense than water and return to the transducer.

The transducer converts the sound waves back into electrical energy that is, in turn, forwarded to the receiver. The receiver amplifies and displays the information onto a screen.

The transducer is a critical part of any sonar unit. A transducer is actually a crystal made from two plates of silver, one on top of another. When an electrical charge strikes

the crystal, the plates expand and contract producing a clicking sound. This is how electrical energy is converted into sound energy.

A housing around the crystal forces the sound waves to travel only out the bottom of the transducer. As the sound waves travel through water the sound waves expand into a cone shape. The deeper the water, the larger this cone angle becomes and the more surface area that's contacted with the sound waves.

This is why sonar is of little use in marking fish in shallow water. The cone angle is so small, only a tiny portion of the water column is covered by the sound waves. In deeper water the cone angle increases and the amount of coverage is greatly increased.

This illustration shows the relative shape of sound waves as they are transmitted into the water and received back at the transducer. Photo courtesy of Lowrance Electronics.

The way sonar functions is amazingly simple. Since it's known that sound travels through water at 4,800 feet per second, the time lapse between a sound wave striking an underwater object and returning to the transducer can be used to calculate how far away the object is. Objects between the transducer and bottom (fish, weeds, brush, etc.) appear as separate marks at the distance they are from the transducer.

This basic fact of sonar function is the same no matter how the information is displayed. However, the way sonar is displayed can make a huge difference in how anglers interpret the data.

FLASHER UNITS

Flashers were the first sonar units and they remain popular even today. Despite major advances in sonar display technology, a flasher unit is still capable of showing an angler everything he or she needs to see. A flasher unit can mark fish, indicate the bottom and even the hardness of the bottom, show weeds and submerged brush and even display changes in bottom contour.

The problem with flasher units is most anglers have a tough time understanding the many bleeps of light they display. Frankly, not one angler in 10 who owns a flasher can identify anything more than bottom depth.

Despite their limitations in displaying useful information to anglers, flashers have remained popular. Flashers continue to sell in part because a number of influential tournament pros endorse them and because boat manufacturers continue to use flashers as the most common factory installed sonar unit. Of course those manufacturers who produce flashers also do their part to promote flasher use.

In defense of this style of sonar, a flasher provides an instantaneous readout of

> *Despite major advances in sonar display technology, a flasher unit is still capable of showing an angler everything he or she needs to see.*

important information. To get the most from a flasher unit requires some training and lots of hours of using these products. The place to start is by learning how to properly adjust the sensitivity on the flasher. If the sensitivity is set too high, the entire screen will be littered with confusing bleeps of light. If the sensitivity of a flasher isn't set high enough the unit will display little beyond the bottom depth.

On most flasher units the on/off switch and the sensitivity adjustment are the same. Turn on the unit and slowly turn up the gain or sensitivity while watching the screen closely. When the bottom signal first appears on the screen the sensitivity adjustment is getting close. Keep turning the sensitivity up until a second bottom echo appears on the screen. The second echo will appear at twice the depth.

This color flasher unit has more contrast than normal flashers and is easier for the average angler to interpret.

At this point the sensitivity of the flasher is adjusted high enough to mark the bottom, fish and weed cover without the screen being littered with unwanted interference. A number of factors will influence the sensitivity adjustment required while fishing. A hard bottom area for example will readily rebound sound waves and a broad band of light will be displayed on the screen. In soft bottom areas sound waves are absorbed into the bottom and the bottom signal displays as a thin band of light.

To achieve the desired level of sensitivity when fishing soft or hard bottom areas, the unit must be adjusted accordingly. Water depth also influences the required amount of sensitivity adjustment. In shallow water the sensitivity is normally set near the low end of the scale. In deep water the sensitivity must be turned up to achieve the desired results.

Recognizing what the bleeps of light represent is the real skill in flasher use. Fish suspended in the water column appear as thin bands of flickering light. The bigger the fish, the wider the band of light that appears on the dial.

Small fish such as bait normally appear as many thin bands of flickering light. Submerged cover such as scattered weed growth produces bleeps of light similar to that produced with bait fish. Telling the difference between these two similar types of information often comes down to intuition more than anything else.

Sloping contours appear as an extra wide bottom signal. The reason the bottom signal widens is because the cone angle of sound waves contact a larger portion of the bottom and return more signals. The steeper the drop, the wider the band of light on the flasher appears.

Flasher units are likely to remain popular despite their limitations and the advancements of both liquid crystal readout

> *Flasher units are likely to remain popular despite their limitations and the advancements of both liquid crystal readout (LCR) and video style sonar units.*

(LCR) and video style sonar units. Those anglers who choose to use flashers have their work cut out when it comes to interpreting them successfully.

OTHER SONAR TYPES

There's another factor that has helped flasher units remain so popular despite the introduction of more user-friendly sonar types. The early LCR style sonar units were poorly designed and they offered anglers less useful information than a flasher unit. The viewing screens on these early units were small and the detail limited.

The primary reason these units were disappointing is because the viewing screens were comprised of large dots or pixels. Groupings of pixels clustered together created less than impressive images. Important information such as fish or cover appeared as blocks or globs that were quite difficult to interpret.

Some of the early LCR units featured only 25 pixels per inch of viewing screen. Today the top LCR units offer 300 pixels per inch of viewing screen.

Obviously, the dot matrix pictures created by current LCR units have dramatically improved. Unfortunately, many anglers were so turned off by early LCR units they have avoided LCR technology all together.

Another problem is associated with early LCR units. Most of these products were designed to be easy to use. Simply turn them on and the automatic function takes over.

This marketing ploy to help sell LCR units backfired. In order to produce a screen with desired images and no interference, a built-in suppression system was used on most models. A suppression system filters out interference at the expense of reducing the unit's resolution or ability to mark objects in the water.

You guessed it, many of these units did a poor job of marking fish, weeds, bait fish and other important information. Then came the fish icon idea that further degraded the respect LCR units received.

Again, in an effort to make LCR units easy to use, manufacturers started displaying fish on the screen as a fish-shaped icon. Big mistake. While these units did a good job of indicating fish on the screen, other objects in the water were also marked as a series of fish icons. For example, a piece of cabbage weed growing up off the bottom appeared on the screen as a vertical stack of fish icons. Anglers quickly lost confidence in these machines as serious fish finders.

Most liquid crystal sonar units are designed with automatic functions that make them easy to use. But to get the most from this sonar technology the user must place the unit on manual and adjust both the sensitivity and grayline to achieve maximum resolution.

In an effort to produce better and easier to interpret sonar units, the manufacturers of these products inadvertently sent the wrong message to their customers. Ironically, many of the LCR units being produced today are outstanding products that clearly mark fish, bait and cover. These units are also easy to use and they offer a wealth of functions that make finding fish an easier task. Some of these units combine both sonar and Global Position System (GPS) navigational information in one convenient product.

Despite introduction of some spectacular LCR sonar products, the sonar market continues to be plagued with questionable entry-level machines that offer less useful information than the original flasher units. It's no wonder so many anglers are reluctant to take the step from flasher units to the latest premium level of LCR sonar technology.

To get the maximum level of resolution from LCR units, anglers need to travel down a few paths. First off, it's important to select a machine that has enough power or peak-to-peak watts to effectively mark fish and cover in shallow or deep water. Most units feature an adequate 500 to 600 watts of peak-to-peak power. The best LCR units feature a full 3,000 watts of fish-finding power.

Extra power enables the LCR unit to do some amazing things. For example, a quality LCR unit with 3,000 watts of power can mark fish laying tight against the bottom, even on soft bottoms. The same unit can show bass feeding among bait fish and clearly show differences in bottom composition. Objects in the water, such as weed cover or brush, can be easily distinguished. Try to get this kind of resolution with an LCR that only generates 500 watts of power.

It's also important to select LCR units that offer enough pixels to generate a detailed picture of what's underwater. Many LCR units still offer less than 100 pixels per vertical inch of viewing screen. To get the kind of detail a serious fisherman needs, an LCR unit should offer 200 to 300 vertical pixels.

The next step is to avoid the automatic function and operate these units on manual. Most quality LCR units enable the operator to run the unit on automatic or manual. By choosing the manual setting, the angler has the opportunity to fine tune the sensitivity and gray line features to achieve maximum resolution. Using the manual mode also eliminates automatic suppression systems that are designed to make the screen nice and clear, but that also rob the unit of resolution.

When setting the sensitivity, adjust it upwards until the screen starts to get cluttered with interference. Now back down the sensitivity slightly so the screen shows a little interference, but not so much it's distracting from the quality of the picture. How high the sensitivity will need to be set depends on the water depth and bottom composition.

To help separate fish from bottom, try turning up the gray line feature a little. When an LCR is operating in the automatic mode, the gray line is normally adjusted to around 20 percent. Raising this setting 30 percent to 50 percent can make a big difference in spotting fish laying close to bottom.

A third feature to explore is the zoom function. Most LCR units offer a 2X or 4X zoom function that essentially enlarges the detail. On zoom it's easier to identify fish close to the bottom, fish feeding among bait and fish holding in cover.

Modern LCR units are capable of providing bass anglers all the information they need in a picture that is easy to understand. The biggest hurdle with using this style of sonar is weeding out the less than desirable units and zeroing in on the serious fish-finding machines.

In addition to flashers and liquid crystal readout style sonar units, anglers can also choose video sonar technology. With video sonar, anglers are treated to color images, high resolution and easy operation. If it

> *If it weren't for one small problem, video sonar would likely become the most popular choice among anglers.*

weren't for one small problem, video sonar would likely become the most popular choice among anglers.

Size is a problem with video units. Unfortunately, video sonar units are like small TV sets and they are too big to be practical in a bass boat. This type of sonar enjoys its most success in larger fishing boats used for Great Lakes trolling or near shore coastal saltwater fishing adventures.

Another style of sonar unit has apparently run its course. Sadly, the paper graph appears to be a thing of the past. Despite the fact that paper graphs provide more resolution than flashers, LCR and video sonar units, this once-popular style of sonar isn't likely to regain any following soon.

Despite some practical features, paper graphs depending on a stylus to burn images into a roll of special paper. The smell of the burning paper was enough to turn off many anglers, but more importantly the cost of buying graph paper and the inconvenience of frequently changing the paper proved to be too many hurdles to overcome.

A few diehards still use paper graphs they have kept in service over the years, but no major manufacturer currently produces a paper graph.

UNDERWATER VIDEO CAMERAS

These days video cameras are everywhere. Even under the water! A wide variety of manufacturers are producing video equipment designed to explore the underwater world.

Essentially these units are downsized camera lenses mounted on a flexible cable. The lenses use infrared technology to display clear images in the low-light situations often encountered under water.

These amazing underwater video systems can provide anglers with a real-life view of what's under their boat. Depending on water clarity, the viewing area can include a considerable piece of real estate or a rather limited look into the gloomy depths.

The practicality of underwater video in bass fishing depends on who you talk to and how much time has been spent exploring with these units. There's little doubt that underwater video provides some not only interesting, but riveting images. The ability to see actual underwater images of fish, cover and bottom types satisfies a natural human curiosity if nothing else.

Underwater video isn't likely to displace sonar as the primary tool used by anglers to find fish. The biggest problem with video units is you have to watch them constantly to get the same information a LCR unit provides at a glance. Also, there is no practical way to swiftly deploy and recover the camera lens which is attached to a cable.

It's safe to say these products are a useful fishing tool, but it's also safe to say they appeal mostly to anglers who are simply curious and willing to dedicate the time to exploring with underwater video.

Should an underwater video camera be part of your bass fishing equipment list? That question is best answered by seeing these products in action and visiting with anglers who have taken the plunge.

A WORD ON GPS

In the electronics industry the real buzz isn't focused on sonar, but a relatively new technology known as Global Positioning Systems. This satellite-based navigational system is accurate, dependable, affordable, easy to use and it works anywhere in the world.

The value of GPS to bass fishermen can't be understated, especially those who frequently fish on large reservoirs or the sprawling waters of the Great Lakes.

Two basic types of GPS units are available: those that are based on a plotter screen and those with a built-in base map.

A GPS unit that uses a plotter screen essentially shows the current location on an otherwise open screen. This location is nor-

mally shown as a blinking icon. As the icon moves on the screen, a dotted line shows the direction of travel.

Other icons that represent important features can be added to the screen as permanently saved waypoints or as temporary icons often referred to as event markers. A waypoint is most often used to permanently mark features such as navigation aids, fishing spots, navigational hazards, etc. Event markers are used to identify features that may or may not be important in the future, such as the spot where a fish was caught or the edge of a weed line, sunken island or other potential fishing spot.

If an angler knows the latitude and longitude coordinates of a specific spot, these coordinates can be entered into the

A GPS unit on a bass boat was a rare event a few years ago. Today more anglers are realizing that GPS technology can help them catch more fish. This hand-held unit cost less than $200 and is fully portable.

machine, saved as a way-point and a compass bearing can be determined. Of course, to navigate to this bearing will require having an accurate compass. The best compass for this work is a deck-mounted and water-filled version that readily shows the compass bearings in degrees.

Plotter-style GPS units are sold in permanent models designed to be mounted to the console of a fishing boat, or hand-held versions that can be used in a wealth of situations.

The second type of GPS units are those with a built-in base map. Generally known as mapping units, instead of a blank plotter screen these units feature a detailed base map that can be zoomed in to achieve great detail or zoomed out to see your location in relation to other landmarks.

Most mapping units come with a fairly detailed base map that covers most of North America. Some mapping units offer more detailed regional maps that can be downloaded onto the GPS and stored as software.

Mapping units have some huge advantages over traditional plotter style GPS units. For one, a mapping unit makes it easier to determine your current location in relationship to other landmarks. Navigating to areas recognizable on the map is simple.

Also, with a mapping unit an angler can navigate to anywhere on the map without the benefit of having a latitude/longitude coordinate. Mapping units are also a safer navigation system for use in fog, darkness or other conditions that limit visibility, because potential hazards show up on the screen.

Commonly traveled navigation routes, marinas and many other points of interest are usually identified right on the mapping screen. Think of a GPS mapping unit as an electronic road map.

As with plotters, GPS mapping units are sold as permanently mounted products or as hand-held versions. Obviously plotter units are less expensive than mapping units. Some basic hand-held GPS units retail for

> *Mapping units have some huge advantages over traditional plotter-style GPS units.*

around $100. making them affordable to just about anyone who enjoys fishing. The more elaborate permanently mounted mapping units can cost up to 10 times as much.

Some GPS units are sold as combined sonar/GPS packages. In many cases these products can be an excellent value, but anglers must be careful to check the resolution of the sonar package. Sometimes the sonar units included in a sonar/GPS package leaves a little to be desired.

Despite the high cost of top-of-the-line GPS units, many anglers are finding these tools are instrumental in their fishing success.

OTHER INTERESTING TECHNOLOGY

Recently Minn Kota, the world's largest manufacturers of electric trolling motors announced they have new technology that allows built-in transducers to be offered as part of a select group of their trolling motors. Known as Universal Sonar, this new technology will allow anglers to use all the major brands of sonar with the built-in transducer provided with the trolling motor.

No more will it be necessary to rig an external transducer and wire to the bottom of the electric trolling motor. Lowrance, Techsonic Industries, Garmin and Computrol, Inc., have all signed working agreements with Minn Kota to make this technology an industry-wide success. The first models of electric motors with Universal Sonar will include the Genesis 55AP and 74AP models, Maxxum 50SC, 65 and 74 models and the AutoPilot 55 and 65 models. Retail on these new products is around $70 and anglers will need an accessory adapter plug that runs around $20.

SUMMARY

Unless some new technology suddenly pops up, bass anglers are likely to stick with flasher and LCR sonar units as their primary fish-finding tools. An angler skilled at using a flasher unit can learn everything he or she needs to know about water depth, bottom composition, the location of fish, bait fish and cover. Quality LCR sonar units provide an easier to interpret viewing screen, and for most anglers, are the practical sonar investment.

Underwater video systems offer a different approach to fishing electronics, but one that's not as efficient as either flashers or LCR units. For the time being, underwater video is likely to remain a supplement to traditional sonar use.

More and more bass anglers are discovering the advantages of owning a GPS system. More than simply a navigation aid, GPS units can be used to keep a permanent electronic record of countless fishing trips. Over time, a GPS unit enables anglers to collect and save invaluable fishing information.

Each year you see more GPS units on bass boats and this trend is no doubt going to continue. Mostly it's anglers who fish large bodies of water that invest in GPS, but anyone who fishes can benefit from this high-tech navigation system.

The next chapter tackles the bulging subject of bass boats.

A new dawn is shinning on fishing electronics. More sophisticated fishing and navigation sonar that's easier to use and less expensive has become the hallmark of the electronics industry.

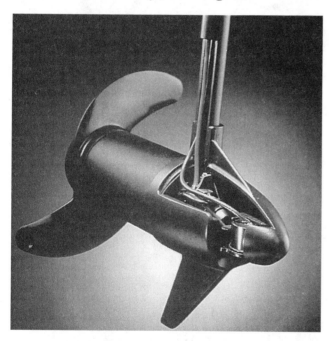

New technology from Minn Kota, known as universal sonar, enables anglers to use most popular sonar brands and models with a built-in transducer supplied with many models of Minn Kota trolling motors.

Scales and Tales   by: Bill McElroy

"YOU BETTER QUIT EATIN' THOSE BUBBLE GUM WORMS, PAL!!"

Bassin' with the Pros

CHAPTER 8

BOATS FOR BASS FISHING

The bass boat is a fishing icon. Recognized even by non-fishermen as a platform for bass fishing, these low-sided craft look like they're going 100 miles an hour standing still. Built to offer shallow draft, a stable fishing platform and water-covering speed, the bass boat can be credited as being the first "species specific" boat. Designed especially for the unique needs of tournament bass fishermen, the bass boat has become one of the most successful fishing boats in marine history.

The image of the bass boat is many things to many anglers. Models range from modest and affordable aluminum boats to fully decked out fiberglass pro tournament specials.

Owning a bass boat is like making a social class statement, not unlike owning a luxury car. For many, the American dream is to own a bass boat and a new pickup truck. Every serious bass angler either owns one of these boats or dreams of owning one. Country music artists sing about bass boats, professional anglers endorse them, dealers load their floor plan with all the popular brands and more than a few anglers mortgage everything they own to buy the ultimate fishing boat.

In some parts of America it appears anglers are lining up to experience the bass boat phenomenon! The strong economy we've enjoyed for the past decade is a major reason anglers have more money to spend and leisure time to justify owning big-ticket items like boats.

All this hasn't gone unnoticed by the marine industry. Take a look around at all the manufacturers producing bass boats. It's staggering how many brands and models are available. Just a few of the popular national brands include Nitro, Ranger, Champion, Bass Cat, ProCraft, Astro, Stratos, Triton, Tracker, Skeeter, Gambler and Fisher. Dozens of other major companies and countless regional boat builders are tapping into the bass boat market.

Aside from the manufacturers, boat dealers and bankers have got to be the biggest fans of bass boats. Even a modest model costs several months' salary and the professional tournament rigs are more expensive than the new pickup that pulls them!

Despite the high cost of owning and operating a bass boat, sales continue to skyrocket. The popularity of national, regional and local tournaments is a major reason why boat sales have continued to expand. Anglers fishing these events often start at the club level, then progress to regional events. A few gifted anglers eventually move up to the pro ranks.

> *Even a modest model costs several months' salary and the professional tournament rigs are more expensive than the new pickup that pulls them!*

As these anglers mature in their bass fishing skills, many upgrade their boats every year or every other year. Some of the top pros purchase, use and later sell two boats per year.

FIBERGLASS OR ALUMINUM?

The first question anyone serious about purchasing a bass boat must ask is, "Do I want an aluminum or fiberglass hull?" The answer to this question depends on how much money can be invested in a boat, how often the boat will be used, what types of water will most often be fished and, to a degree, the level of creature comforts the owner is looking for.

It's a foregone conclusion in the boat building industry that fiberglass boats provide the ultimate in speed, performance and appearance while aluminum boats offer the best value for the dollar. This fact stated, it's also important to note that not every angler needs or would benefit from a performance style bass boat. Aluminum boats fill an important niche in the fishing boat industry.

Aluminum bass boats tend to be entry-level products that are designed either for casual fishing or for smaller bodies of water where long runs are not required to reach the fishing grounds. In terms of the value for the dollar spent, it's tough to beat the practical and functional aspects of these boats.

Most aluminum bass boats range in size from 15 to 18 feet and are rated to handle outboard motors from 25 to 75 horsepower. A few models are designed to accept larger outboards up to the powerful V6 motors.

Anglers can choose from both riveted and welded models. Riveted boats tend to be the smaller and less expensive models. Welded aluminum bass boats are available in all the popular sizes and they cost only slightly more than riveted models.

The features and creature comforts offered inside these boats can range widely. Many models are bare bones jobs that offer little beyond a basic livewell, bolt-on console and rod locker. At the other extreme are elite packages that provide aerated livewells with recirculation systems and timers, marine-grade carpet throughout, built-in charging units, lighted rod lockers and dry storage, molded-in coolers, air-ride seats and just about any other feature offered with professional tournament-grade boats.

Next to price, one of the biggest advantages of owning an aluminum boat is towing convenience. These boats tend to be lighter making them more suitable for small tow vehicles such as a mini-van or a passenger car. Aluminum boats are also a little more economical to operate since they are usually equipped with more modest outboards.

The biggest disadvantage of owning an aluminum boat is felt in the performance category. Aluminum boats simply aren't as fast as fiberglass hulls or as capable of handling rough water smoothly. Also, the horsepower ratings and suggested load limits of aluminum boats tend to be modest compared to similar sized fiberglass boats.

However, these disadvantages are becoming less of an issue as better aluminum boat designs are introduced.

NEW ALUMINUM BOAT TECHNOLOGY

Historically, aluminum boats have been made from panels or sheets of aluminum that are either riveted or welded together. The thickness of these panels ranges from .060 to .100, depending on the size of the boat.

One of the first questions an angler interested in purchasing a bass boat must ask himself is do I want aluminum or fiberglass? Aluminum models range from a modest boat such as this to larger boats with many more features.

The shape of the hull has been limited to flat bottoms and modified "V" designs that tend to be both rough-riding and wet boats.

"Tracker Marine's new Millennium project is changing the way aluminum boats are designed and built," says Bob Goad, Tracker's Project Manager. "Using patented construction techniques developed from the aerospace and automobile industries, we have changed the way aluminum boats are built, the way they look and perform."

Tracker built a whole new factory just to manufacture these boats. The first model to be completed is an 18-foot bass boat to be called the Avalanche. This state-of-the-art aluminum boat looks and performs unlike any other boat ever built from aluminum.

"What sets these boats aside begins with the materials used in construction," says Goad. "Sheets of marine grade aluminum a full .125 (1/8 inch) thick are used in the hull, side decks, transom and gunwales."

A patented process known as Stretch-Drawing is used to form the hull and sides of the boat, adds Goad. "Instead of the traditional flat bottom designs associated with aluminum boats, the Avalanche features smooth lines, curves and radiuses similar to fiberglass boats. Even the keel and strakes are molded into the hulls, not welded or riveted on."

The transom and stringers are formed using another patented process known as Draw-Stamping that yields the ultimate in precision fit and strength. A third manufacturing process known as Stretch-Wrapping is used to extrude the gunwale from one piece of aluminum. All major metal-to-metal parts including the hull, transom, sides, stringers and gunwales are welded using robotic welding machines similar to those used in the automobile industry. The results of these special manufacturing pro-

Inherent strength and the ability to be formed into desired radiuses and curves is the primary reason fiberglass has become the leading material used in performance bass boat design.

cesses yields an aluminum boat that's super tough and one that meets or exceeds the performance of similar fiberglass models.

"Performance on these new boats is something to see," says Goad. "The Avalanche is quick out of the hole, smooth and as fast as compatible fiberglass models. Because these boats are lighter than fiberglass boats, maximum performance can be achieved with smaller and more economical outboards. Also, these boats can be easily towed without having to depend on a full-sized truck, van or SUV."

Automobile paints are used to color match boats and tow vehicles making for a classy look previously reserved for fiberglass hulls. No doubt the Millennium series boats produced by Tracker are going to change the way aluminum boats are built and the way customers look at aluminum. For the first time, aluminum boats offer style, strength, function, value and performance in the same package.

FIBERGLASS

Fiberglass is one tough boat-building material. Amazing as it seems that anything with the word glass in it could be tough, fiberglass is actually stronger than aluminum in many ways. The strength of fiberglass comes from unique properties and overlaying fibers that allow this material to flex repeatedly under stress without damage. When metal, such as aluminum, is flexed over and over again, metal fatigue eventually leads to failures.

Fiberglass also has the advantage of being easily molded to just about any shape. Inherent strength and the ability to be formed into desired radiuses and curves is the primary reason fiberglass has become the leading material used in performance bass boat design.

In addition to being strong and adaptable to a variety of shapes, fiberglass allows the application of the highest quality finishes. Both gelcoat and metal-flake finishes are striking, giving fiberglass boats the edge in the looks department.

Should a fiberglass boat become damaged, the repair work is simply a matter of grinding away the damaged material, then replacing the damaged fiberglass with a matching gelcoat color or metal-flake pattern. A technician skilled at fiberglass repair can return a damaged boat to like-new condition. With aluminum boats, repairing damaged areas to the original strength and finish is all but impossible.

Fiberglass bass boats range in size from modest entry-level boats in the 15- to 16-foot class to monster boats exceeding 22 feet in length and sporting unlimited horsepower ratings. For many years the size of bass boats was somewhat regulated by the horsepower restrictions put in place by the major

bass tournament circuits. Until recently, boats used in many of these tournaments had to have a 150-horsepower motor or smaller.

To achieve the maximum performance from the 150-horse V6 outboard, boat manufacturers put most of their design emphasis into 18- to 19-foot boats. Now that these horsepower restrictions have been lifted, boat manufacturers are designing longer and wider models every year.

As you might expect, the typical tournament bass boat has also jumped in size. Tournament anglers want big boats that are fast, stable, able to run rough water and provide lots of fishing room. Today the most common sizes for tournament boats are 19- to 21-foot models equipped with 200- to 225-horsepower outboards.

As with aluminum boats, the options selected on a fiberglass model have a strong influence on the final price tag. Normally fiberglass boats have more standard

Fiberglass bass boats represent the ultimate in quality, strength and performance.

features than similar aluminum boats. The reason for this is because anglers who purchase fiberglass are normally buying their first boat. When an angler steps up to fiberglass he or she is normally more willing to pay extra for some creature comforts such as storage lids with power piston hinges, lighted dry storage, built-in charging systems, aeration and recirculation systems with timers, deluxe seats, premium carpets, custom covers and a wealth of other options.

Despite the advancements in aluminum boat building technology, fiberglass is likely to remain the leader in performance boat designs. Tournament pros and those who use their boats often are the primary advocates of fiberglass boats. Customer satisfaction is a major reason fiberglass boats aren't likely to become obsolete anytime soon. Tens of thousands of anglers have had satisfying and rewarding experiences with fiberglass boats. Most of these anglers are likely to buy fiberglass boats again.

MULTI-FUNCTION BOATS

The typical bass boat is designed for a specific purpose. Many anglers however are looking for a boat that can be used for a wide variety of fishing and even hunting situations.

In recent years a number of excellent multi-use boats have hit the market. Ideal for fishing bass, panfish, catfish and for duck hunting, this new category of boats has made some major waves in the marine industry.

Most multi-function boats are built on welded aluminum hulls ranging in size from 14 to 20 feet. Some of the leaders in this cat-

This War Eagle boat is an example of a multi-use boat to meet both the needs of anglers and hunters.

egory offer their customers boats that can be easily converted from fishing to hunting machines.

War Eagle is one of the leading manufacturers of multi-function boats. The War Eagle boat accepts a wide variety of accessories including consoles, rod storage boxes, livewells, lights, rod holders and gun boxes. A track welded to the gunwale allows these accessories to be slid into place and secured with wing nuts in minutes. A fully rigged boat for bass or panfishing can be converted to the ultimate duck hunting blind in less time than it takes to change a spare tire.

Multi-function boats are normally offered in an olive drab finish, but many manufacturers offer custom painted finishes featuring the most popular camouflage patterns.

A few of the manufacturers who specialize in multi-function boats include War Eagle, Polar Kraft, SeaArk, Tracker and Go-Devil.

BUYING A USED BOAT

With so many anglers upgrading and purchasing new boats, the boat market is flooded with a wide variety of excellent quality used boats. Buying a used bass boat is no different than buying a used vehicle. Some deals are good and others are problems waiting to happen.

When shopping for a used boat, the most important consideration is how much service the boat has seen. Bass boats and motors wear out just like cars wear out. The more service a boat has had, the greater the chances the new owner will inherit problems.

Like cars and trucks, boats depreciate in value quickly. A 1-year-old bass boat in excellent condition will sell for several thousand dollars less than the same boat would sell for new. Often, the best buys are those nearly new boats that were used for a season and then traded for a newer or larger model. Depending on the manufacturer, some of the warranty features may even be transferable to the new owner.

The older a boat becomes, the more the new owner is likely to experience problems ranging from minor problems with switches, pumps and lights, to major engine repairs and hull damage. All this must be taken into consideration and weighed against the asking price before making a purchase decision.

Buying a used boat from a dealer or professional angler should begin with a test ride to insure everything is working properly.

BUYING DEMOS AND PRO BOATS

Most dealers have a limited number of demo boats for sale each year. Normally these boats see very little time on the water. Many are boats the owner of a dealership personally uses or boats that are used in special events such as celebrity tournaments. Most of the major manufacturers of bass boats host special promotional tournaments, then sell the boats used in these tournaments for a discount after the event.

To a potential boat buyer looking for a bargain, these limited opportunities can spell out major savings. Buying a boat from a professional tournament angler can also be a good way to say a few bucks on an almost new boat. Most professional anglers take great pride in keeping their boats in top condition. Those who don't are easy to weed out. One quick look at a used boat will tell if the owner abuses his boats. Warning signs are lots of gelcoat cracks in the hull, sides and top decks. Look especially close in the corners of the boat near the transom for these stress cracks that indicate hard use.

A few minor cracks are nothing to be concerned with, but if a boat has lots of these hairline cracks look out. With traditional outboards it's impossible to tell how many hours the motor has been operated. Newer motors such as Mercury's Opti-Max outboards have a built-in computer that logs not only the operation hours, but also records the RPM's throughout the motor's life. Any good marine mechanic can check this computer record and tell if the motor was run hard and put away wet.

Go slowly however when shopping. Make sure the boat is in excellent condition before taking delivery.

Like demo boats, only a limited number of pro boats are available. Many pros have their "old" boat sold even before they take delivery of a new one. A simple contract is drawn up between the pro angler and the new buyer that outlines the selling price, boat condition upon delivery and projected delivery date. Normally the buyer pays a 10 percent deposit to secure the agreement.

BATTERIES, PROPS AND OTHER IMPORTANT ACCESSORIES

A fishing boat is only as good as its batteries. It's not gasoline that's the life blood of a fishing boat, but the electric spark made possible by the battery. Without this simple electrical spark, combustion engines would be expensive anchors.

Ironically, batteries are the one area where most dealers and the customers who purchase boats try to cut corners and save pennies. A typical bass boat is equipped with a marine cranking battery that generates around 500 cold cranking amps of starting power. This is more than enough to start the outboard, but what happens when other amp-drawing accessories are added to the picture.

Don't scrimp on the cranking battery used in a bass boat. This battery must not only start the outboard, but also run a wealth of accessories.

The cranking battery must also power navigation lights, livewell pumps, recirculation pumps, bilge pumps and electronics such as sonar units, radios and GPS units. Collectively, the amp draw of these items is more than an ordinary 500 amp battery can withstand. Sooner or later the angler is going to hit the key and realize he's dealing with a dead battery.

To solve this problem anglers are strongly advised to upgrade to a stronger battery. A battery that generates 750 to 1,000 cold cranking amps is more suitable for a full-service bass boat.

The other batteries in a bass boat are used to power the electric trolling motor. These batteries are deep-cycle models that are designed not to offer quick starting power, but rather longevity of power.

Again the more amps of power the battery offers, the longer the accessories linked to it will function. Deep-cycle batteries are rated by the amp hours of service they provide. Cutting a corner here translates directly into less fishing time.

Think of the power in a deep-cycle battery like the fuel in a gas tank. When you're getting ready to leave for a major trip, you want to start out with a full tank and the more gallons on board the better.

If the vehicle you use to tow your boat only had a 10-gallon fuel tank, it would be necessary to stop and gas up constantly. The same is true of deep-cycle batteries. Select a model that offers the maximum amp hours of service and the time you spend on the water will be longer and more trouble-free.

The largest bass boats that are equipped with 36-volt electric motors require three batteries to operate this accessory. It's possible to wire two deep-cycle and one marine cranking battery together to achieve the 36 volts required, but this puts an unusual strain on the cranking battery. It's best to purchase and mount three deep-cycle batteries and wire the electric motor accordingly.

Motor props are another essential item on a bass boat. Most boat performance problems have nothing to do with the motor or the hull. Selecting the wrong prop is the most common reason anglers experience performance problems such as slow hole-shot (initial starting speeds to you going quickly) and porpoising.

The manufacturers of outboard motors provide prop recommendations for each size of outboard. However, these guidelines are just that; guidelines. The total weight of the boat and which hole the outboard is mounted on can make a huge difference in the final performance.

Most performance bass boats are best equipped with a stainless steel prop. Stainless is used on high-torque outboards because steel is stiffer and the blades of the prop flex less under power. An aluminum prop has a considerable amount of flex under power causing the prop to decrease in size and push less water.

Most high-performance bass boats require a stainless steel prop. Stainless props have less flex than aluminum and therefore more ability to generate maximum bow lift, speed and performance.

Aluminum props are a good choice for smaller boats, but full-sized bass boats cry out for stainless props. The three most common types of stainless props are three-, four- and five-blade models.

Three-blade props provide the most top-end speed, while five-blade props have the fastest holeshot and best ability to carry heavy loads. As you would imagine, four-blade props are a compromise of these features.

Props are also rated by pitch, a number that's normally stamped right on the side of the prop. Pitch relates to how far the boat is moved for each rotation of the prop. For example a 21-pitch prop pushes the boat 21 inches forward for each revolution.

The perfect prop is one that runs at or near the outboard manufacturer's RPM recommendations at top-end speed. If the prop turns fewer RPM's, speed and performance are sacrificed. If the prop turns more than the recommended RPM's, damage can occur to the motor.

There's no perfect way to pick props except to bolt one on and give it a try. Unfortunately, props cost upwards of $500 each. Many dealers will let customers try different props, but remember if you ding it, you've bought it.

Setback plates are another performance item commonly seen on bass boats. A setback plate simply mounts to the transom and positions the motor a little farther away from the transom. The overall length of the boat is increased and the boat's ability to maximize speed and performance is enhanced. Most of these plates are adjustable for both the depth the motor rests in the water and also the angle of pitch.

The extra speed a setback plate provides varies depending on the amount of setback, boat weight and type of prop. Normally a setback will allow the boat owner to pick up as much as 5 miles per hour more on top-end speed and a faster holeshot.

Both fixed and hydraulic plates are available that range in price from a few hundred dollars to a couple thousand bucks.

Bass boats and the accessories made for them represent a major investment. It's not uncommon for fully rigged boats to end up costing $40,000! The average tournament-style boat however retails for around $20,000.

In the next chapter we'll investigate the primary senses of a bass. Read on and discover how scent, sound and sight impact on bass fishing.

> *Normally a setback will allow the boat owner to pick up as much as 5 miles per hour more on top-end speed and a faster holeshot.*

This boat features a built-in setback. Bolt on setback plates are now popular after-market items because they improve the performance of most boats.

Bassin' with the Pros

CHAPTER 9

SOUND, SCENT AND SIGHT

Catching a bass boils down to appealing to the one of the fish's three highly refined senses. All species of bass enjoy a highly tuned sensory system that allows them to see, smell and hear their favorite foods. Not only are bass capable predators, their ability to find and catch food in adverse conditions is nothing short of astonishing.

To test the adaptability of bass, researchers have temporarily blinded bass using small disks that fit over the eyes. In only a short time, these fish adjust to the loss of sight and feed effectively by using their remaining senses. These simple experiments prove that bass do not depend on one primary sense when hunting, but rather a complex mix of senses that help them locate food.

It's also important to note that bass are opportunistic feeders. It's often written that bass prefer to eat crayfish. This may be true, but a bass won't turn down a shiner minnow that happens by simply because the lake is full of crayfish.

All primary predators such as bass survive by being opportunistic hunters. If a particular food source is especially abundant or

easy to catch these fish will undoubtedly key on a readily available forage type. However, it's foolish to think that bass become so selective at feeding that they will only strike lures that resemble their primary or preferred forage.

THE LATERAL LINE SENSE

A bass uses every one of its sensory organs when hunting, but one sense ranks as the most unique. The lateral line is a sensory organ that works in cooperation with hearing. The lateral line is barely visible to the eye. Upon close inspection you'll note a faint line runs from the top of the fish's gill cover to the caudal fin.

Beneath the skin the lateral line appears as a thin band of dark flesh. This is the dark meat many anglers fillet away when cleaning a fish.

The lateral line works hand-in-hand with the inner ear, although both sensory organs function separately. The ears of a bass are located under the skin and have no external hole. Sounds are transmitted through the skin, muscle and bone to the inner ear. Primarily the inner ear is used to detect more distant sounds.

Despite some limitations, a bass' sense of hearing is much more acute than that of a human. Also, sound travels through water five times faster than in air. It's safe to assume that bass can hear the common sounds made by anglers at significant distances. Banging a tackle box against the side of the boat, dropping an anchor overboard or slamming the lid on a dry storage compartment is sure to

Bass depend heavily on the lateral line sense when hunting in dirty or off-color water, to navigate among unfamiliar cover and to avoid predators.

alert every bass in the area.

The lateral line sense picks up where the inner ear leaves off. This form of hearing works by absorbing vibrations from the water and transforming them into a highly complex network of information. Open nerve endings located just below the skin collect this information and pass it onto the brain.

The lateral line is primarily used as a short-range tool for determining from which direction sound is coming. Research suggests that the lateral line sense is most acute out to a distance of approximately 20 feet. Other important hunting and survival variables can also be determined with the lateral line.

For example, a bass can tell the relative size of a fish or minnow that's making vibrations in the water. This is a handy tool for determining if the vibrations are the dinner bell or an alert to an approaching predator.

In addition the bass can also tell the distance to the source of the vibrations and the relative direction of travel. In short, to a bass the lateral line sense is like having built-in short-range radar. Bass depend heavily on the lateral line sense when hunting in dirty or off-color water, to navigate among unfamiliar cover and to avoid predators.

EYESIGHT

Bass have good eyesight, but they don't depend on the sense of sight as much as many anglers believe. Bass, most fish for that matter, are nearsighted. In other words, a bass can see

Bass use a combination of hearing, smell, sight and even taste to help them locate and select food.

little in the way of details until the object is right under his nose.

Obviously the clarity of the water determines in part how far a bass can see. Even in clear water it's unlikely that bass can see anything significant beyond 15 or 20 feet.

Bass can however see movement and shadows at greater distances, even those that occur above the water. If the water surface is calm, a bass in shallow water can easily detect an angler casting or moving about the boat at shorter casting distances.

Despite what could be called poor eyesight, bass compensate by having almost microscopic vision at close range. When a bass has the luxury of viewing a slow-moving lure at close range, only the lures with the most natural appearance are likely to stimulate a strike response.

Anglers can benefit from this knowledge by matching up lures and fishing styles. Artificial baits such as grubs, weedless jigs or plastic worms are examples of lures that appear natural in the water and are hard for bass to refuse. Normally these lures are fished rather slowly in an effort to present an irresistible temptation to bass.

More mechanical lures such as spinnerbaits, buzzbaits or crankbaits function best when retrieved quickly enough that the bass doesn't have the opportunity to scrutinize them. Instead of teasing a strike, these fast-moving lures stimulate a reactionary strike response.

COLOR VISION

If bass have microscopic close-range vision, it stands to reason that color can be an important fishing variable. Researchers have determined that bass have the ability to detect even subtle variations in color. Bass have even been trained to strike a particular color of lure.

Despite these interesting experiments, there's no practical way for an angler to

> *We may never fully understand how color impacts bass fishing, but we can adjust when it becomes obvious that one color is working better than another.*

determine which colors are likely to stimulate strikes. There's also no proof that lure color is critical to fishing success. In fact, most knowledgeable anglers have come to the conclusion that color is less important than other fishing variables such as depth, lure speed and lure action.

Taking the practical path to choosing lure color is perhaps the best solution to this on-going problem. When fishing in clear waters it makes sense to use more natural or subdued colors that bass are used to seeing. In very dirty water the brightest fluorescent and dark colors show up best and are therefore most likely to be seen by bass and to stimulate a positive reaction.

Stained water is the middle ground that anglers are faced with most often. It's here that both ends of the color spectrum can be used effectively and no clear choices exist. One way to attack this situation is to select lures that feature two or more colors. Multi-colored lures have more contrast than solid-color baits and are easier to spot.

Regardless of how much care is given to lure color selection, there are going to be days when the rules of common sense don't seem to apply. We've all seen days when fluorescent colors worked better in clear water than more natural and subdued colors. We may never fully understand how color impacts bass fishing, but we can adjust when it becomes obvious that one color is working better than another. Be observant when experimenting with color and don't be afraid to make a change if the situation warrants it.

It makes sense to experiment with color while fishing, but be cautious not to let color become the primary focus of your fishing strategy.

SMELL

We've saved the bass's most refined sense for last. The olfactory region is the largest portion of a bass's brain. Obviously, bass depend heavily on their olfactory sense.

Bass, like many other fish, are able to smell at a level we can only imagine. Two nostrils are located on each side of their snout. Water flowing into these openings is exposed to highly sensitive olfactory nerve endings.

We know that bass and many other species of fish can detect odors down to the parts per million. Not only can a bass detect minute odors in the water, they can also quickly tell the direction from which a scent is coming.

The sense of smell is one of the strongest tools a bass uses to find food, avoid predators, locate spawning sites and find suitable mates. Some biologists believe bass even use scent as a means of finding preferred cover types.

> **More money has been invested in producing "fishing scents" than just about any other aspect of bass fishing.**

More money has been invested in producing "fishing scents" than just about any other aspect of bass fishing. Most of these scent products are either cover scents or attractants. Cover scents are not used solely to attract bass, but rather to cover or disguise unwanted odors that can find their way onto fishing lures. Human scent, gas, oil, suntan lotion and fish blood are just a few of the odors that can prevent bass from striking at a lure.

Attractants are scent products that mimic naturally occurring odors bass are used to. Some of the most popular scents are actually extracted from common bass forages such as shad or crayfish.

The first scent products were liquids. They could be squirted onto the lure or the lure could be dipped into the scent. Scent products today come in a wide variety of easily dispersed forms including liquids, pastes, gels, aerosols and rub-on sticks.

Perhaps the most sophisticated form of fishing scents are the many soft plastic lures with scent impregnated right into the bait. Injecting salt into the plastic was one of the first attempts at making the use of scent more convenient to use and effective. Salt- and/or garlic-impregnated plastic lures are still in wide use today and most soft plastics are produced with added salt, garlic or both.

A few years ago Outdoor Technologies Group (now known

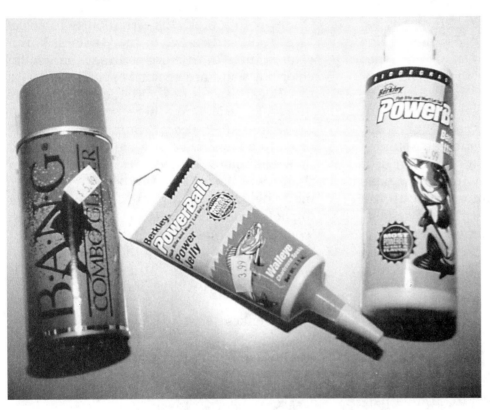

Bass, more so than other species of fish, use their highly developed sense of smell to locate food. Fish attractants are designed to both stimulate strikes and to cause bass to hang onto artificial lures longer.

Scent-impregnated soft plastic lures are widely accepted among bass anglers.

as Pure Fishing) shocked the fishing industry when they released their Berkley Powerbait soft plastic lures. The next step in the evolution of fishing scents, Powerbait was the first soft plastic lure made from a special plastic that includes both scent- and flavor-enhancers. The concept is simple; bass are more likely to strike and hang onto lures that smell and taste like something good to eat.

Powerbait has become enormously successful and a number of other soft plastic lure manufacturers have followed suit with similar products. A few of the most noteworthy include Bass Pro Shops Yum, Chompers G Formula and Gotta Bite produced by Riverside Lures. The same scent used in these soft plastics can also be purchased in bottle form and applied to jigs, spinnerbaits, crankbaits and other lures.

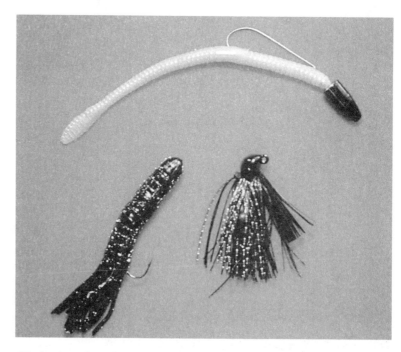

Understanding how bass relate to lure groups can help anglers catch more fish. Jigs, Texas rigs and other soft plastic lures function best when fished slowly and in clear water conditions.

Sound, Scent and Sight

Scented soft plastic lures have made an enormous impact on the bass fishing scene. For many anglers these lures have become the confidence baits they depend on when fishing is tough or when cash is on the line. Scented plastics are offered in virtually every lure type a bass angler could want including grubs, tubes, craws, worms, spinnerbait trailers, jig trailers, lizards and on and on.

THE ZONE OF AWARENESS

Based on all the hype surrounding add-on fishing scents and scent-impregnated

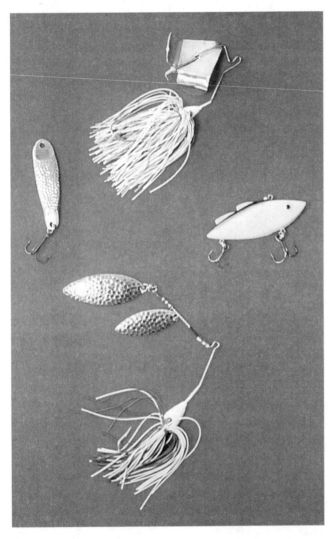

Fast-moving lures such as spinnerbaits, cranks, spoons and buzzbaits are reactionary lures that work best when fished quickly enough that bass don't have the opportunity to get a good look at them.

lures, one might conclude that these products are the answer to catching more bass. Indeed, scent can play an important role in triggering bass into striking and can also stimulate bass into hanging onto these lures longer than unscented models.

Lures that make appealing sounds can also attract bass. The same could be said for lures with colors bass seem to favor. But the problem is the same with all these fishing stimuli: A bass can not detect smells, tastes, sounds or colors at great distances no matter how appealing they may be.

Bass and other fish monitor a limited area surrounding them. This zone of awareness varies in size depending on a number of constantly changing factors such as water clarity, light intensity, surface distortion, and even current. Things within this zone of awareness can be readily heard, seen or smelled by bass. Objects outside this zone of awareness are largely ignored.

No matter how good a fishing lure is, how tasty it smells, what interesting sounds it makes or what color it is, bass are simply not going to detect baits positioned outside this critical zone of awareness. All of the senses a bass routinely uses to locate forage are limited to short-range use.

No matter how you slice it, the angler is ultimately responsible for first locating fish and then presenting a bait close enough to stimulate a strike. Can using lures with appealing scent, sound, taste and color help when bass fishing? Absolutely! Unfortunately, none of these often over-emphasized stimuli are foolproof shortcuts to better fishing.

To catch more bass anglers must accept the limitations of the zone of awareness and strive to present their lures as close to fish as possible.

In Chapter Ten we begin our look at the common lures and presentations used to catch bass. Heading the list is the spinnerbait, which ranks as the most commonly used lure in bass fishing. You'll see why this lure is so popular in the coming pages.

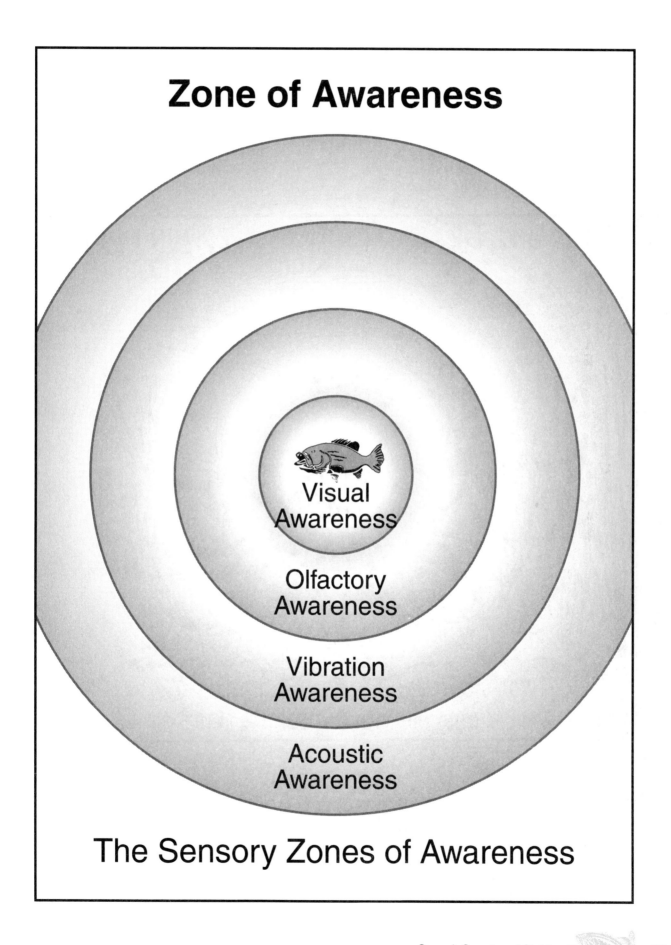

Zone of Awareness

Visual
Awareness

Olfactory
Awareness

Vibration
Awareness

Acoustic
Awareness

The Sensory Zones of Awareness

Bassin' with the Pros

CHAPTER 10

KEVIN VANDAM AND WOO DAVES TALK SPINNERBAITS

Without question, a spinnerbait is the fastest way to contact bass on just about any water. The speed at which these lures are fished has made the spinnerbait the leading choice among tournament anglers who must cover huge amounts of water in pursuit of active fish. No other lure can cover water faster than a spinnerbait. Just ask bass fishing tournament legend Kevin VanDam. This three-time B.A.S.S. Angler-of-the-Year loves spinnerbaits.

"They match my fishing style. I like to move fast and cover water while looking for the most active fish. I consider spinnerbaits to be like little search-and-destroy missiles because they not only cover water quickly, they can be used to fish a wide variety of cover types and just about any type of water from gin-clear to muddy," says VanDam.

In addition to being ideal for covering water, spinnerbaits are deadly in a wide variety of fishing situations. Effective in most types of aquatic vegetation, spinnerbaits can also be worked in and among a wide variety of other cover types.

Getting the most from these lures requires the angler to understand why they trigger so many strikes. Spinnerbaits don't work because they look like something a bass has eaten before. On the contrary, spinnerbaits are perhaps the least natural appearing lures commonly used to catch bass. A spinnerbait is deadly because the flashing blades and vibration created arouses an instinctive strike response.

"Spinnerbaits work best when they are fished in such a manner that the fish only gets a quick look at the bait," says VanDam, who prefers to fish spinnerbaits over all other lures.

A spinnerbait can be fished on just about any type of rod and reel, but most anglers will find a baitcasting outfit the ideal choice. "I use three different rods for fishing spinnerbaits," says Van-Dam. "All three rods are 6-1/2-foot triggersticks. I simply change the action to match the size spinnerbait being fished. For 1/4- to 3/8-ounce lures I favor a medium action rod with a fast tip. If I'm throwing 1/2-ounce or larger baits I'll use a medium/heavy action rod. For the new extra heavy spinnerbaits that weigh an ounce or more, a heavy action rod is required."

When fishing spinnerbaits it's important to understand that water clarity determines the colors, size and types of spinnerbaits that are most likely to produce.

VanDam uses his signature series Quantum 6:1 high speed baitcasting reel for all three rods. "Much of the time when I'm fishing a spinnerbait I'm throwing at targets. Once the lure passes the target I burn the bait back to the boat and cast again. A fast retrieve ratio is the only way to go, even when slow rolling a bait in deeper water."

When it comes to fishing lines, VanDam breaks from tradition. "It's critical to use a

Several years ago the author caught this bass while fishing with Woo Daves on Lake Sam Rayburn. A spinnerbait was used to fish among flooded brush.

Three-time Angler of the Year, Kevin VanDam ranks spinnerbaits as his most important bass fishing lure.

line with low stretch, but high abrasion resistance when fishing a spinnerbait," says VanDam. "You can't beat the new fluorocarbon lines when it comes to these characteristics. Unfortunately, not all the fluorocarbon lines are manageable enough to fish with. I prefer Bass Pro Shops XPS fluorocarbon."

> *"In stained or off-color water I select a larger lure, slow down my presentation, switch to brighter colors and increase blade size."*

The most popular size fishing line for spinnerbait fishing is 17-pound test. "You don't want light line for spinnerbait fishing unless you're trying to reach exceptionally deep water," advises VanDam. "This style of fishing is always taking place around cover that chews line to bits. Since the line diameter doesn't influence on the action of the lure or the number of bites, be safe and use at least 17-pound test."

When fishing spinnerbaits it's important to understand that water clarity determines the colors, size and types of spinnerbaits that are most likely to produce.

"When I'm faced with clear water, I select spinnerbaits that are small, natural in color and I fish them fast so bass don't get a good look at them." comments VanDam. "In stained or off-color water I select a larger lure, slow down my presentation, switch to brighter colors and increase blade size. In dirty water, I use the brightest colors and largest blade combinations fished as slow as possible."

VanDam defines water with less than 6 inches of visibility as muddy, visibility from 6 to 18 inches as stained and visibility greater than 18 inches as clear.

The blade combinations used also have a dramatic impact on spinnerbait success. "You have to understand how different blades function in the water to get the most from a spinnerbait," cautions VanDam. "For example a Colorado-style blade displaces the most water and puts out the most flash and vibration. Because of the water displaced, these baits tend to come to the surface when fished fast. This style of spinnerbait excels best in cold water and slower retrieve speeds."

At the other end of the spectrum, willow leaf blades displace the least amount of water. "A willow leaf blade has the advantage of giving off a lot of flash, but because the water displacement is less the lure can be fished fast and in deeper water," explains VanDam. "I use willow blades during the summer when I'm fishing in warm water and moving the bait as quickly as possible."

VanDam has his own signature series of Quantum rods and reels including several triggersticks ideal for casting spinnerbaits.

Fluttering a Spinner Bait

Just prior to a spinner bait contacting cover such as a laydown, VanDam pauses the bait and lets it flutter downward.

To Rod

Pause
Flutter

On a Cliff or Steep Drop

Daves often uses heavy
spinnerbaits to work cliffs and
other deep water structure.

Bassin' with the Pros

In stained or dirty water VanDam recommends using brightly colored spinnerbaits with large blades. In clear water he downsizes his lures and chooses more natural shades.

These are just a few of the blade types and colors frequently used on spinnerbaits.

The third common style of spinnerbait blade is the Indiana style. "Indiana blades are the in between choice," says VanDam. "I use this blade type mostly in stained water and as a medium-speed bait. This blade type also works well in dirty water when the water is warm."

By varying blade styles, sizes and head weights spinnerbait combinations can be created to fish just about any situation from buzzing along the surface to slow rolling in deep water. "For horizontal presentations I favor a spinnerbait with tandem blades that give off the maximum amount of flash," says VanDam. "Say for example I'm fishing a spinnerbait over the top of weed cover in mid-summer, I'm going to pick one with tandem willow blades that allows me to burn the bait right across the surface. If I'm fishing a shallow-water situation where the water is dirty or cold, I'll pick a Colorado blade model that forces me to fish slower. If I need to fish near bottom in cold and deeper water, I'll use a small Colorado blade matched up to a large size head. The combinations possible are endless."

Selecting spinnerbait colors is similar to choosing the colors for other lure types. VanDam favors more natural colors with lots of tinsel or metal flake to add flash when fishing clear waters. Good examples are shads and the many translucent colors.

In stained waters, brighter colors such as chartreuse or pearl are more visible. In the most stained or dirty waters fluorescent shades including orange, green, yellow and red are going to be the most visible. Black is also a good color to use in dirty water.

The same rules apply to blade colors. Silver chrome is best in clear water, brass or copper the best choice in stained waters and brightly painted blades tops in dirty water.

"If the water is clear or stained, sometimes I'll try and pick a spinnerbait color that matches forage fish," says VanDam. "During the spawn I like to use sunfish or bluegill patterns since these fish are always hanging around bass nests."

It would be impractical to carry enough spinnerbaits to meet every fishing condition an angler may encounter. "I carry a bag full of different blade sizes, styles and colors with swivels already attached," says VanDam. "When I need to make a blade change, I simply bend open the wire on the spinnerbait using a pair of needle nose pliers, replace the blade and swivel and bend the wire closed again."

> *"During the spawn I like to use sunfish or bluegill patterns since these fish are always hanging around bass nests."*

This on-the-water quick change allows Van-Dam to carry and produce hundreds of potential spinnerbait combinations. "At any given time I carry enough components on board to make several hundred spinnerbaits," says VanDam. "To meet all the situations an angler is likely to encounter you'll need at least 75 to 100 different baits."

When traveling on the tour, VanDam carries a huge assortment of spinnerbaits and components. He fishes exclusively Strike King spinnerbaits and has helped to design several models. "With all the blade sizes, shapes and colors I carry, I could make a thousand or more spinnerbait combinations."

Surprisingly, VanDam isn't a big fan of the new Titanium spinnerbaits. "The wire on these baits is softer and they don't give out as good a vibration as steel wire spinnerbaits," says VanDam. "I like Titanium baits for smallmouth because they stay in tune well, but when I'm fishing largemouth around laydowns and other cover types I still favor the traditional steel wire style spinnerbait. I'd say that 75 percent of my fishing is still with steel wire spinnerbaits and only 25 percent with Titanium."

A good first cast is also important. "I strive for a cast that's accurate and that quietly presents the bait into the water," says VanDam. "If I'm fishing an obvious target such as an exposed stump, I target my cast to hit right on the spot I expect the fish to be hiding. When the bait hits, I let it flutter down on a slack line for a few seconds before starting the retrieve. Most of the strikes come within a couple seconds of splash down."

To make blade changes easier on the water, VanDam carries an assortment of blade shapes and sizes with ball bearing swivels already attached. Using a pair of pliers he opens up the wire arm on the spinnerbait, replaces the blade with a different shape, size or color and bends the wire shut again.

Understanding how bass relate to a spinnerbait helps VanDam catch more fish. "It's important to hit the target on the first try," says VanDam. "Don't cast past the target and retrieve the lure into position. As the bait is moving through the water it's displacing water and sending out flash and vibration that alerts the bass something is coming. Spinnerbaits catch more fish when they take the bass by surprise."

VanDam says the secret to better spinnerbait success is making sure the bait

> *A spinnerbait is much like a crankbait in that these lures are most often fished fast and they perform best when the lure hits and rebounds off cover.*

stays in contact with cover as much as possible. A spinnerbait is much like a crankbait in that these lures are most often fished fast and they perform best when the lure hits and rebounds off cover. "I often speed up my retrieve just before the spinnerbait is going to hit a laydown, stump or other visible cover," suggests VanDam. "When the bait makes contact with the cover, I pause the retrieve and let the bait flutter for a couple seconds before resuming the retrieve. Also, it helps to vary the retrieve with some pauses or jerks that break up the rhythm of the bait and helps to trigger strikes."

VanDam explains his theory on spinnerbait fishing by using a school of shad as an example. "When shad are swimming they form into a tight ball," explains VanDam. "Every move the school makes is like a group of sycronized swimmers doing exactly the same thing at the same instant. Moving together as a school is how these fish gain safety from predators. Bass have a tough time picking out a target in such a tight and uniform school. However, when a minnow is injured it gets separated from the school and swims erratically. Every bass in the area is programmed to attack the baitfish that's doing something different."

To sum up traditional spinnerbait fishing, concentrate on target fishing, keep the bait moving so bass don't get a good look at it, fish in contact with cover and select blade and head weight combinations that let you fish various situations as efficiently as possible.

But there's more.

SPINNERBAITS IN DEEP WATER

Spinnerbaits are mostly reserved for fishing shallow water. Legendary for their ability to cover water quickly, the most common spinnerbait sizes are 1/4-, 3/8- and 1/2-ounce. Baits in this size range

Spinnerbaits are versatile lures that can be fished fast, slow, shallow or deep. VanDam is buzzing this bait just under the surface.

simply aren't heavy enough to fish deepwater structure such as ledges, sunken islands, creek channels, the tips of points or flooded timber. To fish these areas and other deep water structure with a spinnerbait the lure must be much heavier.

The blades on a spinnerbait give the lure lift when it's retrieved. Even a fairly heavy 1/2-ounce bait will come to the surface if it's retrieved fast enough. Building spinnerbaits that weight an ounce or more ounces enables these lures to be fished close to bottom in much deeper water.

The 2000 BassMasters Classic Champion Woo Daves is one of many anglers who are excited about one of the newest wave in spinnerbait fishing to come along in years. "Fishing extra-heavy spinnerbaits is fast becoming one of my favorite ways to fish deep-water bass," says Daves. "Sometimes new techniques hit the bass fishing community hard then fizzle out quickly. I feel that in the next couple years heavy spinnerbaits are going to become as common a deep-water fishing tool as Carolina rigs."

One of the biggest reasons these over-sized spinnerbaits are catching on is because they can be used to fish deep water quickly, something few other lures can claim.

"I like throwing heavy spinnerbaits instead of crankbaits," says Daves. "Deep-diving cranks have so much resistance in the water it's hard to fish them all day without getting fatigued. When you start getting tired your concentration wanes and your reaction time slows down. I can fish a heavy spinnerbait all day and still be as fresh for the last bass of the day as I was for the first."

Daves prefers the Ledgebuster spinnerbait produced by Edgebuster Lures. "My favorite model is the single willow leaf," says Daves. "I fish this bait a lot for smallmouth after dark. Also, these heavy spinnerbaits are great for fishing in current where it would be impossible to get a traditional spinnerbait to the bottom."

These oversized lures are best fished on heavier tackle than normally associated with spinnerbaits. A heavy action 7-foot baitcasting rod works nicely. Medium weight saltwater rods are also a good option for fishing heavy spinnerbaits.

Heavy spinnerbait fishing is so new, anglers are just beginning to discover the ways these lures can be used to catch more bass. One thing is for certain, adding more weight to a spinnerbait has made these versatile lures even more useful.

In the next chapter will look at another lure used to find fish. Crankbaits, like spinnerbaits, are one of the best ways to cover water quickly when searching for fish or for working active bass.

The 2000 Bass Masters Classic champion Woo Daves poses with a bass taken on a spinnerbait.

CHAPTER 11

CASTING CRANKBAITS

"Crankbait" says it all. Cast them out and crank them back in. What could be more simple?

It's true that casting crankbaits can be a straightforward means of tempting bass. All the major species of bass are readily taken on these lures and anglers have hundreds of quality crankbaits to choose from. Like any other form of bass fishing, the more you know about these lures and how to get the most from them, the more bass you're going to catch.

Penny Berryman is one of the most popular and colorful bass anglers in America. A national tournament pro for over 15 years, she has won four national titles, was the 1997 Angler of the Year and has qualified to fish in more than 23 different classic tournaments.

One of the Nitro National Tournament Pros, Berryman has fished bass her whole life, but she's not telling her age. "I grew up fishing crankbaits," says Berryman. "My first bass fishing experiences were on rivers, where crankbaits are among the best lure choices. Early on I learned that the most important aspects of crankbait fishing are

fish fast and stay in contact with cover or structure."

The ability to cover water quickly is the strongest attribute of crankbait fishing. No other lure can be used to sample more water in less time. In fact, most crankbaits excel at a moderate to fast retrieve speed that eats up water unlike any other lure type.

"Early in my tournament career I bought and used every crankbait I could get my hands on," comments Berryman. "It wasn't long before I discovered how confusing using crankbaits can be. There are so many types, shapes, diving depths and colors to pick from, it's easy to get intimidated."

In an effort to refine her lure choices to a more practical assortment, Berryman packed up her crankbait collection and headed to the local golf club. That's right, a golf club. The country club had an Olympic-sized swimming pool and Berryman was committed to learning more about crankbaits with her own eyes.

"I started casting with a rod equipped with 10-pound test monofilament," recalls Berryman. "My goal was to make enough casts to get an idea how deep my favorite lures would dive. Also I wanted to see the action of the major crankbait types."

Berryman first noticed even with lures of the same brand and model there were marked differences in how the crankbaits performed. "Unfortunately, not all crankbaits come tuned properly in the package," cautions Berryman. "To get all my lures to run properly I had to spend some time adjusting the line tie so each lure would dive straight down into the water."

> *"To get all my lures to run properly I had to spend some time adjusting the line tie so each lure would dive straight down into the water."*

The best way to tune a crankbait is the trial-and-error method. Make a short cast and watch as the lure is being retrieved. If the bait runs to the left, the line tie will need to be bent slightly to the right. If the bait runs to the right, the line tie will need to be bent to the left.

A pair of needle nose pliers and some patience is required to tune cranks. A little tweaking goes a long way. Even a slight modification to the line tie can make a significant change in how the lure runs.

Crankbaits are one of the best lures when searching for bass. Few baits can cover as much water as quickly as a crankbait.

Penny Berryman has a passion for fishing crankbaits.

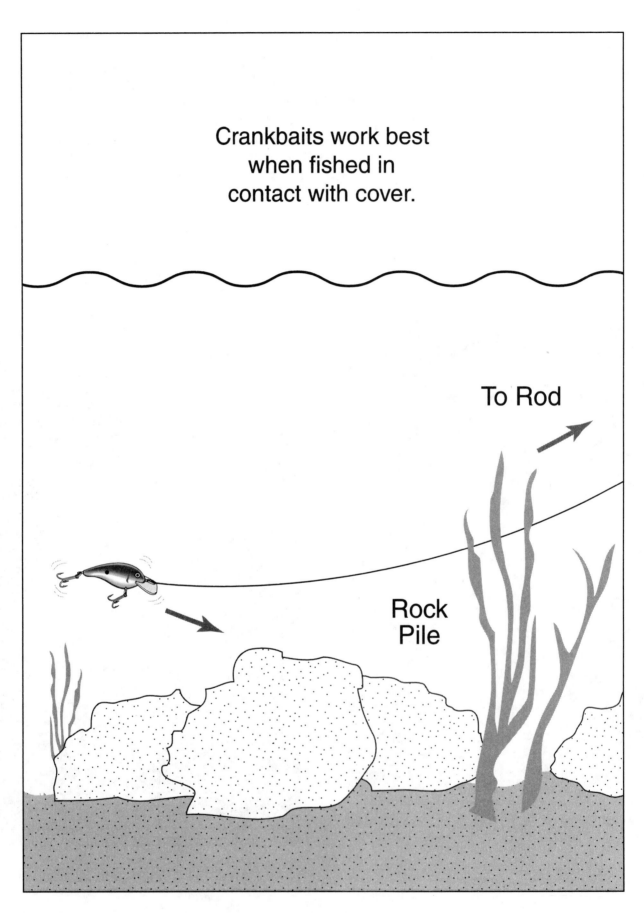

Crankbaits work best
when fished in
contact with cover.

To Rod

Rock
Pile

Bassin' with the Pros

"It usually takes several tries to achieve a 'fine-tuned' crankbait," says Berryman. "This effort is essential however because unless your lures are tuned properly they won't achieve their maximum depth or generate the desired action."

Once a lure is tuned properly most cranks will take a considerable amount of use and abuse before they need to be tuned again. The most common thing that causes a crank to go out of tune is an angler slapping the lure on the water surface to clear the hooks of grass or debris! If a lure gets snagged and is recovered, it's a good idea to check the tune before using the bait again.

Casting into a swimming pool helped Berryman develop a sense for how deep

Casting into a swimming pool help Barryman develop a sense for how deep many crankbaits dive.

many crankbaits dive. "Over the years I've also conducted countless seminars where I cast cranks into the Bass Tub at sport shows," adds Berryman. "In addition to seeing the lure depth and action, I've learned which baits seem to be of interest to bass."

Starting with lures that are tuned and diving properly is critical to crankbaiting success. It's also important to use the proper line-to-lure attachment.

"I prefer to use a small round snap to attach my crankbaits," says Berryman. "The round edges of the snap insures the bait has

Even new crankbaits often need tuning before they can achieve their best fish-catching potential.

Lipless cranks like this Cordell Spot feature a thin profile that can be worked through grass and other cover with amazingly few hang-ups.

freedom to wobble as it was intended to. Avoid snap swivels. The extra hardware only makes it more difficult to tune the lures properly. Also, make sure the snap is on the small side. I use a No. 1 size snap most of the time."

Using a snap makes it easy to change lures as needed. However, anglers can also tie directly to the line tie if the lure features a split ring or snap on the bait. A loop knot is also a good option for those who prefer to tie direct to the lure.

"Some lures have snaps already on them," says Berryman. "Never attach a snap to a snap. This changes the tow point and makes it difficult to get the bait to tune properly. You can attach a snap to a split ring, but not to another snap."

Staying in contact with cover or structure is the other hard and fast rule of casting crankbaits. "The big mistake I see anglers making with cranks is they don't throw them in places where the fish are," says Berryman. "I think anglers avoid throwing cranks into cover because they are afraid of losing their expensive baits."

Crankbait styles such as lipless versions are designed especially to pull through grass and other cover with amazingly few hang-ups. The thin profile of these lures allows them to slip through weed cover without fouling better than cranks with diving lips. Some popular lures in this category include the Bill Lewis Rat-L-Trap, Rapala Rattlin' Rap, Cotton Cordell Super Spot and Luhr Jensen Sugar Shad.

When casting lipless baits, Berryman says the angler should reel until the bait can be felt contacting weeds or grass. The bait is cleared by giving the rod tip a sharp snap that both frees the bait and strips any remaining debris free from the hooks.

> *A loop knot is also a good option for those who prefer to tie direct to the lure.*

Because lipless baits are compact and fairly heavy, they can be thrown great distances. Most models of lipless baits are sinking baits that function best when fishing in sparse to moderate cover and rather shallow water. To reach bass in deeper water a lipped diving crankbait must be used.

Lipped diving cranks come in hundreds of sizes, shapes and depth diving ranges. A pronounced lip causes the lure to dive when retrieved. How deep these lures dive depends on the length of the cast, the size of the lip, angle of the lip, size of the line used and the weight of the lure.

Most lipped diving baits are designed to reach depths ranging from 6 to 20 feet. A few super-deep divers will dive a little deeper.

When a lipped crankbait is retrieved, the lip is the first part of the bait to contact the bottom or cover. The trailing hooks don't snag up as often as you might imagine, said Berryman. Instead, the lure collides with and bounces off underwater objects.

Some classic lipped divers that have produced countless bass for as many anglers include the Bomber A series, Rapala

Some crankbaits like this Timber Tiger use molded wings on the body to enable the bait more freedom to contact structure and brush without snagging.

Shad Rap, Storm Wiggle Wart, Bill Norman N series and Bagley's Balsa Series,

Some other lipped style crankbaits avoid snags by featuring a fat body that helps to prevent the hooks from catching on objects. A couple good examples of baits in this category include the Luhr Jensen Brush Baby and the Worden's Timber Tiger. Both of these lures have a fin-like deflector molded into the side of the bait that helps the lure contact cover without snagging up.

Crankbaits can be fished in and among cover effectively without major snagging problems. If a crankbait does become hopelessly hung, the best way to recover the lure is to use one of the many lure retrievers on the market.

The right rod and reel combination makes casting crankbaits more enjoyable. "A slow gear ratio reel is essential for casting deep-diving cranks all day," says Berryman. "Deeper diving lures have a lot of resistance in the water. An angler can get fatigued very quickly retrieving these baits without the help of a 4:1 gear ratio reel. I match up this reel to a Quantum Tour Edition 7-1/2-foot medium/light action popping rod."

Most anglers use 10- to 17-pound test when casting crankbaits. Lighter line is used most often when trying to achieve maximum diving depths.

Small or very light crankbaits are tough to cast on baitcasting gear. These lures must be thrown using medium action spinning

Penny Berryman recommends using a baitcasting reel with a 4:1 gear ratio and baitcasting rod for fishing crankbaits.

Penny Berryman caught this trophy bass on a crankbait while fishing in the 2000 Legends Tournament held in Nashville, Tennessee.

outfit equipped with 8- or 10-pound test monofilament.

Berryman and other pros who fish cranks frequently prefer to use monofilament line. "Braided super lines have almost no stretch," reports Berryman. "When using super braids, the angler's reaction time is speeded up and it's easy to set the hook before the fish has the bait firmly in its mouth. Also, with braided lines, bass seem to be better able to shake free."

A good quality monofilament with controlled stretch is the best option for casting crankbaits. Berryman uses Excalibur co-polymer line because it has more abrasion resistance than others. "I'm always casting cranks into stuff that tears at my fishing line. You can't have a line that's too tough for fishing cranks in cover."

Over the years Berryman has settled on a handful of baits that get the job done for

> *"When using super braids, the angler's reaction time is speeded up and it's easy to set the hook."*

her. Classics in her tackle box include the Bomber A series, Rebel Wee-R and Cotton Cordell Big-O. The crankbaits she uses most often are compact and easy to cast models that are tough and dependable.

"My single favorite crankbait for some years now has been the Excalibur Fat-Free Shad series," says Berryman. "I consider these baits to be among the highest quality cranks I've ever fished. Each lure has a premium finish, premium hooks, tight shad-like action, a super-loud rattle chamber and they are among the truest running crankbaits on the market."

Understanding what makes crankbaits tick is the secret to being more successful with these lures. Penny Berryman used a swimming pool to determine the diving depth and action of her favorite lures, then took that information onto the water with her.

While Penny Berryman uses and recommends an assortment of crankbaits for bass fishing, her favorite lures are the various sizes of the Fat-Free Shad series by Excalibur. Photo courtesy of Pradco.

Dr. Steven Holt of Ada, Michigan is a fan of crankbait fishing, an avid tournament angler and author of the new book, *Precision Casting*. This book answers the question everyone wants to know about crankbaits, including the diving depth range of more than 140 popular crankbaits.

Like Berryman, Dr. Holt wondered for years how deep his favorite crankbaits would dive. He also wanted to know how variables like line diameter, casting length, retrieve speed and rod position influenced crankbait diving depth. To answer these questions Dr. Holt undertook an ambitious research project that lasted more than two years.

To insure the most accurate and useful information would be provided to avid bass anglers, Dr. Holt carefully developed a method of testing the diving depths of crankbaits. A floating 100-foot long test course was designed that featured marker buoys spaced 15 feet apart. Each marker was equipped with a measuring tape dangling down into the water that could be used to determine the depth of lures as they were retrieved past the markers. Testing was conducted in ultra clear natural lakes where the divers could easily observe the crankbaits as they were retrieved past the measuring tapes.

"We used a scuba diver to document all the depth data provided in *Precision Casting*," says Dr. Holt "Using a diver to record the depth data confirms that the lure is tuned properly, running on course and that there is no debris on the hooks that might influence the lure's action or diving depth. There's no substitute for seeing with your own eyes that a lure is running properly."

After Dr. Holt and several other volunteers made hundreds of measured casts, it was determined that the average cast length is approximately 70 feet. A 70-foot cast would become the baseline for data collection.

At one end of the test course a boat was anchored and the front deck used as a platform from which to cast. From this position crankbaits were cast and retrieved past the marker buoys. Depth data collected was then used to draw a series of "dive curve" graphs that clearly show the path each crankbait tested follows during the retrieve.

In the book *Precision Casting* each lure is pictured life-size for easy identification. Also the "dive curve" chart clearly shows the running path a crankbait makes including maximum depth, how steeply the bait dives

> *"There's no subsititute for seeing with your own eyes that a lure is running properly."*

and how well it holds its depth throughout the retrieve.

"In order to get the most accurate and reliable information we began by hyper tuning each crankbait to insure the lure pulled straight in the water," explains Dr. Holt. "To achieve maximum diving depth and action it's critical that all crankbaits are tuned properly."

Dr. Holt also determined that for consistency every bait would be tested with the rod pointed down towards the water and the tip

Dr. Steven Holt is co-author of Precision Casting *a book that provides accurate diving data for more than 140 popular crankbaits.*

approximately 12 inches from the water surface. This rod position is a normal and comfortable position from which to retrieve crankbaits. He also selected 14-pound test monofilament as standard line to use throughout the testing.

A test line of 14-pound test was selected because this line size is one of the most commonly used among bass anglers. "Because not everyone uses 14-pound test line, each dive curve also features a simple conversion chart that tells maximum diving depth on 8-, 10-, 12-, 17- and 20-pound test lines," adds Dr. Holt. "Ironically, we discovered that line diameter isn't as big a factor in lure running depth as you might imagine.

Precision Casting *answers the question: How deep does this lure dive? Scuba divers were used to document the casting depth of popular crankbaits, then record the data in an easy-to-use graph.*

Line diameter plays a part in running depth, but casting distance is the overwhelmingly dominate factor in crankbait diving mechanics. In short, the farther you can cast a bait, the deeper it's going to dive."

The position the rod was held in during the retrieve also made a significant impact on lure running depth. "Our baseline data was performed by keeping the rod pointed down at the water surface during the retrieve," says Dr. Holt. "As part of our testing we also checked lure diving depths with the rod tip held down in the water, level to the arms, and with the rod tip held up in the air as a comparison. What we discovered is anglers can control the running depth of crankbaits to a certain extent by raising or lowering the rod tip."

Retrieve speed was also tested to determine how this fishing variable impacts on crankbait diving depth. "Surprisingly, retrieve speed had one of the most insignificant impacts on lure running depth," says Dr. Holt. "If anything a slow retrieve allows lures to achieve a slightly deeper depth."

On the water, *Precision Casting* can help anglers select not one but several different crankbait models that dive to a desired depth. No longer do anglers have to depend on one or two familiar lure models. Knowing how deep a crankbait will dive allows the angler to present the lure with more confidence, accuracy and also to minimize problems with snagging.

"It's information like this that can really make anglers more productive when they are throwing crankbaits. The more you know about your lures, the more confident you'll be using them. That confidence will likely help you put the bait in the right place at the right time," said Perryman.

Crankbaits are easy to fish and highly effective at triggering strikes from active bass. In the next chapter another type of crankbait will be explored. Jerkbaits are unique enough to warrant a chapter all their own.

CHAPTER 12

JERKBAITING FOR BASS

Early in the year when bass are most often found in shallow water, one fishing technique demands consideration. Jerkbaiting incorporates a minnow-shaped crankbait that's twitched and jerked with rapid pops of the rod tip. The idea is to imitate a dying minnow by making the bait dart, quiver, pause and twitch in as unpredictable a manner as possible.

Randy VanDam is the older brother of bass fishing legend Kevin VanDam. The VanDam brothers grew up in Southern Michigan fishing tournaments on heavily pressured waters. The pair dominated tournaments in the region for years before Kevin choose a life as a touring bass professional. Meanwhile, Randy dedicated himself to establishing a fishing tackle and marine shop in his home town of Kalamazoo.

One of the things that has made D&R Sports so successful is the huge assortment of bass fishing gear and accessories. Anglers not only from Michigan but also from Indiana, Illinois and Ohio come to shop for their favorite equipment and the latest gear.

Jerkbaiting is one of Randy's favorite ways to fish for bass. Living in the Great Lakes region, he has countless options when it comes to places to fish. Just some of the waters he frequents include Sturgeon Bay, Saginaw Bay, Lake St. Clair and Lake Erie where he caught the state record smallmouth bass.

All of these waters and more are tailor-made for jerkbaiting. "Jerkbaits work best in clear to slightly stained waters," says Van-Dam. "This whole presentation appeals to the eyes and predatory instincts of a bass. The strikes are instinctive and reactionary almost as if the bass can't help itself."

Prime jerkbaiting waters include rock- and gravel-covered flats up to 15 feet deep and areas where weed growth or brush covers the bottom, but the cover doesn't extend to the surface. Bedding bass are also a prime target for jerkbaits and these lures can also be used effectively to fish visible cover. Most deadly during the early season when bass are in shallow water, jerkbaiting can produce fish at just about any time of year when the conditions are favorable.

"I use two basic outfits when fishing jerkbaits," says VanDam. "If I'm throwing smaller baits I'll select a 6-foot medium action spinning rod equipped with a spinning reel and 6- or 8-pound test monofilament. I prefer 8-pound test unless I'm trying to get the bait to run a little deeper. The reel used should feature a large spool diameter. Larger diameter reel spools enable the lures to be cast maximum distances."

The spinning outfit is ideal for throwing smaller baits or for casting when the wind picks up. A 6-foot medium action baitcasting outfit gets the nod when casting larger baits. "I'd rather use a baitcasting outfit if the baits I'm using are heavy enough," says

> *"Larger diameter reel spools enable the lures to be case maximum distances."*

VanDam. "The baitcasting gear is a not only a better tool for fighting fish, I can also control my casts better."

VanDam recommends using 10- to 12-pound test monofilament on baitcasting gear. "I always use clear or green line when fishing jerkbaits," advises VanDam. "It's important to make the presentation as natural as possible. Fluorescent lines are too visible to the fish to be considered for jerkbaiting."

Good Polarized glasses are also essential for jerkbaiting success. "Much of the

Randy VanDam is the brother to fishing pro Kevin VanDam. It seems the ability find big bass runs in the family.

Jerkbaiting is presentation tailor-made for clear-water fisheries, such as those common in the Great Lakes region.

time you can see the fish dart out at the bait," says VanDam. "Sometimes the fish will stop short and a couple more twitches is all it takes to trigger the strike."

A wide variety of minnow-style crankbaits make good jerkbaits. "The first thing I do is replace the factory hooks with premium grade trebles," says VanDam. "Bass swipe at jerkbaits. Often they don't get the bait completely in their mouth. The hooks need to be sharp enough that they literally stick to the fish. Lots of the fish I land on jerkbaits are hooked on the outside of their face. Without ultra-sharp hooks these fish would be missed."

Good replacement hooks include the Mustad Triple Grip, VMC Barbarian, Gamakatsu EWG, Eagle Claw Kahle and Heddon Excalibur. It's best to match the same size hooks provided from the manufacturer to insure the balance of the bait isn't disturbed.

Jerkbaits come in two styles including standard floating/diving and suspending models. "I use mostly suspending lures," says VanDam. "Most suspending baits perform pretty good right out of the package, but I've discovered that not all suspending lures have the same or even predictable buoyancy levels in the water. I even see differences among the same brand and model of lure. Ideally the bait should

> *It's best to match the same size hooks provided from the manufacturer to insure the balance of the bait isn't disturbed.*

suspend or stay at the same depth level when the lure is paused. It's okay if the bait floats upwards ever so slightly. If the lure sinks or floats to the surface quickly it's tough to keep the bait in the strike zone long enough to stimulate strikes from finicky fish."

VanDam checks the buoyancy and balance of his lures and, if necessary, adds weight using Storm's Suspend dots and strips. These handy tools are simply adhesive backed pieces of lead tape.

When modifying a jerkbait, it's important to be sure the bait rests level in the water or with a slight nose-down orientation. Floating baits can be easily converted to suspending models by adding a series of Suspend dots or strips to the underside of the lure or lip. These strips of lead tape can be custom cut as desired, stacked one on top of another and are easy to remove with the tip of a knife blade.

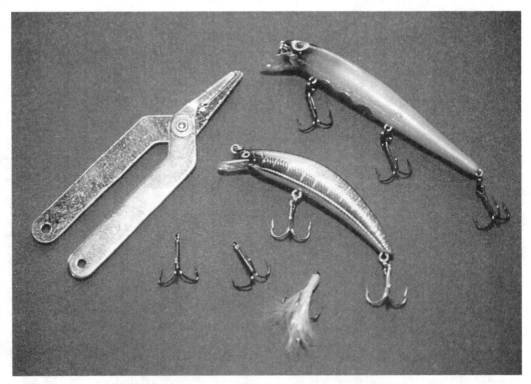

The first thing Randy VanDam does to a jerkbait is replace the factory hooks with premium treble hooks.

Suspending Jerkbait

Jerkbaits are especially deadly on bedding bass. The retrieve must be as eratic as possible, and the bait has to be paused near the outside edge of the bed.

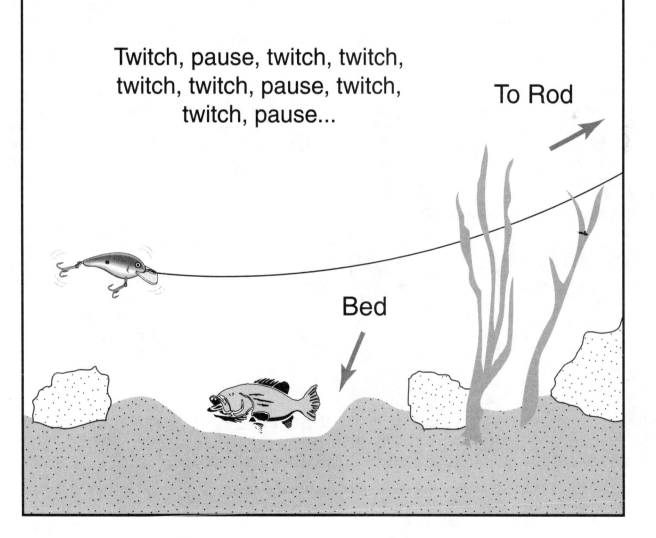

Twitch, pause, twitch, twitch, twitch, twitch, pause, twitch, twitch, pause...

To Rod

Bed

"When you put Suspend dots or strips onto a crankbait, position them so when the hooks wobble back and forth they don't contact these soft strips of lead," cautions VanDam. "The hooks will tear the soft lead tape quickly, causing the bait to loose its critical balance."

You can also modify non-suspending jerkbaits by adding small clip-on weights to the split rings. The tiny 1/32- and 1/16-ounce weights designed for use in tubes are ideal for this purpose. These weights can be cut using a side cutter to customize the weight as needed. Normally these weights are placed on the first hook, but depending on the balance of the lure they may be placed on the second hook.

Some jerkbaits that VanDam considers to be outstanding choices include the Smith-wick Rattlin' Rogue, Daiwa TD Minnow,

> *Floating baits can be easily converted to suspending models by adding a series of Suspend dots or strips to the underside of the lure or lip.*

Rapala Husky Jerk, Lucky-Craft Pointer Minnow, Yo-Zuri Minnow, Storm Suspending ThunderStick, Bomber Long A and Reef Runner RipStick.

All of these popular jerkbaits come equipped with a split ring attached to the lure's wire eye tie. "The split ring actually detracts from the action of some baits," advises Van-Dam. "If a bait has a subtle action to begin with, remove the split ring and tie directly to the wire eye tie. In most cases this will allow the bait to dart more erratically."

"For smallmouth I usually select mid-sized jerkbaits, reserving the larger sizes for largemouth fishing," comments VanDam. "At times the small 2-inch baits can be powerful fishing tools. I like to fish these small baits in June when young-of-the-year minnows become a primary food source for bass."

Often the way a jerkbait is fished is more important than the lure selected. Because this technique is most often used in clear water, it's critical to make long casts that cover water and present the bait out away from the boat.

Blind casting jerk-baits on flats is one of the most popular ways of fishing these lures. "I make a long cast, then reel the bait down by cranking the reel handle hard for a couple turns," explains Van-Dam. "Once I have the bait at the depth level I want, I stop the retrieve and begin the twitching motion that brings the bait to life. The whole key to this style of fish-ing is to make the bait

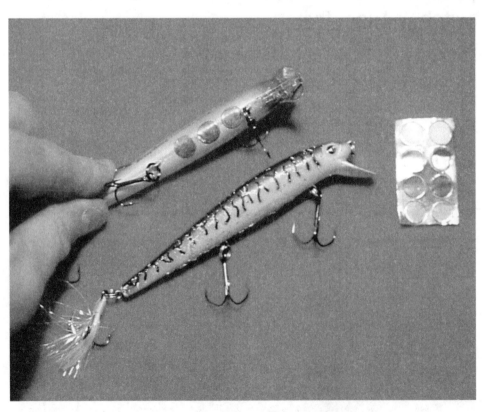

Storm Suspend Dots are an easy way to add weight to non-suspending jerkbaits or to fine-tune suspending models.

move as erratically as possible. Avoid any kind of rhythm or cadence."

According to VanDam, the most common mistakes made with jerkbaits is anglers don't pause them enough. "You have to vary the darting action by snapping the rod tip on a slack line," advises VanDam. "If the bait is jerked on a tight line, the lure simply jumps the direction it was already going. Snapping on slack line causes the bait to change directions every time the lure is twitched."

Sight fishing bass on beds is one of the other ways jerkbaits can be absolutely deadly. "I spend a lot of time fishing smallmouth on the beds," says VanDam. "The key is not to work the bait over the middle of the bed. Instead cast beyond the bed and work along the edge of the bed. This allows the fish a better profile view of the lure."

VanDam also uses another trick to pull bedding bass. "I'll rig a jerkbait to sink slowly by adding a clip-on weight," adds VanDam. "I cast past the bed and work the bait up to the edge of the bed. When the lure is paused it slowly sinks towards the bed. By raising the rod tip I can lift the bait without pulling it away from the bed. It's almost like jigging with a jerkbait."

This unique presentation keeps the lure close to the bed longer than other methods. Every second the bait is in front of a bass

Randy VanDam prefers to use larger jerkbaits largemouth bass and smaller models for smallmouth.

Randy VanDam is especially skillful at catching smallmouth on beds using jerkbaits. This fish is about to be released.

increases the chances the lure will trigger a strike.

When selecting lure colors VanDam goes for baits that are as natural as possible in clear water. "I like lure colors that closely resemble whatever natural forage bass are used to feeding on," says VanDam. "In the Great Lakes I use a lot of chromes and baits with strong flash. In natural lakes where the water may be stained I prefer a painted lure that shows up well against the natural color of the water. Some of my most productive colors are white, gray, pearl and true yellow."

When fishing beds, don't waste a lot of time working the bait all the way back to the boat. If the fish is going to hit the bait it will do so right next to the bed. Instead reel up and make another cast to the same bed or a different bed.

The same strategy holds true when fishing jerkbaits to visible cover such as laydowns. Cast past the target, work up to the target, then retrieve the lure quickly and make another cast. When working visible cover, 90 percent of the fish are taken as the bait passes the target.

SOFT PLASTIC JERKBAITS

Soft plastic jerkbaits have become very popular since they were introduced a few years ago. The original Slug-O made a major impact on bass fishing and stimulated most of the manufacturers of soft plastics to come out with their own versions of these lures.

"The biggest advantage of using soft plastic jerkbaits is the snag-free design of these lures," comments VanDam. "Because these lures are normally Texas rigged, they can be fished right in thick cover you could never penetrate with a traditional jerkbait."

Good places to use soft plastic jerkbaits include weeds or grass that are growing almost to the surface, in the tops of submerged trees, flooded brush, lily pads and around emergent cover such as cane, reeds and cattails. Because these lures are often used to fish in and among heavy cover, anglers need to go equipped with 17- to 20-pound test line in most situations.

Soft plastic jerkbaits can also be used to fish the same types of areas where traditional jerkbaits are most often used. By adding weights these lures can be fished in deeper water with good success. The biggest drawback is these lures are not heavy enough to cast long distances.

Jerkbaits make bass fishing fun for many anglers. This fast-paced technique can be used to cover water quickly and the strikes generated are often explosive. Making long casts and concentrating on developing an erratic darting action are the keys to making this popular technique shine.

In the next chapter we'll look at the bass fishing technique which represents the sport better than all others. Texas rigging a plastic worm, a system that is used almost exclusively to catch bass, is the focus of the next chapter.

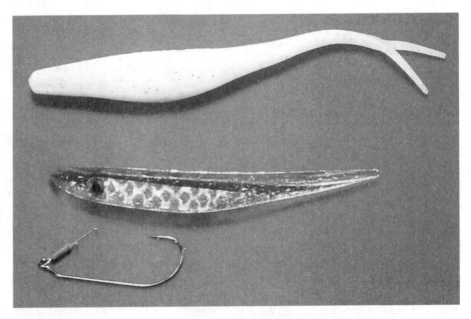

Soft plastic jerkbaits can be worked through heavier cover than traditional jerkbaits.

CHAPTER 13

DAVID WARTON AND BILL DANCE TALK ABOUT TEXAS RIGGING WORMS

Few angling methods are more closely associated with bass than Texas rigging a plastic worm. As distinguished as the Classic itself, Texas rigging ranks at the top of the most popular and productive bass fishing methods. Countless fish have been taken on this simple worm, hook and bullet sinker combination. The simplicity of this deadly rig is part of what makes it so appealing to bass and bass anglers.

Texas rigging has become so popular because this technique is universal enough to apply anywhere. Like jig fishing, Texas rigging a plastic worm is one of those presentations that bass simply can't resist. The ultra-natural appearance of this rig in the water triggers strikes like few other lures.

Originally introduced as an angling technique designed to target bass in heavy cover, Texas rigging produces bass in a wide variety of angling situations.

David Warton is known throughout the bass fishing community as one of the premier worm fishermen in America. A guide on Lake Sam Rayburn in Texas for 25 years, Warton became a full-time professional angler in 1979. To date his career has included 10 trips to the BassMaster Classic and three tournament wins.

"Worm fishing has fallen out of favor somewhat in recent years," says Warton. "I think that most anglers feel worm fishing is too slow. The average guy would rather tie on a spinnerbait and quickly work his way down the shoreline."

It's true that Texas rigging is a slower presentation than many other popular bass fishing techniques. Even though other lures such as spinnerbaits and crankbaits continue to be the workhorses used while hunting for fish, worm fishing often shines once an angler has located a pocket of fish.

"I've always got a Texas rig ready to go, no matter how or where I'm fishing," says Warton. "If I miss a fish on a crankbait, topwater plug or spinnerbait, I'll throw the Texas rig back into the same spot and 90 percent of the time the fish will smack it. A worm is such a natural lure, bass have a hard time telling it's a fake."

> *Even though other lures such as spinnerbaits and crankbaits continue to be the workhorses used while hunting for fish, worm fishing often shines once an angler has located a pocket of fish.*

Worm fishing is a slower presentation compared to some other bassin' methods, but these lures can still be used to cover prime water rather quickly. "I spot fish a Texas rig by making casts to laydowns, brush, rocks or any visible cover." says Warton. "If you play the percentages, 90 percent of the fish that bite are going to be located close to the cover. You don't have to fish the worm all the way back to the boat and waste a lot of time."

Texas rigging soft plastic worms is what bass fishing is all about to many anglers.

David Warton is one of the nation's leading experts at fishing Texas rigged worms.

Texas Rigged Worms

Texas rigged worms are ideal for spot fishing cover such as stumps, laydowns, etc. Work the cover, then retrieve the bait quickly and cast to another target.

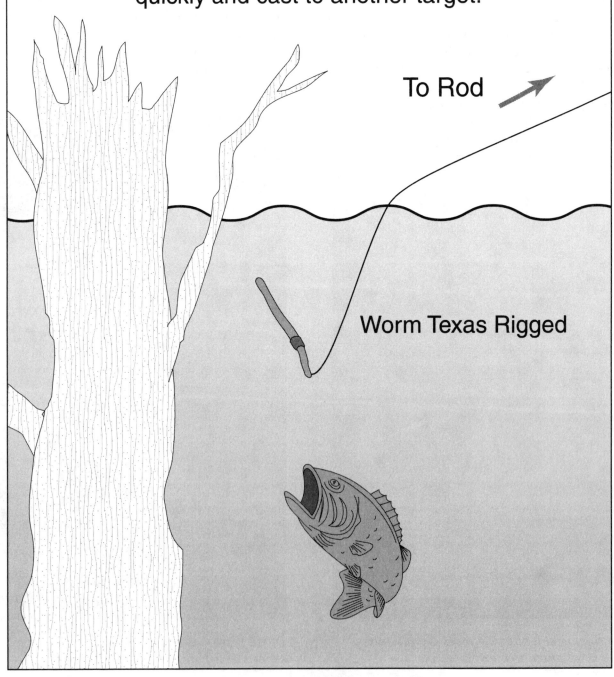

To Rod

Worm Texas Rigged

Getting the most from worm fishing requires anglers to select matched and balanced equipment. "I keep my worm fishing equipment simple and straightforward," says Warton. "I prefer a baitcasting combination with a 6-1/2-foot medium-heavy rod and fast retrieve ratio reel. Most of the time I fish 10- to 12-pound test monofilament unless the cover is exceptionally heavy."

At the business end of his line, Warton prefers a straight shank 2/0 Mustad worm hook instead of the popular offset style hooks. "I'm convinced that a straight-shank hook gives the best hooking ratio. It's also important to set the hook with a sideways sweep of the rod, instead of jerking the rod upwards. A sideways hookset is essential in shallow water. In deeper water the style of hookset used isn't as critical."

A Texas rigged worm must also be balanced properly by selecting the right sized weight, hook and worm. A 4-inch worm, 2/0 hook and 1/8-ounce bullet weight represents a perfectly balanced rig. At the other end of the spectrum a larger 10-inch worm requires a 4/0 hook and 3/8-ounce bullet weight.

"I use three different styles of worms," says Warton. "My favorites include the hook tail, paddle tail and ribbon tail. In open cover I like a worm with a lot of action such as a hook tail. As the cover gets thicker, I switch to worms with progressively less action like ribbon tail and paddle tail."

Warton also has discovered that ring-style worms are deadly on bass. "Ring worms are considerably softer than other plastics," explains Warton. "The extra-soft texture encourages bass to hang onto the bait longer. I'm also a big fan of impregnated plastics. Virtually all the worms I'm fishing are salt-, garlic- or scent-impregnated."

Color can be an important aspect of worm fishing. Warton has settled on a handful of colors that work for him no matter where he fishes. "I only use about five colors," says Warton. "In dirty water I prefer a worm that's mostly black. In clearer water I like plum, June bug, pumpkin and red shad."

David Warton recommends that anglers always keep a Texas rigged worm handy. If you miss a fish on a crankbait or spinnerbait, toss the worm into the same spot and hold on.

The three most popular styles of plastic worms are paddle tail, ribbon tail and hook tail.

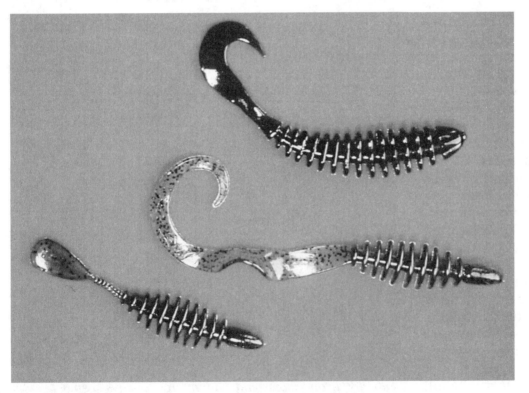

David Warton feels that ring tail style worms feel more natural to bass and that the fish often hang onto them longer than other worm types.

One of the commonly asked questions regarding worm fishing deals with the issue of pegging the sinker. "I don't peg the sinker if I'm fishing in open cover," says Warton. "Leaving the sinker free-sliding makes it easier for bass to suck the worm into their mouth because they don't have to move the weight, just the worm. If you can get away without pegging the sinker, you'll hook more bass."

Pegging the sinker becomes more necessary when fishing worms in very heavy cover such as when flippin'. Pegging the weight allows the weight and worm to act as one unit, instead of the weight ending up on one side of a stick and the worm on the other. This way, pegging helps to reduce snagging problems. A simple trick can significantly increase your hooking ratio.

"Never peg a sinker tight to the worm," warns Warton. "If the sinker is pegged to the worm, the hook can't slip on the hookset and bury into the fish's mouth. Instead leave a little bit of slack between the weight and worm, so the hook can slip and penetrate better when the angler jerks."

> *"I can honestly say that a plastic worm is the most versatile lure I've ever fished for bass."*

BILL DANCE ON WORM FISHING

Bill Dance is one of America's most beloved fishing personalities. A highly successful tournament professional, Dance turned to television with his program Bill Dance Outdoors in 1968. Since that time he has aired more than 2,000 shows, produced 20 educational videos and written seven books on fishing.

A frequent contributor to such popular magazines as *BassMasters*, *Southern Living*, *Bassin'*, *North American Fisherman* and many others, Bill Dance is a leading fishing educator who's knowledge of bass fishing is unsurpassed.

"I can honestly say that a plastic worm is the most versatile lure I've ever fished for bass," says Dance. "Compared to other popular lures, the plastic worm catches not only more bass, but bigger bass. I'm convinced it's the shape of the worm that makes these lures so deadly. The long slender shape of a plastic worm sends a not so subtle message to bass. Because these baits are thin, bass

Bill Dance is one of America's most beloved fishing celebrities.

know they can swallow it and they frequently attempt to do just that."

Stressing fundamentals is the key to becoming a successful worm fisherman. "Don't get bogged down on details such as worm color, style, shape or length," advises Dance. "All the common worm types and sizes catch fish, what's important is to understand the conditions that favor worm fishing and the tricks that insure the most bites."

Plastic worms work best in clear to stained waters. "Compared to spinnerbaits, crankbaits and other lures that make a lot of noise in the water, a plastic worm is a subtle lure," explains Dance. "Bass aren't going to strike these lures unless they can see them."

Even in clear water, plastic worms function best when they are fished in close association with cover. "Bass are rarely far from cover," adds Dance. "To consistently catch bass on worms these lures must be presented to laydowns, stumps, rocks, submerged weeds, brush and other cover types."

The best worm fishing also takes place in warm water. "I don't fish plastic worms unless the water temperature is 55 degrees or warmer," cautions Dance. "Plastic lures have less action when used in cold water. Also in cold water bass tend to be found most often in water that is too deep to be conducive to worm fishing."

The way a worm is Texas rigged also plays an important role in how many strikes

Bill Dance stresses the fundamentals when teaching anglers to Texas rig worms. Like other presentations that incorporate soft plastics, Texas rigging works best in clear to stained waters.

these lures generate. "I like to fish a Texas rig with as light a weight as possible and still maintain contact with the bottom," advises Dance. "Most strikes on a plastic worm occur when the bait is falling. The lighter the weight used, the slower the worm falls. Bass have a greater opportunity to strike a slowly falling lure than one that sinks quickly. Also, a light lure will be easier for the fish to suck completely into its mouth, reducing the chances of missed fish."

Selecting a suitable worm fishing rod is also critical. Rods used for worm fishing should feature a soft tip for accurate casting, but enough backbone to drive the hook through the plastic and into the fish's mouth. "A good worm rod has 20 percent tip and 80 percent backbone," says Dance. "When it comes to rod lengths, I think confidence is the best lure in your tackle box. Fish a rod you're comfortable with. For me that's a 6-1/2-foot triggerstick with a medium action. The extra rod length helps me pick up slack line quickly and gives me more leverage on the fish when I set the hook."

When working a worm Dance said he uses two basic retrieve strategies. "The two most common ways I work a worm are by hopping it or sweeping it," adds Dance. "Hopping is a more aggressive approach and I control the lure by holding the rod in about the 10 o'clock position and snapping the rod tip to lift the bait suddenly off bottom. Between snaps of the rod tip I reel up the slack line. For a less aggressive action I'll sweep the rod smoothly from the 10 o'clock position to about the 12 o'clock position. This motion lifts the worm off bottom and allows it to glide back to bottom on a taunt line."

Regardless of how a worm is worked the point of focus should be where the line enters the water. It helps to visualize the worm below the surface. Stay focused and ready for the subtle tap that indicates a bite.

> *Regardless of how a worm is worked the point of focus should be where the line enters the water.*

The hookset is another area where many anglers struggle. "When a bass hits a plastic worm, the time to set the hook is now," says Dance. "You don't want to have a feeling contest with the fish. Instead, the second you feel the tap, reel down quickly to take up the slack and set the hook hard using an upwards sweep of the rod. Keep the rod tight to your chest so you gain the most power and leverage on the fish."

Many anglers set the hook by raising their arms over their head. "You can't get enough pressure on a fish by using just your arms," cautions Dance. "The average angler only delivers about 6 pounds of hook-setting pressure on a fish. To get more pressure on a fish you need to use as much leverage as possible."

To illustrate his point Dance suggests that anglers try opening a jar of pickles by holding the jar out in front of them at arm's length. Then pull the jar into your chest. You'll be amazed how much more leverage and strength you gain. Plastic worm fishing is no place to go easy when setting the hook.

The hooks used in a Texas rig can also have a big impact on how easily bass are to hook. "I always use an Eagle Claw Featherlight L700 series hook when worm fishing," says Dance. "The thin wire design penetrates the plastic worm and sticks the fish much better than hooks made from larger diameter wire."

You need to select worm hooks that are also balanced to the size worm being used. "A 4- to 6-inch worm is best matched to a 1/0 size hook," says Dance. "If an 8-inch worm is used I'll use a 3/0 hook and a 4/0 hook for bigger worms."

Dance also feels that plastic worms are good lures for targeting big bass. "Adult bass don't spend much time chasing fast-moving prey," explains Dance. "Instead these fish feed more efficiently by selecting larger prey that allows them the luxury of feeding less often. Big bass can be caught using standard 6-inch worms, but a larger worm is going to increase the odds of hooking trophy fish."

To avoid hurting trophy bass, Dance pinches down the barb using a pair of pliers. "The big hooks used in large worms can really mess up a fish," cautions Dance. "Pinching down the barb makes penetration easier and also makes it easier to unhook and release the fish."

The issue of selecting worm colors ranks as one of the least important in Dance's eyes. "I usually select a dark colored

> *"Concentrating on the fundamentals is the best way to catch more bass on plastic worms."*

worm because they show up well in all water conditions. Concentrating on the fundamentals is the best way to catch more bass on plastic worms. "Vince Lombardi used to say, "Winning is achieved through determination," recalls Dance. "The same could be said about bass fishing, especially when Texas rigging."

The subject of plastic worm fishing goes much deeper than Texas rigging. The next chapter goes deeper into methods for fishing plastic worms, including techniques such as jig worms, wacky rigging and many others.

Keeping your arms close to your body gives you more power to set the hook. Here Bill Dance shows perfect form.

CHAPTER 14

JIM SPRAGUE AND BABE WINKELMAN DIG UP MORE ON WORM FISHING

Texas rigging is undoubtedly the most popular way to fish plastic worms and a presentation this widely accepted by the angling public can not be disputed.

While no one disputes the effectiveness of Texas rigging, soft plastic worms can be fished in a number of other productive presentations. Many of these methods excel as niche techniques that no other type of fishing can accomplish.

RIGGED PLASTIC WORMS

Scented and pre-rigged plastic worms are a mainstay for summertime largemouth and smallmouth bass fishing. A classic warm-weather presentation, rigged worms

work best on those days when its already hot and sticky before breakfast.

There's nothing fancy about fishing a rigged worm. Anyone can start catching bass on a rigged worm the first time they fish with it. As essential to summer bass fishing as sunglasses, shorts and T-shirts, these often overlooked bass lures are as easy to use as they are effective.

Jim Sprague of Hastings, Michigan knows rigged worms. His family business, K&E Tackle, is the nation's leading manufacturer of Bass Stopper and Bass Stopper Magnum rigged worms. The Sprague family has spent two generations refining this classic bass fishing lure and presentation.

"The most important thing when choosing a rigged plastic worm is to select a soft and flexible lure," advises Sprague. "Many of the rigged worms on the market are stiff because they are poured with a more durable plastic. Also, some manufacturers use heavy line to rig the worms, further making them stiff and lifeless in the water."

Bass Stopper rigged worms are scented, ultra-soft, flexible and tied using light monofilament. The result are worms that wiggle, squirm, quiver and dart at the slightest movement of the rod tip. This subtle approach is more than bass can stand.

"The best way to fish a rigged worm is over the top of submerged weeds, timber,

> *"These lures also work great for pitching under docks and when casting to bass cruising along the shoreline."*

rocks or other cover," says Sprague. "These lures also work great for pitching under docks and when casting to bass cruising along the shoreline. No weight is necessary, simply tie the main line directly to the loop attached to the worm."

Fishing rigged worms is a form of finesse fishing. Medium weight spinning tackle is the best gear for this style of fishing. In open water situations 10- to 12-pound test line is ideal. If the cover is especially heavy, anglers should switch to 14- to 17-pound test.

"The trick when fishing rigged worms is to go slow," cautions Sprague. "Cast the lure

Rigged plastic worms are deadly on both largemouth and smallmouth bass. Jim Sprague of K&E Tackle produces the Bass Stopper rigged worm so popular among countless anglers.

Sprague recommends fishing the Bass Stopper rigged worm without weight. Cast to weed cover, docks, brush or any type of cover and allow these lures to sink slowly.

out and let it slowly start to sink towards submerged cover. Using short twitches of the rod tip, work the worm gently. The slightest tug on the worm causes the bait to dart and wiggle in a different direction. The action is sort of like a sub-dued form of jerkbaiting."

Most rigged worms feature three exposed hooks protruding from the belly of the worm. These thin wire hooks are exceptionally sharp and they penetrate with only the slightest pressure. Rigged worms also come in weedless versions for fishing in especially heavy cover.

"You can't fish a rigged worm too slowly," stresses Sprague. "The longer you can keep the bait in front of a fish, the better the chances of getting a strike."

Like other plastic lures, rigged worms come in every possible color combination. "We manufacture dozens of different colors, but I find myself fishing two or three choices most of the time," says Sprague. "My favorites include the natural, black with yellow dots and purple with white dots. Other colors work well, but these three keep producing fish for me year after year."

WACKY RIGGING

Sprague and his fishing partners also spend a considerable amount of time fishing wacky rigged worms. "Most of the lakes we fish see a lot of fishing pressure," explains Sprague. "Many of these waters see a tournament every weekend and to make matters worse the water is very clear. Bass quickly get conditioned to any type of mechanical lure such as a spinnerbait or crankbait. The only way to consistently catch fish is by using finesse tactics

> *"I couldn't believe how effective it could be on both largemoth and smallmouth, especially early in the season around spawning time."*

that offer the fish lures so natural and inviting they can't refuse."

Wacky rigging worms is one of those presentations that looks a little silly. "I didn't even try wacky rigging for a couple years because it just looked too much like a gimmick," states Sprague. "Once I finally tried this presentation, I couldn't believe how effective it could be on both largemouth and smallmouth, especially early in the season around spawning time."

Wacky rigging is practiced using finesse worms and other subtle worm styles. The worm is hooked in the middle with a single 1/0 short-shank hook. No weight is used, making light line and spinning tackle the only practical way to fish this rig.

"During the last couple years wacky rigging has accounted for 80 percent of my fish during the early season," admits Sprague. "I use this rig mostly to spot fish visible cover

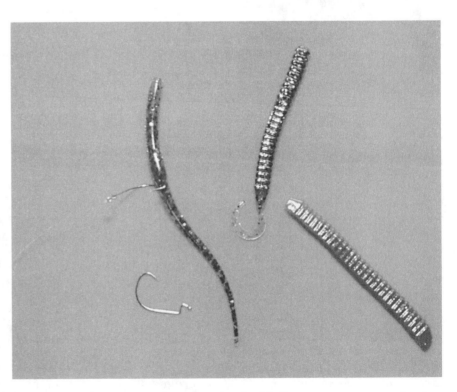

Wacky rigging is most often practiced with finesse worms, centipedes and other subtle-action soft plastics.

including docks, laydowns, emergent vegetation or dark spots on the bottom. I simply throw at the target and let the rig slowly sink. The slightest movement of the rod tip causes the worm to pulsate."

Wacky rigging is a slow presentation that works best in clear water where bass use their sense of sight to find food. You can't fish this rig too slowly, but you can fish it too quickly. It takes patience to let the rig sink slowly.

Babe Winkelman is the host of the popular TV series Good Fishing *and one of the nation's most respected anglers. Targeting bass with jig worms is one of Winkelman's favorite ways to fish. Photo courtesy Babe Winkelman Productions.*

"I've found the best way to work this rig is to cast it to a specific target and let the bait work for 30 seconds to a minute," explains Sprague. "I'll give the bait a little action by shaking the rod tip. If I don't get a bite after about a minute I'll pick up the lure and cast to the next target."

Because wacky rigging is used mostly in clear water, natural colors are the best choices. Shades of green and brown are the best. This technique can also be used with larger worms, but the smaller and softer plastics seem to be the most productive.

JIG WORMING

Jig worming is a modified version of a jig/grub combination. The favorite bassin' technique of one of America's most popular fishermen, Babe Winkelman has been hooked on jig worming for almost three decades. At 53 Winkelman has done it all in fishing. A tournament pro during the early 1980s, Winkelman graduated to television and has since become one of the most beloved fishing celebrities in America. The host of both the *Good Fishing* and *Outdoor Secrets* television series, Winkelman spends countless hours on the water each year in search of exciting outdoor footage.

Winkelman has authored several books on fishing including the popular title *Largemouth Bass Patterns*, and has also produced several videos dedicated to the art and science of bass fishing.

"The main reason I fish jig worms so much is because you never know from one day to the next what mood fish will be in," says Winkelman. "If you choose an aggressive presentation like spinnerbaits you're going to miss a lot of neutral-minded fish. If you choose a more passive type of presentation you'll still catch active bass and have a better chance of catching inactive fish as well."

Jig worming is one of those presentations that works in a wide variety of situations. Winkelman favors this technique early in the year when fishing weed edges, boat channels, black-bottom bays, laydowns, rocks or just about any type of cover that's not too thick to fish an exposed hook through.

"My basic jig worm rig consists of a 1/32- to 1/8-ounce mushroom shaped jighead with a 6-inch Culprit worm threaded onto the jig," says Winkelman. "Because the jighead is a stand-up style that's attached to the nose of the worm, the bait looks much different in the water than a typical Texas rig. The worm stands upright when it hits the bottom instead of tipping over like other worm rigs."

This close-up shows a largemouth that took a jig worm. This technique is equally effective on largemouth and smallmouth bass. Photo courtesy Babe Winkelman productions.

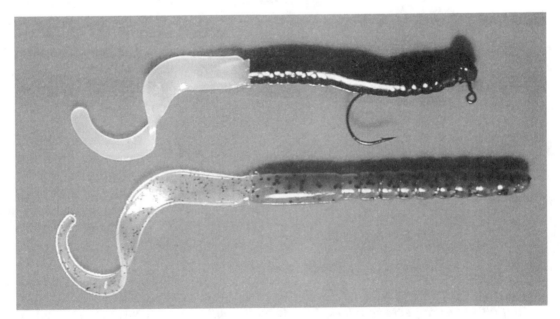

Curl-tail worms are a staple of jig worming, but other worm types can also be substituted.

Because the worm stands upright in the water it becomes more visible to fish, especially in areas where the bottom is covered with moss or short grass that could otherwise hide the lure. Also, the exposed thin wire hook is in position to stick any fish that picks up the bait.

> *Because the worm stands upright in the water it becomes more visible to fish, especially in areas where the bottom is covered with moss or short grass that could otherwise hide the lure.*

"I spend most of my time swimming the jig worm over the tops of emerging weeds, along weed lines, past lay-downs or sunken timber and drift wood," says Winkelman. "If you keep the jig moving you reduce the chances of fouling on bottom debris."

Swimming the jig worm is an excellent presentation when searching for bass. "The beauty of a jig worm is you can swim it, hop it or just let it sit motionless on the bottom," explains Winkelman. "One of my favorite ways to fish this rig is by swimming it over the top of emerging weeds. I cast into the weeds and start the retrieve immediately to keep the bait swimming over top of the cover. When the bait hits the edge of the cover, I'll let the worm sink straight down. Active fish usually hit the bait as it's swimming over the weeds. If the fish are more reluctant to chase, the jig worm dropped right on their nose is more than they can stand."

The most important aspect of jig worm fishing is keeping things light. Use just enough weight to maintain feel of the lure advises Winkelman. In calm conditions a 1/32- or 1/16-ounce mushroom head is ideal. If the wind picks up, switching to a slightly larger 3/32- or 1/8-ounce head will give the angler more control of the lure.

Winkelman's Good Fishing *and* Outdoor Secrets *television programs are broadcast on The Outdoor Channel each week.*

Spinning tackle equipped with 6- or 8- pound test line is ideal.

Depending on if you're swimming or hopping the jig worm, it matters how the bait is tied onto the line. "You can change the orientation of the jig worm as it moves in the water by simply adjusting the knot," says Winkelman. "Tie a clinch knot and pull the knot up tight. Next pull the knot down to the point where the leadhead and eye tie come together. Rigged in this manner the jig will swim more horizontally. To gain a more vertical appearance, slide the knot around to the front of the eye tie for hopping the bait. Each time a fish is hooked the knot must be adjusted."

Like other worm fishing methods, jig worming produces best in clear to stained waters. "Hands down my favorite color is tequila shad, but I also do well fishing June bug, and red shad," says Winkelman.

Other soft plastics that can be substituted for the Culprit worm include finesse worms, floating worms or 4-inch grubs.

Jig worms are easy to fish and productive in a wide variety of situations and water depths.

Jig worms are easy to fish and productive in a wide variety of situations and water depths. Perhaps Winkelman sums jig worms up best. "I like using jig worms because they are fun to fish," adds Winkelman. "The light tackle enables the angler to get the most from each hooked fish. After all, the most successful person on the water is the one who has the most fun fishing."

This chapter just scratches the surface for the many ways plastic worms can be used to catch bass. Moving on to Chapter Fifteen, the subject switches from worms to jigs and the best ways to pitch and flip them for more bass.

CHAPTER 15

PITCHING AND FLIPPIN' JIGS WITH TOMMY MARTIN

Leadhead jigs are one of those universal fishing lures that work on a wide variety of species. Just about everything that lives in fresh or salt water will readily hit a properly presented jig. Bass are no exception. All the major species of bass are routinely taken on a wide variety of jig types.

Many anglers believe that jigs are the single most important lure in a bass angler's tackle box. This is in part because these lures do an excellent job of imitating minnows, crayfish and other common bass forage types. A properly presented jig is very difficult for any bass to refuse because it simply looks too good not to eat! Jigs are also popular because they are effective on all water types everywhere bass are found.

Leadheads also have the advantage of being offered in a wide variety of styles suitable for fishing in heavy cover or open water. These versatile lures can also be used in shallow water, deep water and just about everywhere in between.

Tommy Martin is one of those anglers that feels strongly about jig fishing. A touring pro on the B.A.S.S. Circuit since 1974, Martin won the coveted BassMasters Classic during his rookie year on the circuit. Since then Martin has fished 18 Classics on his way to winning four invitational events and becoming one of the leading money winners in bass fishing.

Prior to becoming a professional bass angler, Martin guided on his home water of Toledo Bend, located on the Texas and Louisiana border. During all the years Martin has guided and fished tournaments professionally he has depended on jigs for much of his success.

"When most anglers think of bass fishing with jigs they think of flippin' in shallow water and heavy cover," says Martin. "Flippin' is a good fishing method, but one that's largely been overplayed in bass fishing. I spend most of my jig fishing time casting or pitching jigs to a wide variety of targets."

Casting to bass helps Martin catch fish that are easily spooked by flippin' and other short-range jig fishing methods. "In the spring of the year I spend most of my time casting smaller weedless style jigs ranging in size from 1/4 to 1/2 ounce," says Martin. "Because the fish are shallow at this time of year, I concentrate on making long casts to laydowns, stumps, clumps of cane, riprap banks and other visible cover. Points, channel edges and sunken islands are other important jig targets."

For casting jigs in shallow water, Martin prefers a 6- to 6-1/2-foot baitcasting combination with 10- to 12-pound test line. This combination offers him the ability to cast both accurately and comfortably all day long.

Because the jig is thrown a considerable distance, the style of leadhead used is also essential. To insure a solid hookset, Martin prefers jigs equipped with thin wire hooks. Stacey's Choice Smallmouth Jig produced by Stanley Jigs is a good example of the type of modest, weedless style, thin-wire jigs in which Martin has faith.

It's essential for casting jigs to feature thin wire and ultra-sharp hooks for two

Jigs are one of the universal lures that work on just about every species of fish; bass are no exception.

Tommy Martin depends on jigs wherever he fishes for bass.

reasons. "A hook that's thin in diameter is much easier to force into the jaw of a bass than the heavy tempered hooks most often used on flippin' jigs," explains Martin. "Line stretch is the other factor that makes it tough to drive anything but the thinnest and sharpest hooks home. The farther the cast and the lighter the line used, the more critical it becomes to use jigs featuring thin and sharp hooks."

Casting jigs requires the angler to concentrate on what the jig is doing at all times. The greater distance between the angler and the fish, slack line, light line, light lures and the effects of wind on the fishing line all make it more difficult to detect bites.

"When casting jigs it's important to understand how slack line impacts on jig fishing," says Martin. "Slack line allows the jig to fall naturally and enables the fish an opportunity to inhale the bait. Unfortunately, slack in the line also makes it more difficult to feel the take. Remember that bass are most likely to bite a jig as its falling. I'd say up to 75 percent of the fish I hook bite the jig on the fall."

This fact in mind, it's important to focus your concentration while the jig is sinking towards the bottom. To control the rate of descent and bring out additional action, a number of jig trailers can be used. By combining different size jigs and various styles of jig trailers, an angler can customize how fast the jig sinks.

In cool water situations it's usually best to use a bulked up jig that falls slowly. During the summer when bass are exceptionally active, a faster fall usually triggers the most strikes.

"I rig up three or four different jig and trailer combinations, then let the fish tell me which ones they prefer on any given day," suggests Martin. "In water colder than 55 degrees I use large pork rind chunks almost exclusively. I feel that in cold water pork has more action than plastic trailers and the jig sinks slower when using big pork chunks."

As the water begins to warm, a wealth of jig trailer options exist. "Pork still works in warm water, but plastic trailers come in a much wider assortment of styles and colors," explains Martin. "Some of my favorite trailers include the Big

Tommy Martin works a jig by casting to a channel edge. Martin prefers to cast jigs whenever possible.

Critter Craw and Li'l Critter Craw produced by Zoom. I also like to use a Big Dead Ringer worm with an inch or so cut off the head end."

Lizards, skirted grubs, twin-tail grubs and plastic pork chunk imitations are all good jig trailers. It's a good idea to experiment with jig trailers and trailer colors. Sometimes it's the trailer that makes the difference.

"I prefer dark colored jigs," says Martin. "Most of the time I tie on a black or blue jig

> *Most professional anglers feel that presentation is more important than color when it comes to fishing jigs for bass.*

with a similar colored skirt. If I want to experiment with colors I'll use the trailer to add a touch of color. It's easier to change trailer colors than to cut and retie different color jigs."

Color is a widely debated topic among jig fishermen. Most professional anglers feel that presentation is more important than color when it comes to fishing jigs for bass.

As the season progresses and bass begin to move into deeper water, Martin follows them with bigger flippin' style jigs and heavier tackle more suited to these lures. "I've taken bass down to 55 feet using jigs on channel edges and sunken islands," says Martin. "When I first started fishing these deep-water areas I had trouble finding jigs heavy enough," says Martin. "I compensated

For casting, Tommy Martin recommends jigs equipped with a thin wire hook. Flippin' style jigs often have heavy hooks that require a lot of pressure to set securely.

Anglers can choose from a wealth of jig trailers. In cool or cold water Tommy Martin recommends pork. For warmer water a variety of soft plastic trailers work well.

by adding a 1/4- or 3/8-ounce bullet weight on the line in front of a 1/2-ounce jig. Today there are a number of good jigs available ranging up to 1 ounce in size."

Martin's overall favorite jig is a relatively new entry in weedless jig technology. The Flat Eye produced by Stanley features extra large rattles and a turned eye tie to help reduce snags. Most importantly however is the unique weed guard design.

"I feel the Flat Eye jig offers a better hook-up ratio than other bass jigs," claims Martin. "The weed guard lays flat against an oversized wide-gap hook. When working the jig through cover the weed guard prevents the hook point from contacting snags. When a fish bites and the angler sets the hook, the weedguard is soft enough to fold out of the

Jeff Denny often finds bass in cover so heavy, flippin' is the only practical way to approach these fish.

way and expose the hook point. I've never fished a jig that did a better job of converting bites into hooked fish."

FLIPPIN' JIGS

No chapter on jig fishing would be complete without some hard-hitting tips on jig flippin'. This short-range and pinpoint presentation is the answer for fishing both dense cover and also for targeting a wealth of visual cover types.

Jeff Denny is a 38-year-old school teacher by day. The moment class lets out however, Denny is most likely to be found bass fishing. A tournament angler for the past nine years, his love of fishing and competitive drive have combined to hone this angler's edge razor-sharpness.

"Jig flippin' ranks as one of those classic presentations everyone should master," says Denny. "Flippin' is effective because the jig can be presented with more accuracy than other jig fishing methods. In addition to accuracy, the jig hits the water so lightly there's barely a ripple on the surface. The stealth and accuracy of this presentation generates reactionary strikes from bass that are surprised by the lure suddenly appearing in front of them."

Flippin' requires some specialized equipment. The rod is the most important tool when flippin'. "I like a 7-1/2-foot rod with a heavy action," says Denny. "If I'm flippin' lighter jigs, sometimes I'll use a 7-foot medium-heavy action rod, but 90 percent of the work is done with the longer and heavier action rod."

Most anglers use a rather inexpensive reel for flippin', the logic being that the reel is primarily used to store line. "I want a high quality reel for flippin', says Denny. "Several times I've stripped the gears out of reels on the hookset. You need a good quality baitcasting reel for this work."

Many reels are designed especially for flippin'. Reels with a flippin' feature enable the reel to shift into direct drive the second the angler removes his thumb from the bail release.

Fishing in Vegetation

Flippin' to open holes in floating vegetation

To Rod

Mats of floating vegetation.

"I'm not a big fan of flippin' features," says Denny. "I'm more comfortable leaving the bail open and controlling the line with my thumb. I feel I can cast more accurately this way and still have control of the fish by pressing my thumb firmly on the spool for the hookset."

Denny breaks from tradition by using much lighter line for flippin' than the 30-pound test many anglers favor. "I usually flip with 17-pound test line because I'm often fishing in clear water and I feel the lighter line allows me better accuracy," says Denny. "I can control most fish on 17-pound test unless the cover is exceptionally heavy. In heavy cover I'll bump up to 20-pound test."

Denny's favorite jigs for flippin' are the Triple Rattle Back, produced by Lunker Lures. "I fish just three jig colors and trailer combinations," says Denny. "I like a black and blue jig with a black pork chunk, a brown and chartreuse jig with a root beer-colored trailer and a white jig with a white trailer. I usually flip 3/8- and 1/2-ounce lures, but in some situations such as docks and other shallow water cover I'll drop down to a 1/4-ounce jig."

Denny identifies four specific applications for jig flippin'. "I spend a lot of time targeting emergent vegetation such as arrowheads, cattails or flooded brush," says Denny. "I also enjoy flippin' to submerged wood, docks and mats of heavy submerged vegetation."

FLIPPIN' EMERGENT COVER

When targeting arrowheads and other vegetation that grows up out of the water, Denny looks for areas that have at least 12 inches of water surrounding the cover. "The more water surrounding this cover the more likely it's going to hold fish," says Denny. "I like to start by flippin' my jig to the outside edges of the cover. The more active fish are most likely to be waiting on the edge. If this doesn't produce I'll go back over the same cover again, targeting the insides of the plant, looking for fish that are literally buried in the slop."

Key spots to hit include anything that stands out as different about a plant or group of plants. "I'm targeting pockets in the cover, little points that stick out, or a group of plants growing out in the open without other cover nearby." explains Denny. "When I'm fishing arrowheads I look for groups of plants that feature a hole in the center. It's amazing how often this tiny pocket will hold a bass."

Denny has also discovered that cover that holds a bass once is going to attract fish year after year. "Some of my best flippin' spots are patches of cover I've fished over and over again," adds Denny. "I think that the bottom composition or perhaps the weed cover growing on the bottom makes these areas more desirable to bass. It's the combination of complex cover that brings fish back time and time again."

Heavy cover, such as these reeds, is the type of vegetation where flippin' out-performs other angling methods.

Flippin' heavy cover is a mainstay for largemouth fishing in many areas. The cover may be weeds, wood or even floating mats of vegetation.

FLIPPIN' WOOD

Submerged wood is another outstanding place for jig flippin'. Wood that holds bass can range from a small piece of driftwood on the bottom to a rotted old tree trunk or relatively new trees that have toppled into the water.

"I feel that submerged wood that's located on an otherwise featureless bottom makes the best jig flippin' cover," claims Denny. "Even a small piece of wood that most anglers would skip right over can hold a good fish. The way I flip this wood depends on how complex the cover is. Small and isolated pieces of wood get one quick flip. If I'm working a tree trunk I'll target the places where limbs and the main trunk come together. Often it takes several flips to com-

pletely cover a piece of cover. The roots of trees toppled into the water are especially good because the water is often a little deeper and there's both cover and shade."

Denny recommends that anglers hit a productive piece of wood several times during a day of fishing. "I believe when you hook a fish, others in the area are spooked," explains Denny. "It doesn't take these fish long however to slip back into the cover. I've hit the same tree as many as three or four times in a day if I'm confident there are good fish in the area."

When fishing wood it's easier to work the shallow water where you can see every detail of the cover. In deeper water anglers must slow down and fish the cover more thoroughly to find the hidden spots that hold fish.

FLIPPIN' DOCKS

There has been stacks of magazine articles written about flippin' techniques for docks. "Docks are pretty straightforward," says Denny. "I target the posts and ladders going down into the water first and then try to reach as far back under the cover as possible. The harder a spot is to hit with a jig, the more likely it will hold fish. I especially like docks near deep water with some weed growth. The lower the dock is to the water the more excited I get because these areas provide maximum shade and not as many anglers are skilled enough to flip into these tight places."

It helps to fish docks with lighter jigs because bass are often suspended in the shade instead of resting tight to bottom. A lighter jig (say 1/4-ounce jig) that sinks slower is going to catch more fish on docks than heavier (1/2-ounce) jigs that make more disturbance in the water and sink quickly.

FLIPPIN' SUBMERGED WEEDS

"I break submerged weeds down into two groups," says Denny. "One group is patches of submerged weeds that have not grown to the surface. Thick patches of coontail and milfoil are good examples of this flippin' situation. The spots that I target are holes in the cover, edges or anyplace where I can get the jig to the bottom. The best fishing usually occurs in water from 3 to 6 feet deep."

This style of jig flippin' calls for heavy jigs that adequately penetrate the cover. Denny recommends using at least a 1/2-ounce jig and often opts for larger jigs. "Keep your line as vertical as possible," cautions Denny. "Don't make long flips. Instead concentrate on short flips that hit exactly on pockets, holes or any opening in the cover.

The second type of weed cover that Denny flips is mats of floating vegetation. This cover can be from loose bunches of weeds dislodged from the bottom by wave action and left floating on the surface or from weed cover that grows up to the surface then lays over and floats on the surface.

"Dense mats of floating weeds give great overhead cover and shade," says Denny. "I use a heavy jig and flip to any hole or opening in the mat. If the cover is really thick I'll yo-yo the jig up and down using the cover to hold the line while I raise and lower the jig. I like to let the jig sink on a slack line then shake it back up to the surface."

Coontail, pondweed, smart weed and other weed types that frequently grow to the surface are good places to find weeds laying over and providing overhead cover. This is the type of cover that calls for heavy jigs and heavier line. A hooked fish must be forced from the cover as quickly as possible before the fish balls up in 10 pounds of weeds!

OTHER FLIPPIN' LURES

Jigs aren't the only lures that can be used effectively in a flippin' situation. Denny often uses three different soft plastic baits for flippin' including tubes, centipedes and crayfish imitations.

"When I'm flippin' a tube or other plastic lure I treat the bait like a jig," says Denny. "I'll select a bullet weight that's heavy enough to penetrate the cover, then peg the weight using a tooth pick so the lure and weight sink as one unit. When you're working thick cover the last thing you need is the sinker on one side of a log and the lure on the other."

A tube is a good bait for this style of fishing because it looks a lot like both a minnow or crayfish. Do-nothing-style plastics like a centipede are another bait that can be Texas rigged and flipped as an alternative to jigs. A Texas rigged plastic craw is also a good option for flippin'.

Flippin' is toe-to-toe fishing excitement. No other form of bass fishing puts the angler closer to the action. Both flippin' and pitchin' jigs are techniques every angler should master.

In the next chapter, we'll look at a different type of jig fishing. The lighter line and jigheads used when fishing grubs and tubes are vastly different angling methods than flippin' or pitchin' with jigs. A separate chapter is required to discuss these light-line tactics in detail.

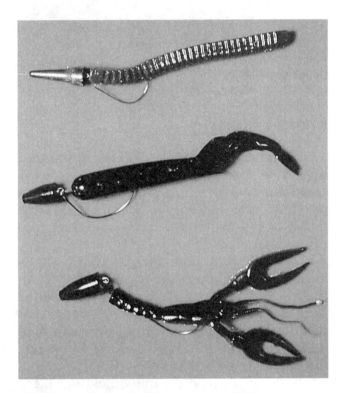

Jigs aren't the only baits that can be flipped. Denny often flips tubes, centipedes or crawfish Texas rigged.

CHAPTER 16

GREG MANGUS
ON FISHING GRUBS AND TUBES

In bass fishing the civil war is still being waged. In the Deep Douth, bass are often fished in large rivers and reservoirs. The water clarity is frequently stained or in some cases downright muddy. The most productive fishing techniques are spinnerbaits and crankbaits. Heavy tackle is the norm and finesse is about the last thing on angler's minds.

Up north, most of the bassin' is done on clear-water natural lakes. Even the rivers usually run clear or are only slightly stained. Lures such as spinnerbaits that are designed to produce reactionary strikes simply don't work as well in water so clear you can see a jig on the bottom in 10 feet of water.

Instead of approaching bass with traditional tackle and techniques, anglers faced with these limitations adjust by using smaller lures, lighter line and baits that look and move like something a bass would eat.

Greg Mangus lives in northern Indiana where he sells bass boats for a living at West Lakes Boat Mart. At 52, Mangus has become one of the most respected tournament anglers in the Midwest. He spends most of his tournament time fishing Tri-State Bass, a respected circuit that holds full field events in Ohio, Michigan and Indiana. In the past few years it's safe to say this soft-spoken angler has dominated the circuit, winning the points championship seven times and the annual Fall Classic three times. Mangus is typical of the brand of northern bass angler who spends most of his time targeting hard-to-catch fish in clear water. His techniques however are anything but typical.

When faced with clear water Mangus spends the lion's share of his time fishing tubes and grubs. "I like to cast tubes and grubs because I can cover water quickly, but still be offering a finesse presentation," says

Mangus. "In order to catch bass consistently in clear water you have to throw something that looks like the food bass naturally prey on. Tubes and grubs do the best job of imitating minnows and crayfish."

Grubs and tubes are standards for fishing clear water, but the tackle Mangus uses and the techniques he has pioneered are anything but typical. The

> *The rod length is also important for making long casts and for picking up slack line on the hookset.*

break from tradition starts with the rods he favors.

"For most of my tube and grub fishing I'm using either a 7-foot or a 7-1/2-foot G-Loomis spinning rod with a moderate action," says Mangus. "When faced with shallow water I choose the shorter rod and 6- to 8-pound test line. When fishing deeper water, the longer rod and 8- to 10-pound test is ideal."

According to Mangus, the rod action is critical to his style of fishing. "It takes a forgiving rod to land a 5- or 6-pound smallmouth on light line," says Mangus. "The extra length and soft action help to tire out powerful fish."

The rod length is also important for making long casts and for picking up slack line on the hookset. Mangus favors Daiwa reels, but he never depends on the drag system to tame a powerful fish. Instead he back reels his fish to insure the line is never stressed beyond its ability.

A third element of Mangus' grub and tube strategy is speed. He typically fishes his lures much faster than other anglers.

Mangus also pours most of his own jigheads because he insists on specific jighead shapes and premium quality hooks. "It's very difficult to find commercially produced jigheads that feature premium hooks," says Mangus. "When you're fishing light line you need the sharpest possible hooks. I use either Owner or Gamakatsu jig hooks on all my leadheads."

Mangus recommends that anglers looking for a commercial head to check out the Bite Me, Nichols and Strike King brand

Greg Mangus has become one of the most feared anglers at tournaments held in the North. His unique approach to fishing tubes and grubs has placed him at the top of his field. Photo courtesy of Louie Stout.

leadheads. "These are the best commercially sold jigs I've found."

For most of his tube and grub fishing Mangus favors open-style hooks with a 60-degree bend on the eye instead of the normal 90-degree turn. This simple feature helps a jig swim better and foul much less on weeds and bottom debris.

The head styles he favors for tube fishing are tear drop, aspirin and barrel-shaped versions. "The aspirin shaped heads give tubes a unique side-to-side wobble you don't get with a tear drop head," says Mangus. "I use heavy barrel heads for another unique presentation."

When fishing grubs Mangus molds a Sparky jighead that's similar to the classic Arky head shape. This is a modified stand-up style head that insures the hook is always riding up-right. He also uses some jigs with fiber weed guards. All these jig styles feature barbs to hold the grub firmly in place.

Mangus started forming his unique grub and tube fishing strategy many years ago when he worked for a sport shop that had a huge aquarium stocked with bass. "It was part of my job to feed the bass," says Mangus. "When I dumped minnows into the tank, most of the small fish would ball up and swim around the tank in one tight group. There were always a few that panicked and headed out on their own. The bait-

> *When fishing shallow water where he has the luxury of watching his lure, Mangus will fish brighter colors to make it easier to observe the bait.*

fish that panicked were always eaten immediately. Meanwhile the group of minnows swimming around weren't even given a second glance by bass in the tank. It was the same every time I fed the fish. I learned that in order to trigger bass into striking I had to make my lures react erratically to draw attention to them."

SPIDER AND ACTION TAIL GRUBS

When fishing grubs Mangus prefers the Chompers and Kalin brands. He fishes 3- and 4-inch single-tails, twin-tails and spider-style grubs in variations of smoke, green and brown with some flake added to give the

This assortment of grub and leadhead styles are among the favorites of Greg Mangus. Mangus often molds his own jigheads using premium hooks from companies such as Gamakatsu or Owner.

lure a little flash. When fishing shallow water where he has the luxury of watching his lure, Mangus will fish brighter colors to make it easier to observe the bait. More important than the brands and colors is the unique retrieve Mangus uses to trigger strikes.

"I strive to make my presentation as horizontal as possible," says Mangus. "I make very long casts so when I'm retrieving the grub it will swim horizontal and in close contact with the bottom for as long as possible. I move my grubs fast, but I'm staying close to the bottom."

Mangus is trying to achieve the most erratic and darting retrieve possible. Instead of swimming the grub and giving the rod tip an occasional lift to hop the bait, he works the rod in a snapping motion that jerks the bait in one direction and then another similar to the way a jerkbait is fished.

"I reel until I can feel the weight of the bait then I give the rod tip a

These Nichols leadheads are designed to enable a tooth pick to be placed through the grub, insuring the grub stays firmly in place on the hook shank.

To help plastic stay put on leadheads, Greg Mangus often uses a wire cutter to rough up the shank of the jig.

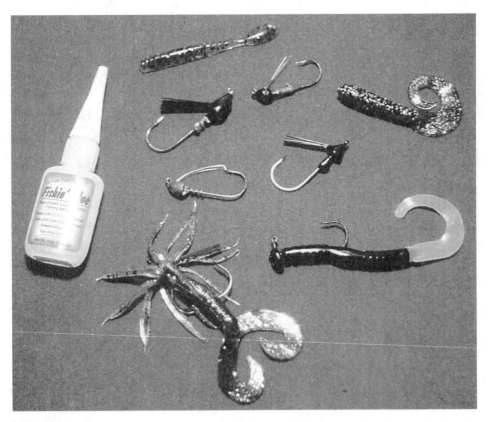

Plastic grubs can also be secured to leadheads using special fishing glues. Simply put a drop of glue on the jig shank and thread the plastic into place. The glue dries in a couple of seconds and makes a secure bond between the leadhead and the plastic bait.

The leadheads used for fishing with tube baits differ somewhat from those designed to be used with grubs.

sharp snap," says Mangus. "The bait squirts forward and I reel up the slack line and snap it again. I'm trying to give the bait a darting motion, but I'm also being careful not to fish the lure in a rhythmic cadence or pattern. I vary both the speed and jerking motion to achieve the most erratic action possible."

Depending on water depth Mangus will use leadheads from 1/16- to 3/4-ounce. Heavier jigs enable him to fish faster while still keeping in contact with the bottom. "I'm convinced that working these baits faster than normal has a huge influence on triggering strikes," says Mangus. "I can also cover more water when searching for active fish."

TUBE BAITS

Mangus uses the same darting and rapid retrieve when fishing tubes. The shapes of the leadheads used inside the tube can help vary the action achieved. "An aspirin-style head will cause the tube to have a more pronounced darting and gliding action," says Mangus. "The center of gravity for this jighead style is higher. When moved in the water the head moves back and forth inside the tube body causing the lure to change directions when jerked. The tear drop-style heads generate a more subdued and predictable action."

Mangus also fishes tubes using a retrieve style that combines heavy jigheads with an aggressive rod sweep. "The retrieve style I'm using is way out of the mainstream," says Mangus. "I use a long rod and heavy barrel-style jigheads in the 1/2- to 3/4-ounce

When fishing a grub or other plastic bait this aggressively, just keeping the plastic lure in place on the leadhead can be a challenge.

range. I cast as far as possible and let the tube sink to bottom. Next I point the rod at the bait and reel up the slack. When I can feel the weight of the bait, I lift the rod in a long sweep that rockets the bait up off bottom, then I let the lure free fall. If I'm fishing in water less than 10 feet the tube often comes up and breaks the surface on the rod sweep."

This aggressive tube fishing technique has produced countless fish for Mangus on Lake Erie and other Great Lakes' waters where smallmouth are often super-aggressive and most apt to strike lures that move in a fast and unpredictable manner.

When fishing a grub or other plastic bait this aggressively, just keeping the plastic lure in place on the leadhead can be a challenge. This is especially true if weeds or other cover complicate the picture. Mangus uses a number of techniques and products to help keep his grubs securely attached to the jig.

"Nichols makes a couple unique jigheads that are designed to hold grubs securely," says Mangus. "The shank of the jighead has a small hole molded into the lead. After the grub is pushed up tight on the jig shank, a toothpick is pushed into the grub, through the small hole and broken off. This pins the grub to the jighead securely. These jigs are offered in both round-head style jigs and weedless style models with weed guards."

Using glue to secure grubs in place is another option. Putting a drop of Super Glue on the nose of the grub, threading it onto the jig and holding it tight against the

Greg Mangus battles a smallmouth hooked while fishing grubs. Photo courtesy Louie Stout.

jig's head for a moment until the glue dries works pretty good. Mangus recommends taking one more step when using glue to secure grub bodies. "I take a pair of side cutters and notch up the lead shank of the jig to increase the surface area," says Mangus. "A little glue is placed on this damaged area and the grub threaded into place. The extra surface area holds the grub in place even when fishing through weeds, wood and other cover."

Grubs and tubes are becoming the standard lures anglers depend on for catching bass in the north, or anywhere the water is clear. Greg Mangus has been instrumental in adding a new twist to the ways these lures are fished. Most of methods used by Mangus are designed to target smallmouth bass, but they also work equally well on largemouth.

Of course, grubs and tubes can also be used in more traditional ways to catch bass. Slower presentations where the lure is hopped along bottom or kept swimming near bottom continue to take untold numbers of smallmouth, largemouth and spotted bass.

Some of the best places to target these lures are open water structure such as shoals, rock piles, sand bars, points, rocky shorelines, ledges, fast-sloping breaks and gravel beds. The leadhead jig is versatile enough to be useful in sparse weed growth or submerged wood and many anglers feel that a simple jig dressed with a grub or tube bait is tops anytime bass are found living in clear water.

Grubs and tubes are light-line techniques, but now it's time to switch gears and talk about a classic bass fishing method that is based on heavy tackle and deep water.

Tubes such as the one used to take this fish excel anytime the water is clear and bass are spooky.

CHAPTER 17

JON BONDY AND RANDY RAMSEY DISCUSS CAROLINA RIGGING

Carolina rigging is to bass angling what Lindy rigging is to walleye fishing. In fact, the two types of fishing are very similar and used for many of the same reasons.

Carolina rigging is primarily used as a deep-water technique that covers water quickly. Effective in natural lakes, reservoirs, ponds, rivers and the Great Lakes, this fishing method can be used just about everywhere bass are found.

BONDY RIGS RIVERS

Jon Bondy of Windsor, Ontario, is a 27-year-old tournament angler, fishing guide, aquaculturalist and bass fishing specialist. Growing up on the shores of Lake St. Clair, the St. Clair River and the Detroit River,

Bondy grew up with three of the most productive bass fisheries in North America at his fingertips. It's easy to see why his passion for bass fishing started early and has grown into an obsession that puts him on the water some 200 days a year.

Carolina rigging is normally associated with deep-water fishing, used most often in reservoirs and natural lakes. Bondy uses a version of Carolina rigging on the Detroit and St. Clair rivers when guiding and during fishing tournaments in the area. His methods are just as deadly on any river where bass relate to channel edges, breaks and hard-bottom areas.

"The ability to cover water quickly is the biggest advantage of Carolina rigging in rivers," says Bondy. "Also, Carolina rigging keeps the angler in contact with the bottom and makes it easy to determine the bottom composition. I'm looking mostly for rocky areas, especially those spots where the river channel is steep."

Most of the bass Bondy catches are smallmouth, but a considerable number of largemouth can also be taken using his unique methods. Bondy's many charter customers are amazed at how easy and productive this fishing method can be.

> *As in any type of fishing, the type of equipment used can make a big difference in fishing success.*

As in any type of fishing, the type of equipment used can make a big difference in fishing success. Medium-heavy action baitcasting gear is required for Carolina rigging. "I use a 7-foot All Star Titanium baitcasting rod," says Bondy. "You need at least a 7-foot rod because most of the time you're dragging with lots of line out. A longer rod helps to take up the slack and line stretch on the hookset better than shorter rods."

Bondy recommends using a monofilament main line from 14- to 17-pound test. "If I'm fishing rather shallow water I opt for the lighter line. In deep water, 17-pound test is about perfect."

The leader is tied using 12- to 14-pound test line. Lighter line gives the bait better

Jon Bondy is an Ontario-based guide who specializes in catching bass on rivers.

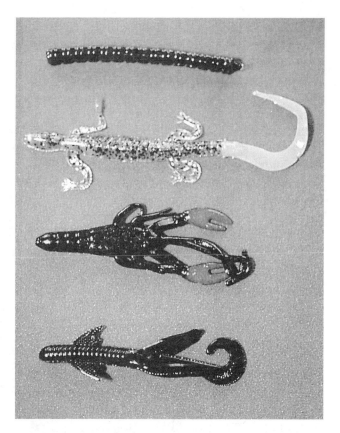

Jon Bondy favors Zoom lizards for Carolina rigging, but a number of other plastic baits can also be used with good success.

action and should the bait become snagged, the leader can be broken off without losing the entire rig.

"The rig I use most often is similar to Carolina rigs used elsewhere," says Bondy. "I start with a bullet weight threaded onto the line, followed by a glass bead and then a good-sized barrel swivel. Tied to the barrel swivel I use an 18- to 36-inch leader tied to a No. 3/0 Gamakatsu Extra-Wide-Gap worm hook. My favorite baits are the Zoom 6-inch Lizard and Fishdoctor, but a wealth of soft plastic lures are productive."

Bondy uses lead sinkers and ties his own rigs because he is usually running a guide trip and trying to keep his expenses down. However, he is quick to point out that brass or steel weights generate more noise when rigging. Pre-rigged Carolina weights like the Bass Pro Shop Carolina Short Cut or the Ultra Steel Carolina Quick Rig are also time savers.

"I let the boat drift naturally downstream with the current and use an electric motor to keep the boat drifting at the desired water depth," explains Bondy. "The trick is to use just enough weight to keep the bait in contact with bottom. If too much weight is used the rig will snag bottom frequently. If not enough weight is used too much line must be let out to make contact with bottom."

A good guideline to go by when matching sinker weights to water depths is to select 1/4-ounce sinkers for depths up to 10 feet, 3/8- to 1/2-ounce weights up to 15 feet, 5/8- to 3/4-ounce up to 25 feet, and 1-ounce weights when fishing down to 35 feet.

"I've discovered that river bass are almost always found on rocky hard-bottom areas," says Bondy. "I've also had my best success by working steep breaks and swift current areas where the rocks are constantly washed free of silt and debris."

Bondy recommends looking for bass at the point where a steep break flattens out into the main channel. If the river you're fishing has shipping traffic, don't overlook areas where dredging is used to keep the shipping channel clear.

Jon Bondy drifts with the current, using his electric motor to stay on sharp breaks.

Light Carolina Rigs on Breaklines

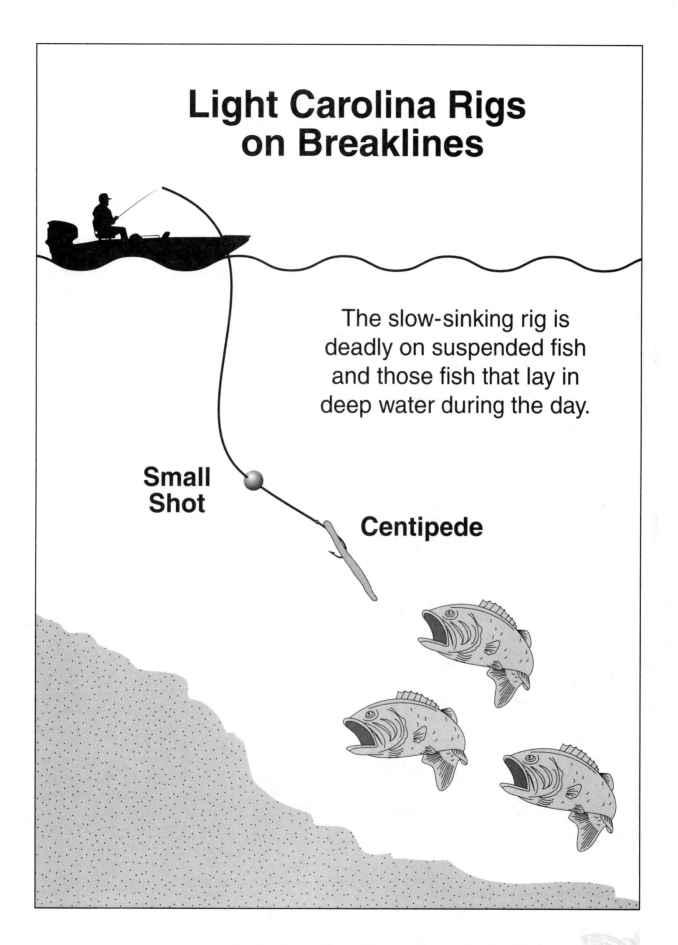

The slow-sinking rig is deadly on suspended fish and those fish that lay in deep water during the day.

Small Shot

Centipede

"River bends, necked down areas and the upstream sides of islands are all good places to find river smallmouth," says Bondy. "When I'm drifting I'm constantly feeling for rocks. If the bottom goes soft, I don't waste any time looking for another spot."

Another tip from Bondy's bag of tricks is to thread the bullet weight onto the line backwards so the cupped end catches in the bottom and churns up more silt.

Most of Bondy's river fishing is conducted on the relatively clear waters of the St. Clair and Detroit Rivers. "In clear water I like to fish natural colors including shades of black, green and brown," says Bondy. "After a rain when runoff turns the water cloudy, I switch to more brightly colored plastic baits."

Bondy has a couple other tricks he uses to trigger strikes. According to Bondy, a short 18-inch leader gives the trailing plastic bait a faster and more pronounced action. This seems to produce best on active fish and in warm water. If the leader is lengthened, the action on the lure becomes softer. Normally a bait with less action works better on fish that are otherwise reluctant to bite.

Another tip from Bondy's bag of tricks is to thread the bullet weight onto the line backwards so the cupped end catches in the bottom and churns up more silt. This simple modification to the standard Carolina rig really works wonders at times.

On the water Bondy helps his clients catch more fish by avoiding common Carolina rigging mistakes. "Never set the hook with an upwards rod sweep," cautions Bondy. "This style of hookset suspends the weight between the rod tip and lure where it bounces around and can actually provide the fish enough leverage to shake free of the lure. Instead, reel up slack line until you can feel the weight of the fish then set the hook with a hard sideways rod sweep."

Here Jon Bondy uses a 3-foot leader from the weight to his bait. By experimenting with shorter leads you can impart a different action on the lure.

The best days for Carolina rigging in rivers is when the wind is blowing the same direction as the current, claims Bondy. "If the wind blows against the current the drift is slower and snagging becomes more of a problem. A fast and consistent drift produces the best results."

Carolina rigging in rivers seems to produce best in waters from 15 to 25 feet deep. Mostly Bondy drifts with the current. Fishing sand bars is one area where drifting isn't the best option. Instead, Bondy positions his boat just downstream of a sand bar and casts the Carolina rig up onto the structure. A slow retrieve is used to drag the rig over

> *The best days for Carolina rigging in rivers is when the wind is blowing the same direction as the current, claims Bondy.*

the sand and back to the boat.

Carolina rigging in rivers is one of those overlooked bassin' techniques. One of the best ways to cover water quickly while learning river structure, Carolina rigging in flowing water works anywhere rivers and bass are flowing together.

LIGHT CAROLINA RIGS

Traditional Carolina rigs feature heavy weights that are dragged along the bottom in deep water. Lightweight Carolina rigs are an important variation on this classic presentation.

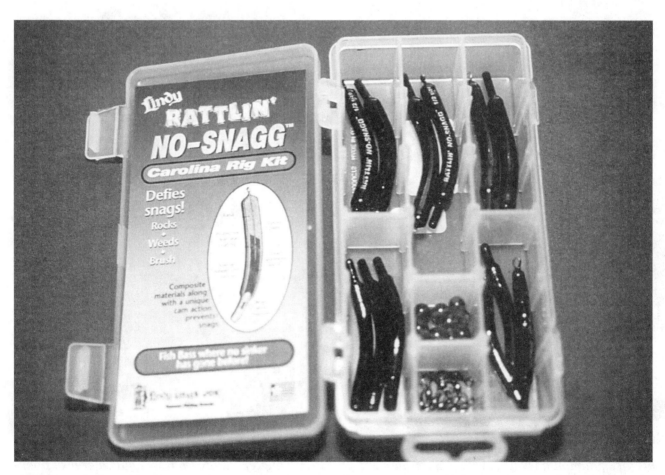

Carolina rig kits, like this one from Lindy, are a good way to insure all the components required are handy.

Made popular by anglers who fish in clear-water fisheries, light Carolina rigs are especially productive when used on heavily pressured waters. Effective at any time of year and in almost any water depth, these lightweight Carolina rigging options are ideal for covering flats, breaklines and weed edges.

Tournament pro Randy Ramsey is a Michigan-based angler who is enjoying tremendous success, especially on heavily pressured waters. Ramsey has been a professional angler for over 15 years. During that time he has fished more than 450 tournaments and won 50 events! In 2000 he was the Tri-State Bass points champion. A fre-

quent face in magazine and newspaper features focusing on bass angling, Ramsey does most of his fishing in the Great Lakes, Canada and Midwestern states.

"I like using lightweight Carolina rigs because the weight allows these rigs to be cast great distances, while the plastic bait enjoys the action of a weightless lure," says Ramsey. "My top pick for tough days, I find this subtle approach shines better the tougher the fishing becomes. I've also discovered that light Carolina rigging is a great way to target big fish."

Clear water, bright sunny conditions and during tournaments when anglers are often forced to fish behind another boat, are

This fat smallmouth is on his way to a tournament weigh-in. Carolina rigging in rivers often produces larger fish than other methods.

Pro angler Randy Ramsey holds a pair of book-end bass he caught using his own version of a Carolina rig.

just a few of the conditions when these pint-sized Carolina rigs excel. Getting the most from this presentation requires spinning tackle, light line and rods a little longer than normal.

"I use a 7-1/2-foot, medium-action G-Loomis spinning rod combo and 8-pound test Magna Thin line," says Ramsey. "You need the extra rod length for making long casts and for picking up slack when setting the hook or moving the bait along bottom. Also, a long rod is a huge advantage when fighting large fish on light line."

Braided lines are a poor choice for this type of fishing because they sink faster than monofilament and because they are more visible to fish in clear water. Stealth is an important aspect of this style of fishing.

"My standard rig features an 1/8- or 3/16-ounce bullet sinker threaded onto the line and tied to a small barrel swivel," explains Ramsey. "Attached to the swivel I run an 18- to 24-inch leader tied directly to a K&E Tackle rigged worm that features

> *The open hooks used with rigged worms are part of what makes this variation of traditional Carolina rigs so effective.*

three thin wire hooks and a monofilament leader molded into the worm."

The open hooks used with rigged worms are part of what makes this variation of traditional Carolina rigs so effective. "When a bass picks up a Texas rigged worm or lizard fished on a traditional Carolina rig, the fish often drops the bait before the angler even knows he had a bite," says Ramsey. "Fishing rigged worms with exposed hooks helps me stick more of the fish that bite. It takes only the slightest pressure to hook these fish compared to the head snapping hooksets required with Texas rigged plastics."

Using lighter weights also has more advantages. "Lighter weights force me to fish slower," explains Ramsey. "Keeping the bait in front of negative fish longer is what triggers the strike. Moving slowly is the only way to squeeze bites out of pressured fish."

One of Ramsey's favorite times to fish these light rigs is during the heat of summer when bass move into deep water. During the day these fish often suspend in open water or tuck into the bottom and wait for night fall. Under the cover of darkness they move up onto flats or edges to feed.

"I target break-lines, but instead of fishing the weed edges like most anglers, I position the boat along the edge and cast into deep water," says Ramsey. "My light rigs sink slowly, often triggering strikes from suspended bass as they fall. When the rig hits the bottom, I work it by using slow sweeps

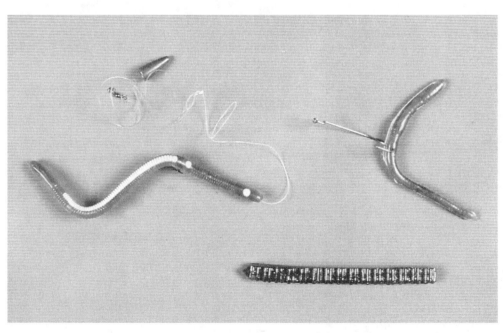

Randy Ramsey uses Carolina rigs for fishing baits that have a tendency to spin in the water such as rigged worms and lizards. The swivel in the system helps to reduce line twist.

of the rod that move the bait a couple feet at a time. In between sweeps it's important to pause the bait and let it settle slowly back to bottom."

This type of fishing requires lots of patience because the lures sink slowly and it's not always easy to tell if the bait is on bottom. Often Ramsey targets this presentation in waters from 20 to 40 feet deep. Strikes are most often detected when you see the line move or feel a sensation of weight at the end of the line.

SPLIT SHOT RIGGING

Split shot rigs are another variation of the Carolina rig. Most often used in cooperation with do-nothing style plastic baits, split shotting is a finesse-style presentation that has merit anywhere bass are found in shallow and clear water.

Ramsey treats split shot rigs somewhat differently than light Carolina rigs. "I use a light Carolina rig for plastics that have a tendency to spin in the water such as rigged worms or lizards," says Ramsey. "The swivel in this system helps to reduce problems with line twist as the bait is worked.

If I'm going to fish a centipede, French-fry worm, or do-nothing-style worm, there's no need to add the swivel. Instead, I simply pinch a split shot onto the line 18 to 24 inches in front of the lure."

Split shot rigs are great for fish-ing transitional bass. "In the post-spawn, when bass are moving towards deeper water, these fish often hold on the inside or outside of weed edges," adds Ramsey. "In this situation I like to cast a Zoom Centipede Texas rigged with a No. 2/0 Gamakatsu offset worm hook. I'll use the smallest split shot I can get away with, usually a 1/32-ounce."

Split shot rigs must be fished slowly and with lots of patience. This rig is an outstanding choice when bass that have been biting one presentation or another suddenly stop feeding. Slowing down and dragging a split shot rig helps Ramsey and many other anglers hook bonus fish that simply will not bite other lures. No matter where you fish bass, rigging, in one of its popular forms, should be a part of your fishing strategy.

In the next chapter we'll focus on deep-water fishing lures, jigging spoons and blade baits. These often overlooked baits can be bass-catching machines.

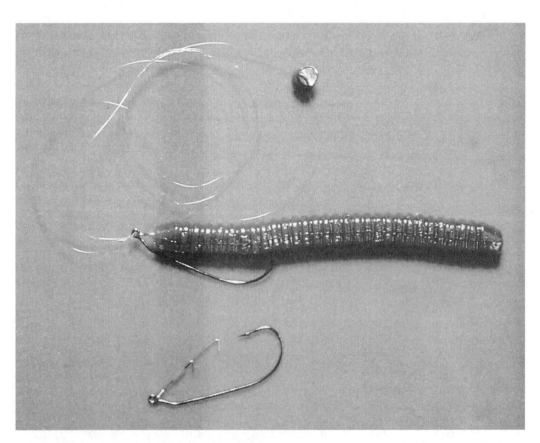

When fishing with centipedes and do-nothing worms a simple split shot on the line and a Texas rigged bait works best.

CHAPTER 18

BEN FELTON SERVES UP SPOONS AND JEFF SNYDER GETS SHARP WITH BLADE BAITS

The heavy metal of bass fishing, spoons and blade baits are two lure types most anglers don't use often enough. Ideally suited for fishing bass in deep and cold water situations, spoons and blade baits also excel in a wealth of other fishing situations.

Ben Felton is a young and aggressive pro who fishes the Red Man, B.A.S.S. and Team USA bass fishing circuits. His innovative approach to bass fishing has helped him earn numerous top-10 finishes and the respect of his fellow anglers.

"I use spoons as an alternative to Carolina rigging," says Felton. "A spoon can be worked faster than a Carolina rig and can also be used to cover a wider range of the water column. I feel that aggressive bass are attracted to the flash and action you can only get with a spoon."

Felton prefers a medium-heavy action baitcasting outfit with a pistol grip for spoonin'. The ideal reel for this style of fishing is a fast retrieve gear ratio baitcaster loaded with 12- to 14-pound test monofilament. At the end of his line he threads on a red glass bead then adds a heavy duty snap.

"The red bead is something I started doing a few years ago to add a touch of color," says Felton. "Most of the spoons I fish are solid silver or gold and the red bead provides some needed contrast. I feel the bead helps, especially when fishing smallmouth in clear water."

The marketplace is loaded with dozens of brands and models of jigging spoons. These lures are produced in a wide assort-

> **"Most of the spoons I fish are solid silver or gold and the red bead provides some needed contrast."**

ment of shapes, finishes and weights. After experimenting with many types of spoons, Felton has settled on three styles that he feels do the best job on a wide variety of water types. He carries four sizes including an assortment of 1/4-, 3/8-, 1/2- and 1-ounce spoons.

"I have the most faith in the Cordell, Hopkins and Strata spoons," says Felton. "The Cordell spoon is a wider spoon that sinks a little slower than either the Hopkins

Ben Felton often uses jigging spoons in place of Carolina rigs for quickly covering water.

Jigging spoons are one of the most overlooked baits for fishing all species of bass.

or Strata spoons. Unfortunately, this spoon is hard to find. The Hopkins spoon is readily available at most sport shops and works equally well on largemouth, smallmouth or spotted bass. The Strata spoon is similar to the Hopkins in shape and action. Produced by Bass Pro Shops, this spoon and can be ordered through the mail or purchased from any BPS retail outlet."

Other classic jigging spoons anglers may want to consider include the Swedish Pimple, KastMaster, Krocodile and Crippled Herring.

Like many other professional anglers, Felton demands that his lures are equipped with premium quality hooks. "The first thing I do when I buy a new spoon is replace the factory treble hook with a Gamakatsu Extra-Wide-Gap treble hook," says Felton. "Depending on the size of the spoon I use a No. 6, 4 or 2 sized hook."

Unlike most anglers who treat spoons as vertical jigging lures, felton spends most of his time pitching and casting spoons. Some of his most productive fishing spots are metal or concrete sea walls, ship docks, breakwalls, piers and other cover that rises up vertically from the bottom.

"The best walls are those that have deep water right up tight to the edge," explains Felton. "I like to target areas with at least 4 feet of water and I'll often find fish as deep as 20 feet. The best walls are usually those with some sort of wave action or current flowing across them. When you get inside protected marinas, boat slips and other areas out of this current, you don't find as many fish."

When pitching to walls, Felton prefers to position his boat to work into the current or wind. "Working into the wind makes it easier to hold the boat in one position," explains Felton. "I like to position the boat parallel to the wall and out about 10 feet. I make short pitches, targeting my first casts tight to the

> *"Most of the bass encountered along these man-made walls are located close to the point where the vertical cover contacts the horizontal bottom.'*

edge formed between the wall and the bottom. It's important to let the spoon fall on a slack line. Often I'll feed the lure line as it sinks to insure the spoon slides straight down the wall."

Most of the bass encountered along these man-made walls are located close to the point where the vertical cover contacts the horizontal bottom. Bass lay at this transition point with their tail towards the wall and their nose out in the current. If the spoon falls on a tight line, it will pendulum out away from the wall and may miss this narrow strike zone."

Ben Felton likes the Cordell spoon, but he replaces the factory hook with a Gamakatsu Extra-Wide Gap treble before fishing.

While most of the fish will be taken close to the wall, some will relate to rocks or other bottom debris located out away from the edge. It only takes a cast or two to cover the water out away from the edge.

"Once the spoon hits the bottom, I bring it to life by snapping the rod tip sharply with my wrist," says Felton. "Each snap of the rod tip jerks the spoon a foot or so off bottom and allows the lure to sink on a slack line. After giving the spoon several jerks, I'll reel up and pitch the bait a little farther down the wall."

This style of spoon fishing is best treated as a fast-paced presentation designed for targeting aggressive fish. Felton moves quickly until he contacts bass, then he slows down and fishes the area more thoroughly. He often switches to other techniques such as grubs or tubes to milk out a few extra bites from fish that aren't aggressively feeding.

"When you're fishing smooth metal or concrete walls that offer little cover, the fish tend to be scattered along the edge," admits Felton. "Usually I find that fish concentrate on rocks, drift wood or other debris submerged near the base of the wall. If the wall has a bend or corner these spots are prime locations."

Breakwalls and piers made of broken stone or concrete pieces offer bass a wealth of small pockets and places to hide. With so much good cover to work, covering these areas takes more time than smooth walls. Short, but accurate flip casts are the way to cover this water efficiently.

"Pay attention to the bass you catch and you'll have learned how to catch more," says Felton. "When I catch a fish I take note of the water depth and if there's anything unique about the spot that produced the fish. Sometimes the pattern is as simple as combining a particular water depth and cover type. Other times, the fish are keying on some specific aspect of the cover such as corners or turns."

Felton most often selects a 1/2-ounce spoon because it allows him to maintain contact with the bottom while moving the bait quickly. "If I feel the fish aren't very active, I'll often switch to a smaller spoon and slow down a little. On the other hand if I'm catching a lot of small fish, I'll switch to a larger spoon and speed up."

In clear waters Felton favors a silver spoon. In stained waters he switches to a hammered gold finish.

Pitching to sea walls and other vertical cover is just one way Felton uses spoons to catch bass. Blind casting to structure is another

Ben Felton sticks mostly with silver and brass spoons that he feels do the best job of imitating baitfish.

favorite method Felton uses to cover water quickly.

"I spend a lot of time watching my electronics and looking for anything different on the bottom that may hold a few fish," says Felton. "Shoals, rock piles, sand bars and breaklines are just some of the areas I target with spoons."

Spoons are ideal for casting because they can be thrown much farther than conventional search lures such as spinnerbaits. For casting chores Felton recommends selecting 6- to 7-foot medium-heavy triggerstick with a fast-retrieve baitcasting reel. Monofilament line in the 14- to 17-pound range is recommended.

"When I'm casting a spoon I let the lure sink to the bottom then work it back to the boat using a rod snapping action similar to that used when working a jerkbait," explains Felton. "The retrieve is fast and it's important to use a spoon that's heavy enough to maintain contact with bottom between rod twitches. Each time the rod tip is snapped the spoon hops and scoots along the bottom."

When fishing rock piles, shoals or other isolated spots on the bottom Felton recommends casting across the structure and working the spoon back to the boat. When more linear targets such as breakline or weed edge is targeted, the spoon must be cast parallel to the edge.

"When you're fishing a breakline, the active fish are most likely to be near the lip of the break," cautions Felton. "Work the lip with the first cast then make succeeding casts along the break in deeper water. With weed edges, the fish are going to be tight to the edge or just inside the weed cover. To trigger strikes the spoon has to be worked close to the weeds."

Jigging spoons are not exactly weed-free lures. To keep fouled lures to a minimum Felton recommends swimming the spoon along the edge, making contact with bottom only occasionally.

Felton uses jigging spoons early in the season before bass move shallow to spawn. After the spawn, when bass again head for deeper water, spoons again become a useful tool.

"I fish spoons all summer long and right into fall," says Felton. "Anytime I expect to find bass in water deeper than 10 feet, I'm willing to try a spoon."

Spoons are equally effective on largemouth, smallmouth and spotted bass. These lures produce best on active fish, but there are times when a spoon will trigger strikes from fish that simply won't hit conventional lures.

BLADE BAITS

Blade baits are the second half of the heavy metal one-two punch. Like spoons,

Spoons like the one used to catch this smallmouth are outstanding search lures. A spoon can be cast farther than just about any other lure, making them top choices for covering water quickly.

these lures are great baits for searching out active fish and they are most effective when bass are found in deep water.

"I break down blade baits into two categories," says Jeff Snyder an Ohio-based pro angler who has been fishing tournaments since 1974. "Blade baits with curved blades such as the Cicada or Ripple Tail have good vibration and action when fished slowly. Blade baits with a straight blade such as the Gay Blade, Sonar, Silver Lucky and Silver Buddy must be worked more aggressively to bring these lures to life."

Snyder spends much of his time off the water conducting seminars at fishing clubs, sport shows and retail tackle dealers. In addition to winning numerous tournaments, Snyder still holds a Lake Erie tournament record set in 1984. His six-fish stringer weighed an amazing 34 pounds, 4 ounces and they were caught on a blade bait.

For fishing curved blade style baits Snyder recommends using spinning tackle. "I use a 7-foot spinning rod and reel combination

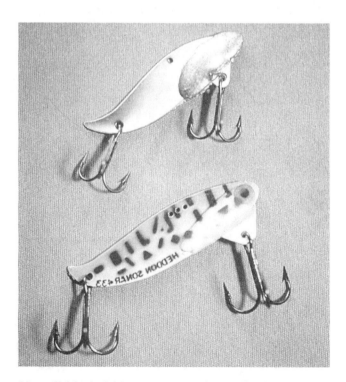

Not all blade baits are created equal. This Silver Buddy and Heddon Sonar are straight-blade models that must be worked aggressively to produce the desired action.

with 6- or 8-pound test Berkley XT monofilament," says Snyder. "The 7-foot rod is important for making long casts and also for picking up slack line when working the bait and setting the hook. I also feel that an abrasion-resistant line such as XT is very important. Blade baits are constantly in contact with the bottom and the line takes a beating."

Blade baits with a straight blade must be fished more aggressively to bring out the flash and vibration these lures are known for. "You need baitcasting tackle and heavier line when fishing the Sonar, Silver Buddy and other straight blades," explains Snyder. "I personally favor a 6-foot medium-heavy baitcasting outfit with a pistol grip handle. I like the pistol grip because I use my wrist to work the baits."

Heavier line is also in order when fishing these lures. Snyder recommends using 14-pound test Berkley XT and a fast-retrieve-ratio baitcasting reel.

When using curved blades Snyder favors the 1/4- and 3/8-ounce sizes and fishes slowly. When using the straight-blade models he jumps up to the 3/4-ounce and fishes very fast.

Before Snyder makes his first cast he modifies his lures slightly. "Instead of tying to the snap that comes on many of these lures, I remove the snap and replace it with a split ring," adds Snyder. "Snaps have a tendency to catch on the line when the lure is worked. A split ring is a smoother and more trouble-free connection."

When fishing blade baits Snyder usually starts out with the Reef Runner Cicada. "I reach for the Cicada first because you never know what mood fish are going to be in," explains Snyder. "If you fish too fast you're going to miss a lot of neutral fish. I'd rather start out slow and speed up the presentation once I determine that the fish are active."

The Cicada works best when fished slowly. Because the flash and vibration are generated at the slightest movement, these unique lures can be fished more like a jig than a blade bait.

"It's important to realize that a blade bait is designed to be worked horizontally," cautions Snyder. "I start out by making a short underhand flip cast and letting the lure sink to bottom. I reel up the slack line and with the rod parallel to the water, I pop the tip just enough to pull the bait a few inches off bottom then let the lure fall back to bottom on a slack line. The slack line is then reeled up and the lure popped again."

Snyder calls this technique "burping the rod" because you can feel a rumbling in the rod the second the lure starts to move. Most of the time the strike occurs when the lure is settling back to bottom. "I tell folks who come to my seminars not to expect a smashing strike," says Snyder. "Instead they are more likely to feel a sensation of weight."

Another retrieve seems to work especially well on smallmouth bass that are hanging around sand or gravel flats. "I point the rod right at the lure and sweep the rod a foot or two to the side," says Snyder. "This causes the bait to shuffle along the bottom then suddenly stop. Smallies seem to go nuts over this retrieve."

The Cicada is a great lure for casting on flats, along sea walls, to submerged islands, rock piles and other bottom structures that hold bass. In clear water Snyder uses silver lures. He switches to gold in stained waters. In low-light conditions black is a good color. In dirty water conditions he feels that more aggressively worked baits produce better.

Snyder uses more aggressive techniques when fishing straight blades. "Before I tie on a Sonar or Silver Buddy I'm looking for something that suggests the fish are active," says Snyder. "If I see a school of shad being forced to the surface that's a good indication that bass are feeding actively. I also use my sonar to find baitfish that are adjacent to good cover or structure. If I see baitfish and gamefish marks right in among the baitfish I'm certain these fish are feeding actively."

The approach is a simple but aggressive one. "Cast the lure out about 50 feet and let it sink to the bottom," advises Snyder. "I reel up the slack line then turn my reel so my thumb is pointed straight up. With an aggressive snap of my wrist I pop the bait a

couple feet off bottom and let the bait crash back to bottom. The slack is reeled up and the lure popped again."

Heavy blade baits are used so the lure can be moved quickly and still remain in contact with the bottom. Snyder favors the 3/4-ounce size. Shallow water is one of the few situations where blade baits are not practical. "I don't fish blades during the spawn," says Snyder. "The action these lures produce is just too aggressive for spawning fish. I catch the most fish on blades during the summer, fall and winter when bass are most likely to be found in water 8 feet or deeper."

Spoons and blade baits work equally well on largemouth, smallmouth and spotted bass. These frequently overlooked lures are especially well suited to fishing open waters where heavy cover isn't a problem. These lures are also well suited to fishing in rivers. The heavy metal of bass fishing, spoons and blade baits rock when it comes to bass.

Top-water is undoubtedly the most exciting way to catch bass. In Chapter Nineteen we'll delve into the finer points of catching bass on the surface.

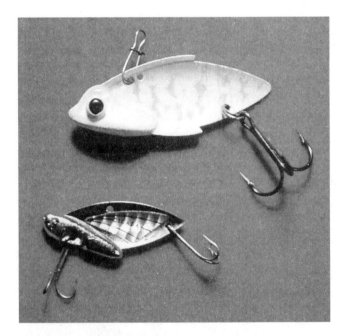

Blade baits with curved blades such as this Reef Runner Cicada and Luhr-Jensen Ripple-tail have good vibration and action even when worked slowly.

CHAPTER 19

CHARLIE CAMPBELL AND JIM MORTON TALK TOP-WATER TACTICS

Bass fishing is an exciting game, but never more so than when the game is played on the surface! Nothing in fishing beats the rush of a lunker largemouth exploding on a surface lure!

Surface fishing is ultra exciting because the angler's attention is focused on the bait from the time it hits the water until it's time for another cast. With other forms of bass fishing the lure is rarely so visible to the angler. An intense concentration forms between the angler and the surface lure. When the strike occurs the angler sees it right before his or her eyes!

Often bass are missed on top-water lures because the angler sees the fish and sets the hook before the bass actually has an opportunity to grab the lure. The hard

and fast rule of all surface fishing is to wait until the weight of the fish can be felt before setting the hook. This is rarely an easy task!

Charlie Campbell is a living legend in the world of bass fishing. He began his career guiding more than 40 years ago. In the early 1960s he started fishing tournaments professionally. Along the way he has won 163 tournaments and fished in the BassMasters Classic five times.

A school teacher by trade, Cambell also worked for many years at Bass Pro Shops where he spent most of his time testing and evaluating their extensive product line. These days Campbell is officially retired, but he still fishes regularly and participates in a wide range of promotional and charity fishing events. Recently at the Legend's Tournament sponsored by Nitro Bass Boats and Bass Pro Shops, Campbell outlined his strategy for fishing top-water lures.

"Top-water is my favorite way to fish bass because I can see the lures, watch them work and see the strike," says Campbell. "It's tough to beat top-water action both for fun and productivity when the conditions point to top-water fishing."

A list of several conditions must be met before top-water fishing becomes productive. "Clear to slightly stained water is mandatory for surface fishing," advises Cambell. "Top-

> *Even in very clear water a bass isn't likely to leave the bottom in 20 feet of water to strike a surface plug.*

water fishing is a visual presentation. If the water is too dirty, bass simply can't see the lures well enough. Bass must also be in relatively shallow water. Even in very clear water a bass isn't likely to leave the bottom in 20 feet of water to strike a surface plug. Lastly the water must be warm enough that bass are actively chasing prey. Generally speaking the best top-water fishing occurs once the water is above 55 degrees."

Top-water fishing is most often thought of as a spring presentation. It's true that

Charlie Campbell is a bass fishing legend who has spent over 40 years refining the art of bass fishing.

Charlie Campbell recommends trying top water fishing when the water is between 55 and 80 degrees and clear-to-stained in color.

top-water fishing produces best on most lakes before warm weather sets in and the water column starts to stratify. "Top-water fishing remains good all summer long on certain waters," says Campbell. "This is especially true in creek arms of major reservoirs and northern lakes where the water remains cool all summer long."

When bass feed on the surface they are amazingly efficient. "Bass attack schools of baitfish from below, forcing them to the surface," says Campbell. "The surface is a convenient barrier that allows bass to corner the bait and feed at will."

It's important to note that bass also use structure and cover to help them corner baitfish. "Anything a bass can use to trap baitfish makes the spot better for top-water fishing," explains Campbell. "I look for lay-downs, stumps, rocks, steep banks, the back ends of pockets, corners in walls or anything that bass can use to narrow down the escape routes baitfish can take. These are the spots that produce the best top-water fishing, not simply casting out over open water."

The equipment Campbell favors for top-water fishing includes a 5-1/2-foot graphite casting rod with a pistol grip, fast-retrieve ratio baitcasting reel and 14-pound test monofilament. "I prefer a rod with a soft tip for working surface baits and a medium-

Top-water fishing isn't just a spring pattern. Here Charlie Campbell checks a map to locate creek arms where a cool creek dumps into the main impoundment. This cool water will keep bass shallow most of the summer, making for an ideal area to try top-water fishing.

The best topwater action takes place in or near cover. Bass use the surface to corner baitfish. They also use logs, rocks, stumps, brush, the bank, or any other object to restrict the escape route baitfish can take.

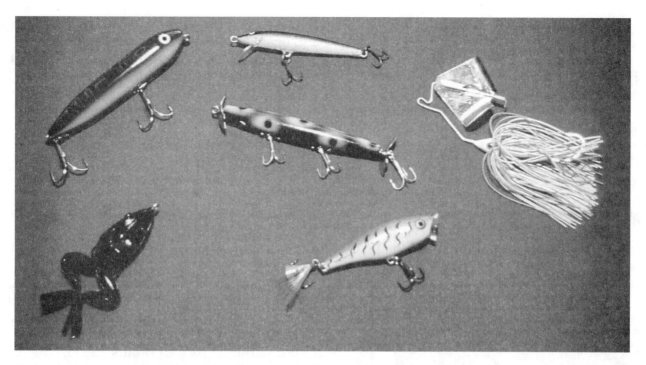

Top-water baits can be broken down into several categories. Some of the major types include buzzbaits, chuggers, prop baits, minnow baits and plastic frogs.

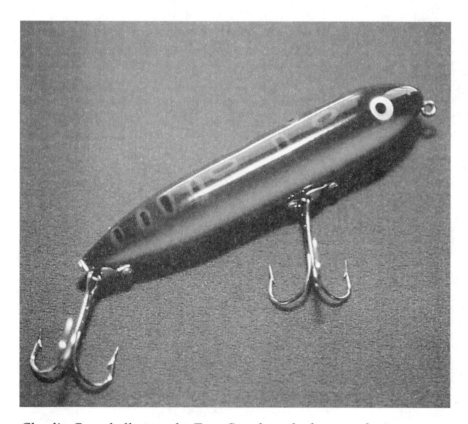

Charlie Campbell rates the Zara Spook as the best-producing top-water bait of all time. The classic walk-the-dog retrieve made famous by this lure has produced countless bass.

light action," says Campbell. "A rod with a little softer action helps in slowing up the response time."

Setting the hook too soon is a major problem with top-water fishing. Some anglers favor ultra-slow action fiberglass rods that further slow up the reaction time and help to prevent the bait from being pulled away from the fish.

With some smaller top-water lures spinning tackle is the best choice. A 6-1/2-foot medium-light action rod, and spinning reel with a large-diameter spool allows light lures to be thrown maximum distances. The ideal line for spinning tackle is 8-pound test monofilament.

Campbell breaks down most surface baits into several categories including chuggers, prop baits and plastic frogs. One bait has earned a category all its own, the Heddon Zara Spook.

"I feel the Zara Spook is what top-water fishing is all about," says Campbell. "Undoubtedly this lure ranks as the single most popular top-water bass lure in history and my experience suggests this bait is also tops for producing trophy fish."

The Spook is fished differently than most other types of top-water baits. "When I'm fishing a top-water lure I normally try to make the retrieve as erratic as possible," says Campbell. "I start and stop the retrieve suddenly, pause often and do anything I can to surprise the fish and trigger a reactionary

Chuggers come in a number of brands, shapes and sizes. Effective on largemouth and small-mouth bass, chuggers rate a close second to the Zara Spook in popularity and productivity.

strike. A Spook is fished a little differently. The "walk-the-dog" action made famous by the Spook is a very rythmic and predictable side-to-side jumping and darting action. The Spook is worked by snapping the rod tip on slack line in much the same way a jerkbait is brought to life. The major difference is the Spook stays on the surface and is kept moving throughout the retrieve."

Long casts are an important aspect of fishing top-water lures such as the Spook. Not only do long casts help to cover more water, presenting the lure away from the boat helps to avoid spooking fish in clear water.

The Spook has been copied by a number of lure manufacturers, but none of these baits have risen to popularity. Recently Excalibur, a division of PRADCO, the company that owns and builds the Heddon Zara Spook, introduced a Super Spook which is essentially the same lure as the Zara Spook with premium hooks and a fancy paint job. A smaller version of this bait is called the Spook Jr. Also the orginal Zara Spook is offered in a smaller version known as the Zara Spook Puppy.

It's unlikely that any top-water lure design will ever top the sales or number of fish produced by the original Zara Spook. Sometimes there is no topping the original.

CHUGGERS

A number of quality top-water baits fit into a category known as chuggers. All these baits feature a concave face that is designed to spit water, pop and gurgle when the bait is snapped forward sharply. The leading bait in this category is undoubtedly the Rebel Pop-R, but there are many other baits that work equally well. A few of the chuggers available include the Excalibur Pop'n Image, Rapala Skitter Pop, Storm Rattlin' Chug Bug, Bass Pro Shops XPS Z-Pop, Strike King Spit'n King, Fred Arbogast Hula Popper and Cotton Cordell Pencil Popper.

Other classics such as the Fred Arbogast Jitterbug and Heddon Crazy Crawler also fit into the chugger category. These baits however aren't jerked to bring out a spitting action. The blade on the front of these lures moves water best with a slow and steady retrieve. The steady retrieve often favored with these lures makes them a top choice for fishing bass after dark. Faster moving lures are harder for bass to key in on and catch.

Campbell recommends that chuggers be fished with stops, long pauses and sudden starts. "Chuggers do a great job of attracting bass, but these fish don't always strike immediately," explains Campbell. "Often the angler must trigger the strike by making the bait come to life then lay motionless for long pauses. The pauses seem to unnerve the fish."

PROP BAITS

Prop baits are surface lures with rotating blades mounted on the nose or tail of the lure. Most of these baits are thin minnow profiles. The two most popular lures in this category include the Smithwick Devil's Horse and the Heddon Tiny Torpedo. Both of these lures are fished in a similar way.

"I fish a prop bait by pulling the bait forward in spurts," says Campbell. "The action I use most often can be described as ZURP, ZURP, ZURP, PAUSE... ZURP, ZURP, PAUSE... These baits can also benefit from an occasional rod snap that changes the lure's direction of travel."

PLASTIC FROGS

Designed to fish the surface where there's plenty of heavy cover, plastic frogs can go places no other surface lure can go. Because frogs are often used to fish lily pads, hydrilla, moss and other floating vegetation, heavy line is more essential than with other top-water lures. Fishing with at least 17- to 20-pound test is recommended and even heavier line can be used if the cover is especially nasty.

The most popular soft plastic lures in this category include the Mann's Legends Frog, ScumFrog, Snag Proof Frogzilla, Mustad Swamp Frog and the Bass Pro Shops

Lazer Eye Tender Toad. Each of these baits have enough surface area to keep them afloat and the snagless designs to walk over pads, stumps, moss or virtually anything floating in the water.

The best way to fish these lures is to skitter them across the surface, pausing frequently on the edges of cover. Because the cover is often very thick, bass often strike at and miss these lures several times before zeroing in for the kill. The excitement can be unnerving, but worth every second.

Jim Morton of Oklahoma is another leading tournament pro who relishes top-water fishing for bass. He fished in the B.A.S.S. Eastern and Central tours, Top 150 events and was fortunate enough to win a

Jim Morton is a tournament professional and also works to coordinate the promotional efforts of more than 40 individuals for the Rapala and Storm Lures pro staff teams. This 13-pound, 4-ounce brute was taken on a Storm Rattlin' Chug Bug.

BassMasters Invitational event in Oklahoma in 1992. "I won the Oklahoma tournament on a buzzbait and have been fishing professionally every since," says Morton.

As the promotions manager for Rapala, Storm and Blue Fox lures, Jim's job is to manage a staff of 43 professional anglers who participate in a number of tournaments, special promotions, shows and other events.

The gear Morton favors for top-water fishing is similar to that used by Campbell and other leading pros. "I usually select a 6-1/2-foot baitcasting outfit with a 5.1:1 gear ratio reel," says Morton. "I'm tall enough that a 6-1/2-foot rod works well for me, but I'd recommend that anglers pick a rod length that suits both their height and the fishing situation. "For example, when I'm fishing in flooded timber or brush, I use a shorter rod that's easier to maneuver in the cover."

Even in clear water Morton doesn't believe in using light line for top-water fishing. "Thin lines sink too quickly," says Morton. "I want a line that will float on the surface and help me give my baits the maximum action when the rod tip is popped. The size I use the most is 14-pound test, but if the cover is heavy I'll switch to 17- or even 20-pound test without hesitation."

Morton is quick to point out, however, that anglers need to match the size line used to the lures fished. "If I'm fishing a large top-water bait like a Spook or Rattlin' Chug Bug, I prefer heavy line," explains Morton. "However, if I'm throwing a Baby Chug Bug or other small top-water lure I'll drop down to 10- to 12-pound test to achieve more casting distance and accuracy."

Morton recently field tested and helped develop two new fishing lines produced by Rapala known as Tough Line, an abrasion-resistant line for fishing cover and Finesse Line, a softer and more limp line for casting with spinning tackle. "Tough Line has a different formula that resists the memory so common with abrasion-resistant lines," claims Morton. "Without a doubt this is the best high-abrasion line I've ever handled for bass fishing," claims Morton.

Morton considers buzzbaits to be one of the most versatile types of surface baits because they can be fished through so many cover types and in a wide range of seasonal situations. "I fish buzzbaits year around," says Morton. "Even in water as cold as 40 degrees I'm confident that bass will strike a buzzbait."

One of Morton's most productive buzzbait patterns goes unnoticed by most anglers. "Most guys who fish a buzzbait are working it in cover, around brush, near lay-downs or anything a bass may be hiding in or near," says Morton. "I like to target featureless banks where bass often push shad up against the shore. The best areas are banks that have a sharp drop or lip that acts

When possible, Jim Morton prefers to fish top-water baits on heavy line. This Rattlin' Chug Bug is heavy enough to cast easily on 14- to 17-pound test line.

like a wall bass can use to corner baitfish. To hold fish the spot only needs a couple feet of water, but deeper areas are also good. The edges of sandbars are another great place to find this same pattern."

Morton also fishes minnow baits such as the classic Rapala Floating Minnow, as surface lures. "I use minnow baits early in the year before the spawn and during the spawn," adds Morton. "What I like about these lures is they are so natural looking they will catch fish even when sitting still. I often cast them to a laydown or other cover and simply let the bait sit motionless in the water for a few moments. By just lightly shaking my rod tip I can make these lures quiver, shake and twitch without hardly moving. What makes them so deadly is they have action without having to move the bait from the strike zone."

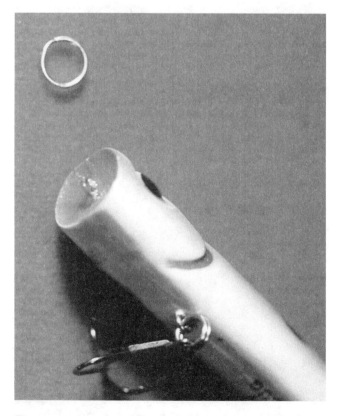

By removing the split ring that comes on the lure and tying directly to the eye tie, Jim Morton reduces the action of the Rattlin' Chug Bug so he can fish the bait more quickly.

Morton also uses minnow baits to catch those bass often spotted cruising the shallows during the post-spawn. "Minnow baits are deadly on cruising bass that are all but impossible to catch on more aggressive top-water lures," says Morton. "I like to cast ahead of the fish and simply let the bait rest motionless. If the fish passes by and doesn't notice the lure I'll cast again and this time work the bait with a subtle shake or quiver. It's amazing how often a bass will simply slurp up a minnow bait that's just resting on the surface."

When faced with lots of prime cover such as boat houses, docks, grass, laydowns and other visual targets, Morton usually reaches for the Storm Rattlin' Chug Bug, a lure he helped design and field test. "What makes the Chug Bug so useful is this bait can be fished in several ways," explains Morton. "You can fish the Chug Bug like other chuggers by popping and pausing the lure, or if you prefer you can walk the dog like you would fish a Spook."

Morton modifies the Chug Bug slightly to fish a unique top-water technique. "Most anglers use a snap or loop knot when fishing top-water baits," says Morton. "This is a good idea most of the time because it allows the bait to enjoy more freedom of movement. In the fall I like to speed up my retrieve while at the same time reducing the side to side jumping action of the Chug Bug. To accomplish this I remove the split ring and tie my line directly to the wire eye coming out the front of the bait. Now when I'm jerking the bait it moves straight at me instead of darting back and forth. I pick up the retrieve to the point the bait is literally skipping across the surface. Largemouth literally explode on this action."

In calm water Morton favors baits without rattles such as a Rapala Skitter Pop. When the surface of the water is rippled by the wind, baits that generate more noise and action tend to produce better.

For smallmouth bass Morton favors smaller baits. "A smallmouth will hit a large top-water lure, but the number of missed fish skyrockets," advises Morton. "Generally speaking I like to fish smallmouth with smaller lures and faster retrieves. Largemouth tend to favor bigger baits moved more slowly. However, right after the shad spawn in late spring and early summer, small baits like the Baby Chug Bug can be outstanding largemouth lures while these fish are feeding on young-of-the-year baitfish."

Those anglers who have an opportunity to fish trophy bass waters will want to upsize their baits. Using big baits helps to increase the odds of catching larger bass and also plays a role in keeping smaller and more aggressive fish from striking. Even muskie sized top-water lures are used to catch lunker largemouth out west, in Florida and in Mexico where bass grow big.

Morton also had some interesting tips that anyone fishing top-water lures could benefit from. "Setting the hook too soon is the biggest problem anglers encounter when fishing top-water lures," says Morton. "No matter how much experience you have, it's tough not to set the hook when a bass breaks the surface, especially if you haven't had a bite in awhile. I recommend that folks avoid watching the lure. If you focus too much on the bait, you're going to react too quickly."

When a fish strikes, the hookset is also important. "You want to avoid the typical cross their eyes type hookset you would use when fishing a Texas rig," cautions Morton. "Instead use a more subdued rod sweep to pick up the slack and pull tight against the fish. Ultra sharp hooks are essential on all top-water baits. Either sharpen the hooks on the lure or replace them with premium quality hooks."

When working a top-water bait, let the rod do the work, advises Morton. "The reel is only used to pick up slack," explains Morton. "For most fishing situations a 5:1 ratio reel is ideal for top-water fishing. Some faster retrieves require a 6:1 gear ratio reel."

"I'm often asked, 'Why are top-water baits painted with patterns on the sides and back,'" comments Morton? "Logic seems to indicate that bass can only see the belly of the lure. Actually, the rocking motion of the lure in the water and refraction in the water enable the bass to see the sides of the lure clearly. When I'm fishing in clear skies I like to use chromes that maximize flash from sunlight. In cloudy weather, I feel painted lures are more visible to the fish."

The important thing to remember with top-water lures is these baits most often perform best when fished in close association with some type of cover. Anything that narrows the escape routes a minnow might take can potentially be a great spot to catch a bass on top-water lures.

It's also important to take the time to enjoy this unique fishing strategy. Few other species of fish are as susceptible to top-water fishing as bass. Get out and have fun.

In the next chapter we'll take a look at some finesse fishing techniques that will give you a subtle approach to catching big bass.

This Jitterbug is another classic top-water lure that is deadly on both largemouth and smallmouth bass.

CHAPTER 20

MARK ZONA AND JIM SPRAGUE SHOW THEIR FINESSE

Finesse fishing exploded onto the bass fishing scene as a light-line, small-lure presentation that could be used to catch fish on beds or fish in clear water. Since being introduced in the early 1990s this fishing revolution has become one of the hottest topics in bass fishing. Initially, the focus of this technique was on tube baits. Today anglers are using a wide variety of soft plastic lures to finesse more bites from largemouth, smallmouth and spotted bass.

Finesse fishing is about light lures and light lines, but this style of fishing is also about triggering strikes from bass that see lots of fishing pressure. The more a body of water is fished, the more deadly finesse tactics become.

FINESSE DOCK FISHING

Dock fishing is a popular way to target largemouth bass, but most anglers approach docks with an attitude. Their goal is seemingly to fish each dock as quickly as possible so as to get to the next dock before another boat gets there first. The most common lures used are spinnerbaits or jigs on flippin' tackle.

This strategy works to a point. Active fish are readily caught on docks, but bass soon become conditioned to fishing pressure. The more pressure these docks receive the less bites anglers are likely to get on conventional tackle. In clear water this situation is compounded to the point that few bass are caught near docks.

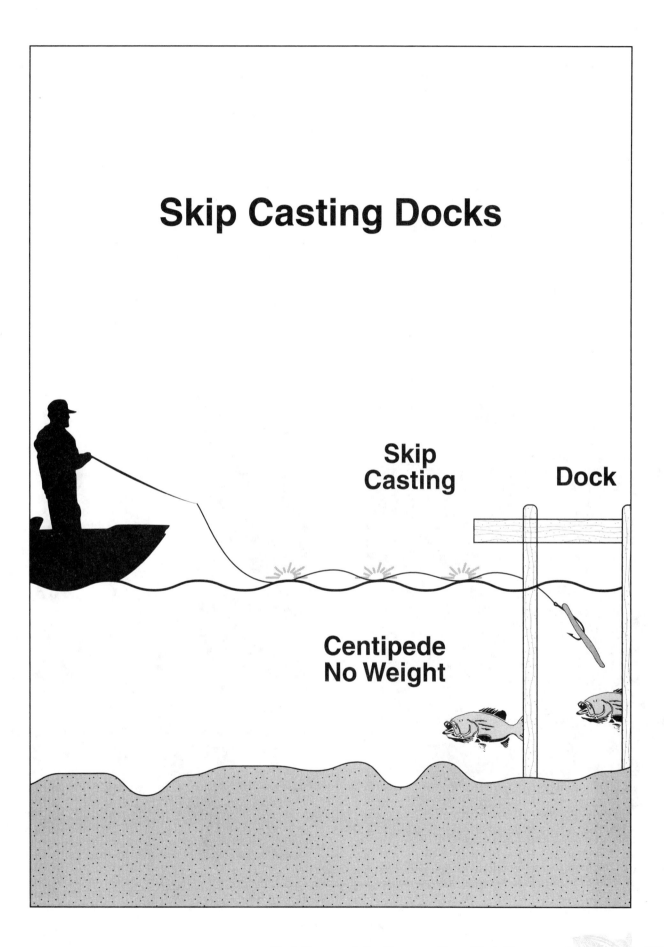

Skip Casting Docks

Skip
Casting

Dock

Centipede
No Weight

Mark Zona is a frequent competitor on the B.A.S.S. and FLW circuits. His approach to dock fishing could be described as ultra-finesse. Not only does Zona use light line and light lures, he fishes much more slowly than most anglers.

"I grew up wading and fishing docks on clear-water lakes," says Zona. "It didn't take me long to notice that most anglers only scratch the surface when it comes to dock fishing. I'd watch intently as a boat fished a dock. After the boat left without catching a fish, I'd sneak up quietly to see if any fish

> *Not only does Zona use light line and light lures, he fishes much more slowly than most anglers.*

were under the dock. More times than not I discovered that there were fish under the dock that simply didn't bite."

Zona also made another observation that has helped him catch countless bass from docks. "I started to notice that bass would frequently swirl under a dock," says Zona. "Upon closer observation I discovered that the bass were feeding on very small minnows that cruise along the shoreline. Most of the minnows are smaller than your little finger."

Gradually Zona put together the pieces of the puzzle. He knew that he would have to

Mark Zona thrives on dock fishing with finesse tactics behind other anglers using more traditional methods.

This largemouth was taken by skip-casting a plastic bait with no weight up under a dock.

select a bait that closely resembled these small minnows. He also felt that fishing more slowly would tease these fish into biting.

After years of experimenting with different baits Zona settled on two soft plastic lures for most of his dock fishing. "I use either a Texas rigged Zoom centipede on a 3/0 hook with no weight or a Venom tube rigged on a 1/64-ounce Bite Me jighead," says Zona. "I fish these lures on a 6-1/2-foot medium action Falcon spinning rod, Shimano 2500 series reel and 8-pound test green Stren Super Tough line."

One of the keys to presenting these lures under docks, boat lifts and moored boats is using a technique known as skip casting. "When I'm trying to teach someone how to cast under docks, I tell them to imag-

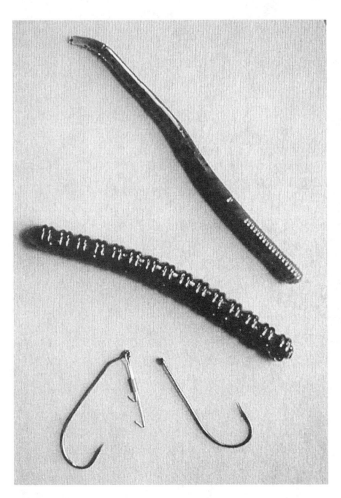

The plastic baits best suited to finesse dock fishing include centipedes and finesse worms.

ine they are skipping a stone," explains Zona. "The key to this casting technique is to use your elbow and wrist to move the rod. If you use your arm, you lose casting accuracy."

Mastering skip casting takes a lot of practice and patience. Eventually you should be able to hit targets the size of a coffee cup and skip the lure into position with hardly a sound.

"I believe the bait skipping on the surface is a big part of what makes this pattern so deadly," says Zona. "To bass under the dock the centipede or tube skipping over the surface looks like a minnow trying to escape from a bass or other predator. When the lure stops moving and starts to slowly sink to the bottom it looks like a dying minnow."

Rigging is especially important when fishing the centipede. "I rig the hook through the thin side of the bait so it's straight and sinks level in the water," explains Zona. "You don't want the bait to sink with the nose or tail down because it glides instead of sinking straight down where you want it. The bait sinks very slowly and with the slightest lift of the rod I can coax the bait back to the surface. During the entire time the lure is under the dock, I barely move it. Too much action is going to turn off the fish."

Getting the bait positioned and sinking slowly is only part of the puzzle. The other important aspect of this fishing style is keeping the lure in front of bass for as long as possible. "Heavily pressured fish are the toughest to get to bite," admits Zona. "A lot of bass will bite after 15-30 seconds, but some fish take a minute or two before they can be teased into striking."

Obviously fishing this ultra-finesse method takes patience. "When the fish bites you can't over-power the fish and jerk him clear of the dock," says Zona. "Instead you have to keep just enough pressure on the fish to lead him out from under the dock. If you pull on the fish too hard he will run and tangle the line around dock posts and other cover."

As you might imagine lure colors need to be subtle and as natural as possible. The

Zoom centipede produces best for Zona in the Cucumber Seed color pattern.

"The most amazing thing about this dock fishing technique is once you start doing it, you find yourself fishing docks other anglers pass up," says Zona. "Most anglers work the docks that feature the most water under them. I've discovered that even docks in shallow water can hold fish."

This unique technique works best in the spring when bass are more likely to be shallow. Also, because you're fishing in shallow water largemouth bass are the most likely targets. This ultra slow technique also works well when fishing beds.

TARGETING CRUISING FISH

How many times have you seen big bass cruising along the shoreline in shallow and clear water? You can throw spinnerbaits, cranks and top-water lures on these fish all day without so much as generating a follow. Usually this phenomenon occurs after the spawn, but before the heat of summer forces bass to seek out deeper water.

The same rig Zona uses to fish docks is deadly when sight fishing cruising bass. "I feel like I can catch 75 percent to 90 percent of the bass I spot," says Zona. "The key is to anticipate where the fish is going and cast ahead of the fish. If you throw right on the fish you're going to spook him most of the time."

As in dock fishing, the centipede works best when fished with no weight and allowed to sink slowly in the water. You'll only be able to cast this rig about 50 feet, but that's far enough to lead cruising bass.

DROP SHOTTING

Drop shotting is one of the newest methods being used to trigger strikes from hard-to-catch bass. A finesse tactic that works well in both shallow and deep water, the basic rig is so simple it's

amazing this technique didn't surface years ago.

A weight such as a bell sinker, egg sinker or split shot is secured to the end of the line. Spinning tackle and 6- to 10-pound test line is ideal for this presentation. Above the weight a straight shank thin wire worm hook is tied directly to the line. This hook can be positioned close to the weight or several feet above the weight depending on the type of cover growing on the bottom or where the fish are suspended in the water column.

"One of the ways I use drop shotting is for spawning bass," says Jim Sprague of K&E Tackle. "Once bass are exposed to fishing pressure on their beds, the fish become

Targeting cruising fish is another way that finesse rigging plastics can pay off in more bass.

reluctant to leave the bed. In order to trigger strikes the lure has to almost dangle inside the bed. With a drop shot rig, I can keep the weight outside of the bed while positioning the bait right in front of the fish. With just a little wiggle of the rod tip, I can make the bait move and dance without pulling the bait out of the bed."

Drop shotting is also a great way to fish bass in water ranging from 10 to 30 feet deep. Because the lure is

> *Useful as a means of fishing the deep sides of weed edges, drop-offs, deep-water structure and flats, drop shotting is undoubtedly going to become more popular as more anglers discover this unique finesse fishing method.*

rigged above the weight, the bait is positioned above the bottom weeds and debris where bass can more easily spot it. Also, since the bait doesn't actually contact the cover, the lure is fishing 100 percent of the time, compared to other deep-water fishing methods where the bait frequently catches on weeds or debris.

"The best hook for drop shotting is a 2/0 thin wire worm hook with a couple notches on the shank to hold plastic lures in place," says Sprague. "The hook isn't Texas rigged, but simply threaded into the plastic lure. The most popular lures for this rigging technique include finesse worms, centipedes, lizards, curl tail grubs and swimming-tail worms."

Drop shotting has another benefit. This rigging method allows anglers to detect light strikes because the bait is positioned ahead of the weight. Also, as the weight hits bottom anglers can get a sense for the type of bottom they are fishing on, helping then key on more productive spots such as rock or gravel.

Useful as a means of fishing the deep sides of weed edges, drop-offs, deep-water structure and flats, drop shotting is undoubtedly going to become more popular as more anglers discover this unique finesse fishing method.

Anglers who enjoy drop shotting will find Gamakatsu's new Pre-Tied Drop Shot Rigs are the fastest way to get fishing. "These new pre-tied rigs feature a 3-foot tag attached midway on a 6-foot length of leader material that can be custom cut to whatever length the

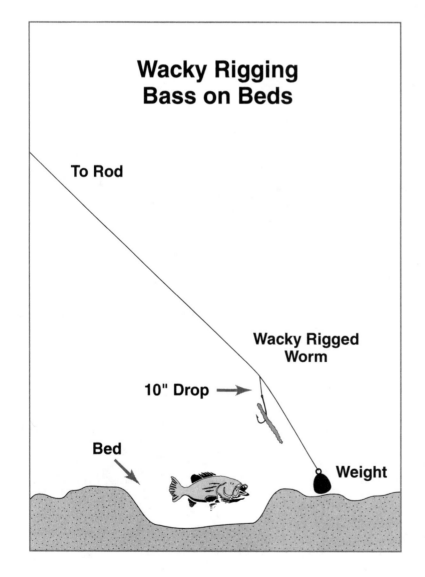

Wacky Rigging Bass on Beds

To Rod

Wacky Rigged Worm

10" Drop →

Bed

Weight

anger desires," says Glenn Young, Regional Sales Manager for Gamakatsu. "The hook supplied is the popular split shot hook so many finesse fishermen use and depend on. The angler simply adds a split shot or other weight on the end of the leader."

Anglers can use almost any combination of tag length, but Young recommends attaching the hook 8 to 10 inches from the leader. "I've had the most success fishing these rigs with wacky rigged Bass Assassin finesse worms," says Young. "The slightest twitch on the line causes the bait to fold in half and then pop back into shape. It's deadly."

Anglers can cast this rig or drift fish if the wind is coming from the right direction for the lay of the cover or structure. While we can't explore every facet of finesse fishing here, the slow subtle approach is one of the fastest growing areas of bass fishing. Going light and small has proven itself as the best ways to catch pressured bass and bass in clear water.

In the next chapter we'll part with traditional bass fishing methods and venture into live bait fishing tactics. Most anglers start their fishing careers fishing live bait. A lot of folks never find a reason to fish anything else.

This commercially prepared drop shot rig makes it fast and easy to get started using this new and unique fishing presentation.

While drop shotting is one of the newest finesse fishing tactics, anglers all over the country are catching on quickly.

CHAPTER 21

LIVE BAIT TACTICS FOR BASS

The mere mention of live bait in some bass fishing circles is enough to provoke a brawl. Tournament pros are among the many anglers who take great pride in their ability to catch bass on a wide variety of artificial lures. In fact, many of the most popular lures were designed with feedback and suggestions from the leading tournament anglers. Using live bait is like a form of cheating to these anglers! The only way to raise a tournament fisherman's hackles faster is denouncing catch-and-release or claiming you have a faster boat!

The fact is, tournament pros are prevented from fishing with live bait because the rules of many events strictly forbid it. Banning live bait from tournaments dates back to the early years of competitive fishing. When bass tournaments began to gain popularity in the 1960s angling ethics weren't exactly a common topic at the barber shop. At the time, most anglers fished

not just for recreation, but also to provide food for their families. No one questioned the use of live bait or anglers who kept the fish they caught.

Tournaments, however, applied fishing pressure on popular bodies of water like never before. With the focused pressure tournaments generated, it didn't take long for the organizers of these events to realize fish mortality was becoming a major problem. Competitive fishing had reached a critical point. If these events were to survive, the bass caught and brought to the scales would have to be released unharmed. The concept of catch-and-release was born and one of the largest and most successful conservation movements in history started.

The widespread acceptance of catch-and-release fishing has undoubtedly done more to insure the future of bass fishing than any other issue in sportfishing. The marine industry rallied behind this movement by designing and building boats with better livewells, complete with aeration and recirculation systems.

As catch-and-release practices picked up momentum, live bait fishing methods were doomed

Soft plastic lures are the most commonly noted example of fishing products that were introduced as a direct result of this phenomenon.

to fall from favor. Live bait and bass tournaments simply didn't mix. First off, bass caught on live bait tended to be hooked more deeply. Mortality on these fish was significantly higher than bass caught on artificial lures.

Secondly, using live bait didn't support the marketing concept behind tournaments. Fishing tournaments have always been and will always be about promoting fishing and stimulating the sale of products used in fishing. Using live bait didn't do much to promote product sales for the sponsoring manufacturers.

The positive twist is that banning live bait stimulated lure manufacturers to take a more active role in product development. Newer and better fishing lures were soon developed to take the place of live bait. Soft plastic lures are the most commonly noted example of fishing products that were introduced as a direct result of this phenomenon. Fishing scents and scented lures are also good examples of products that were developed to bridge the gap between artificial lures and live bait.

All of this insight into tournaments and the use of live bait makes for interesting reading, but it doesn't make much of a case for anyone who's interested in using live bait. Before we become too critical of the use of live bait, perhaps we should revisit our own fishing roots. Just about anyone who owns a fishing rod started out with live bait dangling from the end of it. The lessons learned fishing with live bait as a child spill over into adulthood. Countless anglers prefer to fish with live bait.

Even the suggestion of using live bait is an insult to some bass anglers. The author believes live bait methods are among the best ways to catch all species of bass.

I credit my own youthful experiences with live bait for fueling the passion I still feel for sportfishing. I doubt that I would have ever developed as keen an interest in fishing had I not had the opportunity to use live bait. No doubt I would have caught few fish and lost interest in fishing.

As a kid I enjoyed collecting bait almost as much as using it. Netting minnows, digging worms, catching grasshoppers with the help of my mother's bed sheets were just some of the ways live bait found its way into my budding fishing career.

> *"Netting minnows, digging worms, catching grasshoppers with the help of my mother's bed sheets were just some of the ways live bait found its way into my budding fishing career."*

One of the most unique methods I used to catch live bait was targeted at the population of frogs that lived in a pond near my home. I used a bamboo rod with about three feet of monofilament line attached to the end. I tied a small dry fly pilfered from my father's trout vest on the end of the line. Slowly I'd wade around the marshy pond in hopes of spooking a leopard frog into giving away his location. Once I located a frog, the fly was lowered until it was only a couple inches from the frog. A quick twitch of the rod tip was usually all it took to stimulate the frog into snapping at the fly and

Professional tournaments turned bass fishing away from live bait in an effort to prevent injury to hooked fish and also to stimulate more product sales for lure manufacturers.

hooking itself. Instant fish bait!

I don't know about the ethical — or legal — ramifications of such bait collecting techniques, but I can attest to the effectiveness. I'd store my frogs in a mason jar with an inch of water in the bottom and half a dozen air holes in the lid. Some of my fondest childhood memories are of the largemouth bass live frogs allowed me to catch.

Frogs are just one of many live baits that can be used to catch bass. The most common choices include minnows, crayfish, nightcrawlers and leeches. Some less noted live baits include salamanders, mud puppies, helgramites and grasshoppers. Some of these baits you can purchase at your local tackle shop and others you'll have to collect yourself.

> *Early and late in the season it's tough to imagine anything more effective at catching bass than a live minnow pinned to a jig or Carolina rig.*

MINNOWS

Minnows are the ideal cold water bait. Early and late in the season it's tough to imagine anything more effective at catching bass than a live minnow pinned to a jig or Carolina rig.

Just about any species of minnow an angler can get his hands on is potentially a good bass bait. However, some types of minnows are easier to keep alive and frisky. Among the most durable minnow species are fatheads, dace and small suckers. It is a little more difficult to keep spottails and chubs perky, and emerald shiners, golden shiners and shad are quite tough to keep alive in a bait bucket.

Unfortunately anglers don't often have the luxury of choosing a minnow species from their bait dealer. Certain species of

Minnows are a natural for jig fishing. To keep the minnow from falling off the hook when casting, place a small piece of plastic over the hook point after hooking the minnow through both lips.

minnows are simply more readily available in some parts of the country than others.

Keeping the bait in your bucket wiggling and interesting to bass boils down to keeping the water cool and well oxygenated. The amount of dissolved oxygen available in water decreases as the water temperature increases. In other words minnows aren't going to live for long in warm water.

Charter captains on Lake Erie often depend on live bait rigs baited with minnows to catch early- and late-season smallmouth.

Changing the water frequently or adding ice chips to the water are ways to help keep your bait fresh. Putting your minnows in the livewell of your boat and running the aeration pump is the best way to keep any minnow lively.

There are dozens of productive ways to fish with minnows, but a couple key methods deserve special consideration. An ordinary leadhead with a minnow hooked lightly through the lips comes as close to the perfect fishing presentation as any. The most useful jig sizes are 1/16-, 1/8- and 1/4-ounce. To insure the minnow stays on the hook, push a small piece of soft plastic over the hook point after baiting up. A small chunk of a grub or plastic worm works best. This piece of plastic acts like a washer that prevents the hook from working free of the bait.

Rigged in this manner a minnow can be cast over and over again without tearing free of the hook. Medium spinning tackle is the best way to fish a jig and minnow combination.

Drifting with Carolina rigs is another popular way to catch bass on minnows. While this method can produce bass at any time if year, the fall is the best time to catch trophy fish.

Standard tackle and a Carolina rig equipped with a No. 1 short-shank hook works best. Select a hefty 4-inch minnow. Bass are instinctively looking for bigger forage at this time of year. Hook the minnow through the nose or just in front of the tail and drag this rig on flats, along breaks, deep water points and other hard-bottom areas.

Slip bobbers are a good technique for fishing with minnows in weeds or other cover. Instead of using a single hook at the business end, try a 1/32- or 1/16-ounce leadhead jig like those often used for fishing tube baits.

Set the bobber stop so the bait rides just above emerging weeds or submerged brush. Cast the bait using a delicate under-hand flip and let the wind drift the bait into position.

NIGHTCRAWLERS

Viewed by many as the ultimate fish bait, nightcrawlers have earned this reputation by being effective on just about any fish that swims. Crawlers are also relatively easy to keep alive. So long as the bait remains cool, a supply of crawlers can be kept for weeks.

The best way to keep nightcrawlers for extended periods is in a cooler filled with commercial worm bedding. The dirt in which crawlers come packaged at the bait shop is messy stuff and it has little food value for the crawlers. Most commercial worm beddings are made from recycled paper with a special food mixture already added.

To insure the bait stays in good condition the temperature in the bedding should not exceed 55 degrees. The worms will die quickly if exposed to warmer temperatures. Ice packs are the most practical way to keep nightcrawlers wiggling.

One of my favorite ways to fish with nightcrawlers for large-mouth is also one of the most simple. Select a spinning outfit equipped with 8-pound test line. Tie on a single No. 4 short-shank hook and hook a nightcrawler once through the collar. No weight is added to the line.

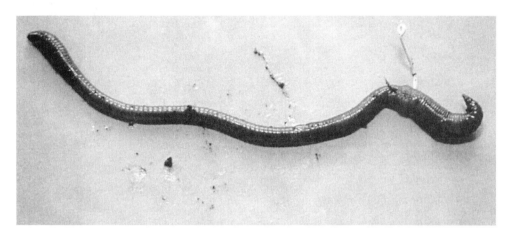

Nightcrawlers are believed by many to be the ultimate fish bait. Using a live crawler, hooked once in the collar is a good way to fish over the top of emerging weed growth. No weight is required. Just cast the bait into position and let it sink slowly.

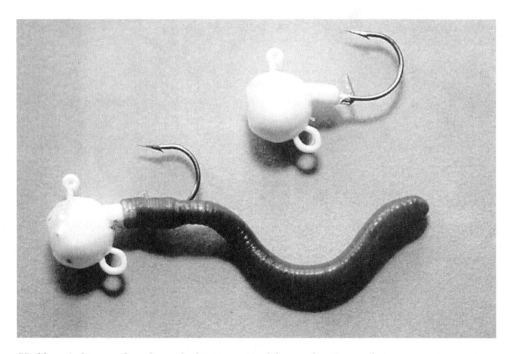

Half a nightcrawler threaded onto a jig like a plastic grub is a great way to trigger strikes from smallmouth found living in rivers.

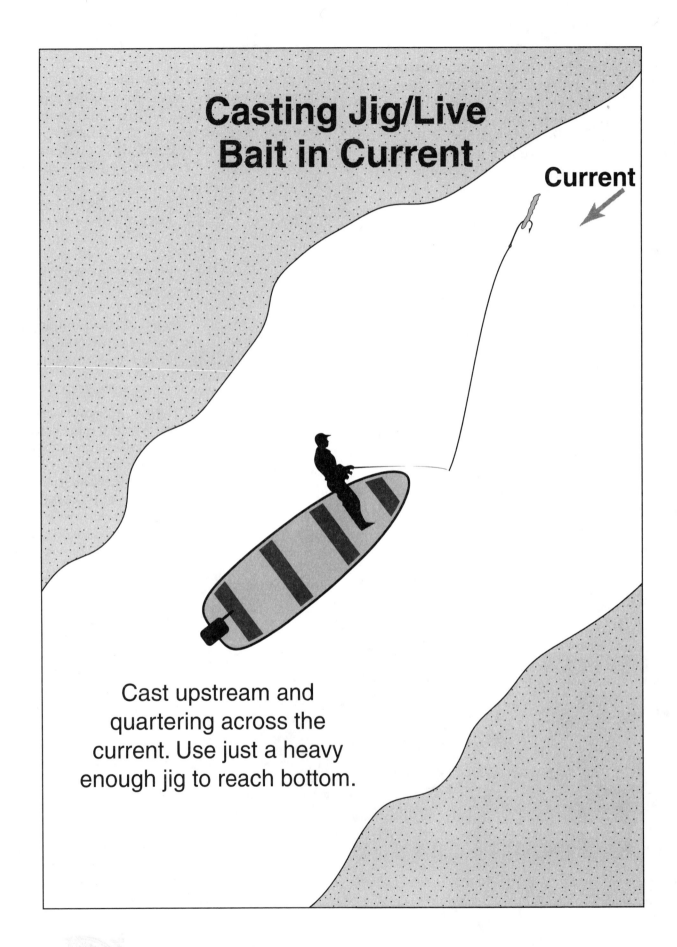

Casting Jig/Live Bait in Current

Current

Cast upstream and quartering across the current. Use just a heavy enough jig to reach bottom.

Cast this bait to submerged weeds and let the worm sink naturally. As it sinks the worm squirms and wiggles in a manner than no bass can ignore. Any largemouth within sight of this simple rig is doomed to be caught. This is a great technique for introducing kids to bass fishing because the fish will rarely drop the bait. Also, the small hooks used make it

> *This is a great technique for introducing kids to bass fishing because the fish will rarely drop the bait.*

easy to hook fish even without the benefit of a healthy hookset.

Half a nightcrawler threaded onto a leadhead jig is also a great way to target bass. The crawler is threaded onto the hook in exactly the same way as a grub body. Jigs with a barbed collar help to hold the bait in place on the hook. A jig and crawler can be fished in the same places you would throw a grub. This simple presentation is especially deadly when fishing rivers for smallmouth. The swirling eddy currents below dams are especially good places to fish a jig and crawler.

Select a jighead that's just heavy enough to make contact with bottom. Cast quartering upstream, retrieve slowly and use the rod tip to lift the jig slightly off bottom. Each time the jig is lifted, the current will sweep it downstream a foot or two. When the bait has been washed downstream of the boat, reel up and cast again.

LEECHES

A leech could be described as the perfect finesse bait. The undulating and swimming motion of a leech has been the undoing of countless bass and other game fish.

The leeches most commonly used for bait aren't the same species as those seen swimming along the shores of natural lakes. Ribbon leeches are the species most commonly trapped and commercially sold as fish bait.

Leeches, like nightcrawlers, are relatively easy to keep alive and perky. So long as the water

Dr. Steve Holt believes night crawlers can be one of the most effective fishing baits around.

is changed every few days and kept cool, leeches will do fine for weeks.

The best way to hook a leech is through the sucker or the wide end of the animal. The head of a leech is the narrow end. When hooked through the sucker the leech will swim naturally and stay on the hook cast after cast.

An ultra-thin hook is required for leech fishing. If the hook is too heavy it will sink the leech and destroy the delicate swimming action this bait is noted for. A No. 4 Aberdeen-style hook is perfect for leech fishing. Many anglers also favor floating jigheads with thin wire hooks that help keep the bait up off the bottom where bass can easily spot it.

> *Most anglers also favor floating jigheads with thin wire hooks that help keep the bait up off the bottom where bass can easily spot it.*

One of the most productive ways to fish a leech is on a simple split shot rig. Place the shot on the line about 18 inches in front of the hook and use just enough weight to enable the rig to be cast on medium action spinning gear. The best line for this style of fishing is 6- or 8-pound test premium monofilament.

Cast this rig to docks, laydowns, rock piles or any visible cover. To get the best action from a leech it must be fished slowly. If the bait is retrieved too quickly the leech will simply ball up on the hook.

Leeches are at their best in water warmer than 50 degrees. In cold water a leech looses a lot of its desire to swim and wiggle.

Prop jigs like this one can be used to fish minnows, crawlers or leeches effectively.

FROGS

Many farm kids have spent the morning catching frogs and the afternoon catching bass. Both activities are character builders.

Frogs are exceptionally good bait for fishing largemouth bass in heavy cover, but they are delicate and difficult to keep alive. It only takes a few casts to whip the life out of one of these amphibians.

Bull, green or leopard frogs are the most common species used for bait. Many states regulate the capture of frogs, so it's best to check your local regulations before heading out to catch a supply of bait.

Small frogs in the 2-inch range make the best bass bait. The best way to fish a frog is with a single weedless hook in the nose. The Eagle Claw 449WA Weedless Worm Hook in a size No. 4 or 2 is ideal for this style of fishing.

Flippin' is a good way to cast frogs without hurting them. The top places to fish frogs include lily pads, the edges of cattails, rushes or reeds, around heavy pockets of arrowhead and other emergent vegetation. You'll need 20-pound test line to wrestle bass out of the cover.

Keep a tight line on the frog and prevent him from swimming down and tangling the line around the stems of lily pads or other cover. The trick is to keep the frog out in the open where a bass can spot it silhouetted against the surface.

HELGRAMITES

A helgramite is the larval stage of a dragonfly and is about twice the length of a mayfly nymph. To catch these aquatic insects you'll have to wade shallow streams turning over rocks and logs on the bottom. Essential gear includes a small mess seine net and something to help turn over rocks such as a shovel.

Place the seine net downstream of a rock or log and then dislodge the rock from the bottom. The current will carry the helgramites downstream where they are collected in the net.

Be careful when handling these insects. They have sharp pinchers that are capable of painful bites. Handle them by the neck being careful to get a solid hold on them.

The best place to fish helgramites are the same streams from which they are captured. Smallmouth absolutely love these insects and will rarely pass up a chance to slurp one down.

A simple split shot rig with a No. 4 thin-wire Aberdeen hook is all it takes to have a fun and productive fishing experience. Wad-

> *Perhaps it's fitting that the live bait that's the toughest to come by is often the most productive.*

ing is the easiest way to fish small streams with helgramites. Work your way slowly upstream, casting into the current and letting the flow of water naturally sweep the bait downstream. Use a small split shot that's heavy enough to hit the bottom every few feet. If you use too much weight the bait will hang up on the bottom. If too little weight is used the bait will be quickly washed downstream.

CRAYFISH

There's little doubt that the crayfish ranks high on the menu for largemouth, smallmouth and spotted bass. The biggest problem with crayfish is finding a supply of bait. Few tackle shops carry crawdads and those that do normally charge a premium for them. You can catch your own by wading the shoreline of rocky creeks, ponds or lakes, but filling a bait bucket isn't easy.

Perhaps it's fitting that the live bait that's the toughest to come by is often the most productive. If bass have an appetite weakness for anything, crayfish top that list.

The summer and fall months, when bass are most often found in deep water, are prime time for fishing crayfish. Some good places to target include riprap bank protection, along piers and breakwalls, rock sea walls, limestone ledges, gravel flats, hard-bottom shoals, the edges of bluffs and areas of shale rock.

A Carolina rig with about 24 inches of leader and a No. 2 thin-wire hook is one of the best ways to fish with crayfish. Hook the bait through the tail and lob cast into position. Drift or use a slow dragging retrieve. Don't let the crayfish sit too long on the bottom or he'll crawl under a rock and snag the line.

Live bait fishing comes with a responsibility. In some situations bass populations can be seriously damaged if anglers don't take care to release all or part of their catch. This is especially true below dams and other areas where large numbers of fish often concentrate into small areas. Where it is practical, pinch down the barb on hooks to make it easier to unhook fish without hurting them.

There's no sin in keeping a few fish for the table. Try to limit your harvest to those fish that are hooked deep or bleeding. Also, consider limiting your take to that which can be eaten fresh. Filling the freezer with fish simply because they are readily available and easily caught isn't ethical or in the best interest of bass fishing.

Unlike many other species of fish, bass are rarely stocked or planted. In most cases the fish you catch are wild creatures that survive and thrive under sometimes harsh conditions. Growth rates are often slow, especially in northern regions, so ethical anglers will do their best to release most of their bass unharmed.

While using live bait for bass may be controversial in some circles, there is little doubt that going natural is a great way to get your line stretched.

In the next chapter we'll focus on the growing popularity of tournaments and spend some time helping anglers understand how the game of professional fishing is played.

Pro angler Woo Daves kisses this fish goodbye before releasing it. Anglers can catch-and-release bass taken on live bait, as long as they set the hook immediately to prevent the fish from swallowing the bait.

CHAPTER 22

PRO FISHING IS JUST PART OF THE MIX

The popularity of fishing tournaments cannot be denied. From club-sponsored events and regional tournaments, right up to and including the top-level B.A.S.S. Top 150 and Wal-Mart FLW events, interest in tournaments has never been higher. The pay-outs are big. The media attention continues to grow and bass anglers are gaining more and more celebrity.

Just as we've used well-known pro anglers to show you new and effective ways to catch more bass, tackle companies use pro anglers and fishing tournaments to promote their wares. It's part of the business of fishing... but is it for you? You may love to fish and you may be really good at it, but when it comes to turning pro, there's a lot more to big-time bass fishing than just slapping a decal on your boat at throwing a crankbait at few stumps.

A REALITY CHECK

There's one undeniable fact about professional fishing: it is expensive. Big-ticket items like a boat and tow vehicle cost upwards of $50,000. Tacked on top are entry fees, travel, gas, food and insurance expenses not to mention the investment of rods, reels, terminal tackle and accessories.

It's a common misconception that bass pros get all their boats, motors and gear given to them. Not true. In fact, the majority of professional anglers receive far less in sponsor products and cash than they spend in pursuits of tournaments each year.

Fishing bass tournaments is a lot like traveling the rodeo circuit. You move from town to town following a tour of events. Each event requires a cash entry fee. Contestants at these events are competing mostly for their own entry fees. Expenses such as travel, food and required gear are the responsibility of the contestant. When the contest is over, only a handful of contestants earn a check. Except for the top couple of places, the money awarded doesn't even cover the invested expenses.

Tournament fishing and rodeo are forms of gambling pure and simple. Like the state lottery, for everyone who strikes it rich, there are many more who never win a dime. Anglers justify the lousy odds by reasoning that their fishing skills are better than the competition. Angling skill and experience is, no doubt, a factor in increasing an angler's chances of doing well at a tournament. Unfortunately, these competitions are frequently based as much on luck as skill.

Luck is one of those intangible elements of fishing that's ever-present. Is it luck or skill when an angler blunders onto a school of big bass and wins a tournament? Is it luck or skill when an angler makes a cast

Tournament fishing appeals to men and women alike. Interest in tournaments has skyrocketed in recent years.

Tournament bass pros are a lot like rodeo stars. Both groups travel the country from event to event, both groups pay their own entry fees and in most cases the participants spend more than they win!

and catches a 5-pounder, while the angler in the back of the boat catches a 4-pounder? Is it luck or skill when one angler lands a big bass while another loses the fish at the side of the boat?

No one can measure how much luck influences the outcome of tournaments, but anyone who has fished many of these events can attest that luck does indeed play a role.

Being versatile is the best skill a bass angler can have. Rick Clunn is the ultimate example of versatility. The only angler to qualify for all 27 BassMasters Classics, Clunn has also been the Classic champion four times.

Just about every angler competing at the national tournament level has the necessary knowledge and angling skills to win any tournament. It's the element of luck that makes winning these events so elusive and interesting.

The single most important skill a tournament angler can possess is the ability to consistently locate fish regardless of the type of water, time of year or weather conditions. This is as much an intuitive skill as a learned behavior and few anglers become truly proficient at finding the types of bass it takes to win tournaments. Hard work and experience are the only ways to achieve this level.

The next skill a tournament angler must master sounds obvious but few anglers make the cut. A tournament angler must become skillful at all the popular fishing presentations. Versatility is a skill that can't be over emphasized.

Most anglers excel at one or two favorite types of fishing, but few develop exceptional skills at all the major presentations. Even if you become the best worm fisherman on the tour, that won't help you if the bass are biting on crankbaits.

The final skill a tournament angler must develop has to do with the business of bass fishing. To become a successful tournament angler, one must learn how to market himself both to sponsors and the fishing public.

"The most successful tournament pros achieve their status in part because of their on-the-water successes and in part because of their unique personalities and ability to share their knowledge with the public," says Mike Finé, Manager of Press and

Public Relations for Tracker Marine. "At Tracker we view professional anglers as valuable assets to our marketing and public relations goals."

Tracker has three levels of sponsorship they offer to tournament fishermen, says Finé. "The entry level is called State Team and these are anglers who are well known and respected locally," explains Finé. Normally these anglers work through a local dealer who offers them a discount on a boat, accessories and service."

The next level of tournament pros are called National Team. "Our National Team members are anglers who have had significant tournament fishing successes and who work closely with us to promote our products at consumer shows, special promotions and photo shoots," adds Finé. "These anglers are compensated with deeper discounts on boats, delayed payment plans and in some cases modest retainers."

Tracker and Nitro's coveted Pro Team is the top level in tournament sponsorship. "Only the cream of the crop ever achieve Pro Team status," says Finé. "To achieve this level an angler must have significant tournament success and help the company market and promote our products in many other ways. Guys like Kevin VanDam, Rick Clunn and Woo Daves bring major accomplishments to the table. VanDam is a three-time Angler of the Year, Daves is a Classic winner and Clunn is the only man to have qualified for all 27 BassMasters Classics. In addition, these anglers frequently work with the print, television and radio media to further promote bass fishing."

Pro Team members receive more significant retainers and special discounts on boats. In some cases these individuals are compensated for personal appearances.

"Sponsors have to be sharp enough to understand how they can best market their fishing talent," adds Finé. "All too often I see companies who view pro staff members as a liability instead of a marketing coup."

Top pros like Kevin VanDam and Rick Clunn are an inspiration to thousands of anglers who dream of turning pro. Unfortunately, only a tiny percentage of those anglers who fish tournaments ever make enough money to earn a living at the sport.

ATTRACTING SPONSORS

Almost every angler who fishes in tournaments is interested in attracting sponsors. The cost of fishing tournaments is staggering, especially at the regional and national levels. Without financial help from cash and product sponsors, most anglers would not be able to compete for long. Sadly, too many anglers let the pursuit of tournaments destroy their family lives and lead them to financial ruin.

Like I said before, tournament fishing is a form of gambling. Those anglers who don't learn how to balance the desire to fish and compete with other personal and professional priorities will soon face troubles they never dreamed of.

Most anglers have no idea where to begin when it comes to securing sponsorships. It's tempting to think that once you win a tournament or two, sponsor money will start flooding in. This rarely happens. Opening a dialog with potential sponsors is the responsibility of the angler.

Anyone serious about becoming a professional angler would be wise to consider joining the National Professional Anglers Association. A group of tournament anglers and supporting sponsors, the NPAA was formed to identify, recognize, honor and promote professional anglers. Simply reading the bylaws of this organizations and understanding what makes a professional angler is a major step in the right direction. You can contact the NPAA at 605-223-2136.

A resume that summarizes your fishing career in one or two pages is often the best way to open a line of communication with potential sponsors. Be sure to list the tournaments you fish, wins and other major accomplishments such as big fish honors, angler-of-the-year awards, etc. It's also important to show you're willing to earn sponsorship rewards by showing your willingness to work at consumer sport and boat shows, participating in retail promotions, by doing seminars and offering members of the press fresh scoops and insights into bass fishing.

Remember, a sponsor is going to want to know what you can do to help them sell or promote their products. It's that simple. No one gets a major sponsorship simply because they have won a tournament, or dozens of tournaments for that matter. Being a successful angler is important, but equally important is developing the skills it takes to promote and sell the products your sponsor produces.

Simply putting manufacturers' decals on your shirt, boat and truck isn't going to cut it. You may look like a pro, but sponsors won't be fooled or impressed.

In order to attract sponsors, anglers must be willing to share what they know about fishing with members of the public. Here, Gary Klein takes the time to sign an autograph at a national tournament.

These days, walking into a potential sponsor cold turkey and selling yourself into a major sponsorship deal is exceptionally tough. Even modest sponsorships are rarely easy to achieve. The number of aggressive tournament anglers seeking sponsorships is staggering. Many major manufacturers receive dozens of resumés from hopeful tournament anglers every day. In order to compete in this environment, you must be willing to work harder than the next guy.

While this outlook may appear bleak, it's accurate and realistic. Only a tiny frac-tion of the anglers who want to become pro-fessional anglers ever achieve enough success to earn a full-time living in the fish-ing industry.

Many anglers take a more realistic approach to the task of attracting sponsors. These anglers depend primarily on their respective careers to provide the funds nec-essary to fish and treat tournaments as a serious hobby or recreational pursuit. Many go so far as volunteering their time to help out at shows, promotions and other events as a means of getting their foot in the door. Once they have proved themselves as useful sales and marketing tools, the next step towards achieving that all-important com-pensation is addressed.

HOW SPONSORSHIPS ARE AWARDED

Most manufacturers will only pay cash to their highest level of pro staffers. These funds are normally paid out as monthly retainer checks, but some companies prefer to pay pro staffers in one lump sum to sim-plify accounting. Contracts are normally awarded year to year, but some longer agree-ments are negotiated.

Many companies, however, are willing to provide compensation in the form of dis-counted or free goods. Anglers can also earn some limited sponsorship funds by inquiring about promotional budgets established to pay for modest expenses such as appear-ance fees, meals, lodging and travel expenses. Usually only the large manufac-turers have these promotional funds avail-able to them. Smaller manufacturers simply can't afford this luxury.

Major sales and marketing firms that handle the distribution of products for a number of manufacturers sometimes set aside money to pay tournament anglers for helping at trade and consumer shows. Nor-mally to tap into this cash the pro must first be approved by the manufacturer.

On the flip side, many sponsorship con-tracts require the angler to provide a num-ber of "work days" as part of his sponsorship

Tournament anglers who land promotional contracts with sponsors are normally required to provide a certain number of "free work days" as part of their contract. These work days are often used to conduct seminars, take members of the press fishing or conduct other special promotions.

and must do so for no additional compensation. The sponsor can use these "work days" to secure help at shows, in-store promotions and special events.

In the last few years the funds available in the fishing industry to support professional anglers have taken a nose dive. Take a look around at the fishing industry. Even some of the biggest manufacturers are being bought and sold like trading cards. This doesn't portray a very healthy financial environment for these companies or the fishing industry in general.

When business is slow and profits are meek, the first budgets to get cut are promotions and advertising. This is a reality of business. The very fact that the fishing tackle and marine industries have been stagnant for some time, has forced professional anglers to seek funding outside the industry.

Non-industry sponsorships are the most lucrative, but also the hardest to secure. Most of these dollars go to high-profile anglers, especially those that command a lot of press or who have their own television programs.

When a non-industry company or manufacturer looks at a sponsorship proposal, they want to know how many potential customers are going to be influenced by the association. Non-industry sponsorships are like advertising. You buy an ad in a magazine and the magazine is distributed to 100,000 households. The cost of this promotional ad is rated by how many dollars were spent to reach a determined number of customers. It's called cost per thousand. To achieve a large non-industry sponsorship contract you have to have a lot to offer in return. Smaller deals, however, can be achieved. Bottling companies are a good example of a local non-industry sponsorship. These local businesses often have access to national marketing funds that can be used to sponsor local events and promotions.

When your local town sponsors a festival in cooperation with a major beverage company, the money for this relationship comes from funds set aside in national advertising campaigns. It's the local bottling company however that does the legwork and recommends sponsorships. These are the people to make contact with for local sponsorships.

The process of becoming a professional angler is an uphill battle all the way. Very few anglers ever earn enough at fishing to make a living. To become a successful professional angler you need a rare combination of angling skills, personality, salesmanship and the burning desire to share what you know about fishing with others.

In our final chapter, we'll look at the future of bass fishing. The sport we enjoy so much has grown at an alarming rate during the past two decades. One has to ask, what's next for bass fishing?

Non-industry sponsors are the toughest to land. Most of these contracts go to anglers who have been established for long periods of time, and those who have a high profile, such as TV personality and tournament pro Roland Martin.

CHAPTER 23

THE FUTURE
OF BASS FISHING

To understand where bass fishing is going, it helps to know where the sport has been. The bass fishing opportunities available in the United States are currently at an all-time high.

Bass fishing has enjoyed phenomenal growth during the past three decades. But this American success story didn't just happen. A number of factors must be credited for enabling the sport of bass fishing to prosper and mature the way it has.

The success of bass fishing can be traced to the development of Tennessee Valley Authority impoundment projects across the South. The U.S. Army Corps of Engineers was also responsible for building a number of major reservoirs in the western and southwestern parts of the nation. These projects created millions of acres of prime bass habitat where none existed before. Throughout the eastern, southern and southwestern parts of the country huge res-ervoirs make up the vast majority of the bass water available to anglers.

The motivation for building these water control structures wasn't to improve recreational opportunities. The TVA projects began during the depression as a means of creating badly needed jobs. Since that time, most reservoirs have been established in the name of flood control and also to create water reserves to attract industry and for agricultural purposes.

Despite the fact that these bodies of water weren't formed with bass fishing in mind, the recreational benefits that have developed as a byproduct are immeasurable.

The adaptable nature of these fish also enabled largemouth, smallmouth and spotted bass to expand their historic ranges. Today, these primary bass species are more widely distributed and available to anglers than at any time in history.

In 1967 another major milestone occurred in bass fishing. Ray Scott started professional fishing on a roller coaster ride that would eventually grow into the world's largest association of anglers. The BassMasters tournament trail and later the *BassMasters* magazine and television program brought the world of bass fishing into millions of homes.

The unprecedented success of BassMasters spawned a wealth of other vertical format magazines and television pro-

> ***Ray Scott started professional fishing on a roller coaster ride that would eventually grow into the world's largest association of anglers.***

gramming targeted at bass fishing. Other tournament circuits, both regional and national, also began to grow in popularity. It wasn't long before the professional anglers who competed in these events started to become household names. The sport of bass fishing was never going to be the same.

A firestorm of new and better products for bass fishing began to hit the marketplace. Many of these products came about as a direct result of the involvement tourna-

To know where bass fishing is going, it helps to know how it began. Tennessee Valley Authority dam projects created countless reservoirs that currently support some of the finest bass fishing in the nation.

Bill Dance was one of the original heroes of the B.A.S.S. circuit. Dance won eight of the first 20 pro events. He later went on to star in his own television program, Bill Dance Outdoors.

ment anglers have with the sportfishing industry.

Since then, bass fishing has continued to grow and prosper, but many wonder if the roller coaster Ray Scott started can keep up the pace in the future.

It's safe to say that the future of bass fishing is stable, but future growth is not something many manufacturers are willing to bet on. The stable and prosperous economy we've enjoyed for the past decade has been instrumental in encouraging the popularity and growth of bass fishing. There's nothing like having a few bucks in your pocket to make a person think about ways to spend it.

While the immediate future appears to be stable, the long-term health of the fishing industry is in question. At this point the only practical way to increase the number of anglers who participate in sportfishing is to increase the number of youth who are exposed to fishing. The major manufacturers of the bass fishing industry have recognized this fact for some time.

A number of sportfishing manufacturers, conservation groups and the American Sportfishing Association are working together to solve this problem. Unfortunately, the solution will require a lot more than committees, business meetings and even industry-wide support.

The biggest threat to sportfishing is the dysfunctional family lives many children lead. Millions of children grow up in single-parent households where they are unlikely to be exposed to fishing. Remember the demographics quoted earlier; 73 percent of anglers are male and 80 percent of bass anglers are male. Kids who grow up without a father in the house are far less likely to discover the pleasures of fishing than those kids who have a dad at home.

What's worse, research indicates that children who aren't exposed to fishing by age 12 are unlikely to develop an interest in the sport, even once they reach the magic age of 24 to 54 that marketing agents drool over.

The future of bass fishing boils down to getting kids involved in the sport. Outdoor television programs such as Babe Winkelman's Good Fishing *are a strong tool for getting kids interested in fishing. The* Good Fishing *TV series frequently features young people enjoying fishing.*

The window of opportunity we have to expose and ultimately hook kids on fishing is narrow indeed.

The burden of passing on the privilege of sportfishing falls to those who enjoy and participate in the sport. Anyone who fishes and feels that fishing is a wholesome and beneficial recreational activity has a responsibility to share the gift with others. Together, the millions of anglers in America are ultimately the ones who can insure the continued growth and prosperity of sportfishing.

You can't wiggle out of this responsibility by writing a check to your favorite fisheries and wildlife foundation or even by paying

If we are all to avoid signs like this, we must be good stewards of the environment and do our part to introduce others to the excitement of fishing. TV game show host Chuck Woolery is a Tennessee native and avid bass angler who took time out here for a few laughs while fishing a tournament in Nashville.

more for fishing licenses and excise taxes on products. The problem isn't lack of money. The problem is lack of participation.

If you have children, do your part to involve them in fishing at an early age. Take them fishing often and keep the fishing trips simple and fun. Leave the bass boat and your expensive gear at home in the beginning. With young kids it's best to target abundant and easily caught species such as crappie, bluegill or perch. Even rough fish such as carp, bullheads and drum will light the fire of enthusiasm in a young angler. These species can often be targeted from shore and caught using very simple and inexpensive fishing equipment. It doesn't matter how big the fish are or what you catch, just so long as something pulls on the other end of the line.

If you don't have kids, pick a relative, friend or neighbor kid and share the gift. Finding a kid who's interested in trying fishing shouldn't be a problem. I've yet to meet a kid who didn't enjoy the thrill of fighting a fish.

A number of individuals do more than their part to pass on the message of sportfishing. Two fishing celebrities featured in this book, Babe Winkelman and Bill Dance, are legends in the fishing community. Each of these men use their respective programs as a means of promoting sportfishing as a whole, not simply as a business. The programming format may be different, but the message is the same. Fishing is one of the purest forms of fun and entertainment on Earth.

Kids and family members are frequent parts of both programs. This helps to spread the message that the love of sportfishing is something best passed on from loved one to loved one. We can't sit back and wait for someone else to do the job. It's up to us as anglers to insure the future of bass fishing.

The wealth fishing brings to the soul supersedes race, age, income levels, religious beliefs and social classes. Fishing for any species is pure, unadulterated fun. Bass fishing just happens to be a little more fun! Pass it on.

RESOURCE GUIDE

BOAT/OUTBOARD/MARINE MANUFACTURERS

Brunswick Marine Power
W6250 W. Pioneer Road
Fond du Lac, WI 54936
414-929-5039

Outboard Marine Corporation
200 Seahorse Drive
Waukegan, IL 60085
847-689-7625

Ranger Boats
P.O. Box 179
Flippin, AR 72634
501-453-2222
www.rangerboats.com

Suzuki Motor Corporation
3251 E. Imperial Highway
Brea, CA 92821
714-996-7040

Triton Boat Company
15 Blue Grass Drive
Ashland City, TN 37015
615-792-6767
www.tritonboats.com

Yamaha Marine Group
1270 Chastain Road
Kennesaw, GA 30144
800-248-9687
www.yamahamotor.com

Honda Marine
4900 Marconie Drive
Alpharetta, GA 30005
678-3392600
www.honda-marine.com

Bass Hunter Boats
1617 James Rodgers Drive
Valdosta, GA 31603
1-800-345-4689
www.basshunter.com

Trojan Marine Batteries
12380 Clark Street
Santa Fe Springs, CA 90670
1-800-367-7670
www.trojan-battery.com

Lund Boat Company
P.O. Box 248
New York Mills, MN 56567
218-385-2235
www.lundboats.com

Tracker Marine (Tracker/Nitro)
2500 E. Kearney
Springfield, MO 65803
1-417-873-5962
www.trackermarine.com

Marine Group (Pro Craft, Astro, Fisher boats)
2500 E. Kearney Street
Springfield, MO 65803
888-776-5520
www.procraftboats.com
www.astroboats.com
www.fisherboats.com

Champion Boats
P.O. Box 763
Mountain Home, AR 72653
501-425-8188
www.championboats.com

TACKLE MANUFACTURERS

The Producers
326 West Kalamazoo Ave., Suite 105
Kalamazoo, MI 49007
616-345-8172

Sampo, Inc.
P.O. Box 328
Barneveld, NY 13304
315-896-2606

Slider Co.
511 East Gaines Street
P.O. Box 130
Lawrenceburg, TN 38464
800-762-4701
www.sliderfishing.com

Snag Proof Manufacturing
11387 Deerfield Road
Cincinnati, OH 45242
800-762-4773
www.snagproof.com

Top Brass Tackle
P.O. Box 209
Starkville, MS 39760
601-323-1559
www.topbrasstackle.com

Lindy Little Joe, Inc.
P.O. Box C
1110 Wright Street
Brainerd, MN 56401
218-829-1714
www.lindylittlejoe.com

Precision Angling Specialists, LLC
P.O. Box 317
Tustin, MI 49688
1-800-353-6958
www.precisionangling.com

Ed Cummings Inc. (fishing nets)
2305 Branch Road
Flint, MI 48506
810-736-0130

Fishing Hot Spots Inc. (fishing maps)
2389 Airpark Road
Rhinelander, WI 54501
1-800-500-6277
www.fishingmaps.com

Frabill, Inc.
P.O. Box 49
Jackson, WI 53037
1-800-558-1005
www.frabill.com

Gamakatsu USA, Inc.
P.O. Box 1797
Tacoma, WA 98401
253-922-8373
www.gamakatsu.com

Gemini Sports Marketing
100 Northwest 3rd Street
Grand Rapids, MN 55744
888-604-6644

Hart Tackle Company, Inc.
P.O. Box 898
Stratford, OK 74872
1-800-543-0774
www.harttackle.com

K-C Tackle Manufacturing
P.O. Box 210
Hollsopple, PA 15935
814-479-4323

KL Industries, Inc.
1790 Sun Dolphin Drive
Muskegon, MI 49444
616-733-2725

Kulis, Inc.
725 Broadway Ave.
Bedford, OH 44146
440-232-8352

Bill Lewis Lures
P.O. Box 7959
Alexandria, LA 71306
800-633-4861
www.rat-l-trap.com

Hildebrandt Corporation
P.O. Box 50
Logansport, IN 46947
219-722-4455
www.hildebrandt.net

Hopkins Fishing Lures, Inc.
1130 Boyssevain Avenue
Norfork, VA 23507
757-622-0977

Attwood Corporation
1016 North Monroe Street
Lowell, MI 49331
616-897-9241

Costa Delmar
123 North Orchard Street
Ormand Beach, FL 32174
1-800-447-3700
www.costadelmar.com

Bear Claw Tackle Company
4904 Arrow Park Drive
Bellaire, MI 49615
231-533-8604

Billy Baits Inc.
P.O. Box 501402
Marathon, FL 33050
305-289-1211

Blakemore Lure Company
P.O. Box 1149
Branson, MO 65615
417-334-5340
www.blakemore-lure.com

Zipper Worm Company
1540 Countryshire
Lake Havasu City, AZ 86403
520-855-6928

Lucky Strike
2287 whittington Drive, RR #3
Peterborough, Ontario K9J 6X4
705-743-3849
www.luckystrikebaitworks.com

Mister Twister, Inc.
PO Drawer 996
Minden, LA 71058
318-377-8818

Axial Technologies, Inc.
4972 North Highway 169
New Hope,MN 55428
612-535-6339
www.axialtech.com

Worden's Lures
P.O. Box 310
Granger, WA 98932
509-854-1311
www.wakimabait.com

Normark Corporation
10395 Yellow Circle Drive
Minnetonka, MN 55343
612-933-7060
www.rapala.com

O. Mustad & Sons
P.O. Box 838
Auburn, NY 13021
800-453-4540
www.mustad.net

Owner American Corp.
3199-B Airport Loop Drive
Costa Mesa, CA 92626
714-668-9011

Yo-Zuri, Inc.
GBS Distribution
513 NW Enterprise Drive
Port St. Lucie, FL 34986
1-888-336-9775
www.yo-zuri.com

Reef Runner Fishing Lures
Box 939
Port Clinton, OH 43452
419-798-9125

K&E Tackle
2530 Barber Road
Hastings, MI 49058
616-945-4496
www.stopperlures.com

Luhr Jensen & Sons Inc.
P.O. Box 297
Hood River, OR 97031
541-386-3811
www.luhr-jensen.com

Stearns, Inc.
1100 Stearns Drive
Sauk Rapids, MN 56379
800-328-3208
www.stearnsnet.com

Strike King Lure Company
174 Highway 72 West
Collierville, TN 38017
901-853-1455

Thunder Bullets
17515 Territorial Road
Osseo, MN 55369
612-420-4191
www.thunderbullets.com

Tite-Lok
P.O. Box 219
Topeka, IN 46751
219-593-2277
www.titelok.com

Tru-Turn Daiichi Hooks
100 Red Eagle Road
Wetumpka, AL 36092
800-77-HOOKS
www.tru-turnhooks.com

Water Gremlin Company
1610 Whitaker Avenue
White Bear Lake,MN 55110
800-328-1440
www.watergremlin.com

Witchcraft Tape Products, Inc.
P.O. Box 937
Coloma, MI 49038
800-521-0731
www.wtp-inc.com

Creme Lure
5401 Kent Dr.
Tyler, TX 75707
903-561-0522

Eagle Claw Hooks
Wright & McGill Company
4245 East 46th Avenue
Denver,CO 80216
1-800-628-0128

Yamamoto Kogaku Company
25-8 Chodo-3
Higashiosaka City, Osaka 577-0056
Japan
816-6783-1104
www.biz.nifty.ne.jp/yamamoto.com

Yum
P.O. Box 60368
Lafayette, LA 70506
318-984-1986
www.fishyum.com

Bagley Bait Company
5719-1 Corporation Circle
Fort Myers, FL 33905
941-693-7070

Apex Tackle Corp.
P.O. Box 988
South Sioux City, NE 68776
402-494-3009

Bass Assassin Lures Inc.
Route 2 Box 20
Mayo, FL 32066
904-294-1049
www.bassassassin.com

Bay De Noc Lure Company (Jigging Spoons)
P.O. Box 71
Gladstone, MI 49837
906-428-1133
www.baydenoclure.com

Nils Master Lures
17240 Kalkkinen/Finland
+358-3-7674 153

Airguide, Inc. (Marine Compasses)
706 Holly Road
Mankato, MN 56001
1-800-227-6433

Uncle Josh
P.O. Box 130
Fort Atkinson, WI 53538
920-563-2491
www.unclejosh.com

Mann's Bait Company
1111 State Docks Road
Eufaula, AL 36027
800-841-8435

Bullet Weights, Inc.
P.O. Box 187
Alda, NE 68810
308-382-7436
www.bulletwts.com

Northland Fishing Tackle
3209 Mill Street NE
Bemidji, MN 56601
218-751-6723
www.northlandtackle.com

Bait Rigs Tackle Company
P.O. Box 44153
Madison, WI 53744
1-800-236-RIG1

Pradco, Inc. (Rebel, Smithwick, Excalibur, Bomber, Fred Arbogast, Riverside brands)
P.O. Box 1587
Fort Smith, AR 72902
501-782-8971
www.lurenet.com

Pure Fishing (Berkley, Fenwick Abu Garcia, Red Wolf brands)
1900 18th Street
Spirit Lake, IA 51360
877-502-6482
www.purefishing.com

VMC, Inc.
1901 Oakcrest Avenue
Saint Paul, MN 55113
612-636-9649
www.vmchooks.com

FISHING ROD/REEL MANUFACTURERS

Shakespeare Fishing Tackle
3801 Westmore Drive
Columbia, SC 29223
803-754-7000
www.shakespeare-fishing.com

Marado Inc.
19247 80th Ave. S
Kent, WA 98032
253-395-3355
www.marado.com

All Star Rods
9817 Whithorn
Houston, TX 77095
281-855-9603

G. Loomis
1359 Down River Drive
Woodland, WA 98674
800-662-8818

Lamiglas, Inc.
P.O. Box 1000
Woodland, WA 98674
800-325-9436
www.lamiglas.com

St. Croix Fishing Rods
856 4th Avenue
Park Falls, WI 54552
1-800-826-7042
www.stcroixrods.com

Daiwa Corporation
P.O. Box 6031
Artesia, CA 90702
www.daiwa.com

Okuma Fishing Reels
Ultra-Com International Tackle Corporation
580 W. Lambert Road
Suite F
Brea, CA 92821
1-800-GO-OKUMA
www.okumafishing.com

South Bend Sporting Goods
1950 Stanley Street
Northbrook, IL 60065
847-715-1400
www.south-bend.com

Cape Fear Rod Company
1-888-886-2064
www.capefearrodcompany.com

Penn Fishing Tackle Manufacturer
3028 West Hunting Park Avenue
Philadelphia, PA 19132
215-229-9415
www.pennreels.com

Zebco
6101 East Apache
Tulsa, OK 74115
918-836-5581
www.zebco.com

ELECTRIC MOTOR MANUFACTURERS

MotorGuide, Inc.
6101 E. Apache
Tulsa, OK 74115
610-323-9402

Minn Kota, Inc.
1326 Willow Road
Sturtevant, WI 53177
www.minnkotamotors.com

TACKLE STORAGE SYSTEMS

Plano Molding Company
431 East South Street
Plano, IL 60545
800-874-6905
www.planomolding.com

Woodstream
1093 Sherwin Road
Winnipeg, Manitoba R3H 1A4
800-665-0258

Tackle Logic
500 Duvick Street
Sandwich, IL 60548
630-552-9737
www.tacklelogic.com

Flambeau, Inc.
P.O. Box 97
Middlefield, OH 44062
1-800-457-5252
www.flambeau.com

FISHING ELECTRONICS

Lowrance Electronics
12000 E. Skelly Dr.
Tulsa, OK 74014
800-324-1356
www.lowrance.com

Magellan Corp.
960 Overland Court
San Dimas, CA 91773
800-669-4477
magellangps.com

Cobra Electronics (Lowrance/Eagle)
6500 West Cortland Street
Chicago, IL 60707
773-889-8870
www.cobraelec.com

Aqua-View (Nature Vision Incorporated)
1701 College Road
Baxter, MN 56425
218-825-0733

Eagle/Lowrance Electronics
P.O. Box 669
Catoosa, OK 74105
1-800-569-4509

Techsonic Industries, Inc.
#1 Humminbird Ln
Eufaula, AL 36027
334-687-6613
www.humminbird.com

FISHING LINES

Berkley (see Pure Fishing under rods/reels)

P-Line
P.O. Box 140
Brisbane, CA 94005
800-537-2394

Ande, Inc.
5409 Australian Ave.
West Palm Beach, FL 33407
561-842-2474
www.andemonofilament.com

Seaguar Fluorocarbon
GBS Enterprises
513 NW Enterprise Drive
Port St. Lucie, FL 34986
888-336-9775

Mason Tackle Company
P.O. Box 56
Otisville, MI 48463
810-631-4571

Maxima America
3211 South Shannon Street
Santa Ana, CA 92704
714-850-5966
www.maxima-lines.com

Stren Fishing Lines
870 Remington Drive
Madison, NC 27025
336-548-8700
www.stren.com

JWA Fishing and Marine
1326 Willow Road
Sturtevant, WI 53177
1-800-884-2JWA

TOURNAMENT ORGANIZATIONS & MAGAZINES

B.A.S.S, Inc.
5845 Carmichael Road
Montgomery, AL 36117
334-272-9530

BASSIN , Inc.
5300 City Plex Tower
2448 East 81st Street
Tulsa, OK 74137
918-491-6100
www.natcom-publications.com

Operation Bass
88 Moors Road
Gilbertsville, KY 42044
502-362-4304

MAIL ORDER COMPANIES

Bass Pro Shops
2500 E. Kearney
Springfield, MO 65898
417-873-5618
www.basspro.com

Cabela's, Inc.
One Cabela Drive
Sidney, NE 69160
308-254-6691
www.cabelas.com

GLOSSARY OF TERMS

Aluminum: The material used to make the majority of the value-priced boats on the market today. Aluminum boats provide great value and can serve the average angler well in many applications.

Aluminum Oxide: The material most often used to line the insides of rod guides.

Aluminum Props: Propellers made from aluminum are not as strong as stainless steel, but they do offer good value, especially in areas where the chance of hitting underwater obstructions in high. Aluminum props will give way before damage is done to the lower unit of the motor.

Backlash: A term used to describe the line tangle that occurs when a baitcasting reel spool continues to rotate once the lure has splashed down and stopped moving.

Baitcasting Reel: A level-wind style reel usually equipped with a centrifugal braking device to reduce the problem of backlashing.

Blade Bait: A type of lure fashioned from metal that is most often used to fish in deep water or heavy current.

Braided Lines: A class of fishing lines that use Spectra fibers braided to form a thin but very strong fishing line.

Bunk Board: A measuring stick used to insure caught fish are above the minimum size limit.

Butt Seat: A backless seat that is most often mounted on a tall seat pedestal in the bow of a fishing boat.

Buzzbait: A spinnerbait-like lure that's designed to be fished on the surface. The blade gurgles along the surface creating a reactionary strike from bass.

Carolina Quick Rig: A manufactured Carolina rig that allows the angler to simply tie the main line on one end and the leader on the other.

Casting Deck: An elevated deck on the front or back of a boat that provides an angler with a convenient fishing platform.

Chime: The point on a fishing boat hull where the sides meet the running surface.

Chugbait: A topwater type plug that features a concave face that pops, spits and gurgles water as the bait is moved.

Circle Hook: A hook style where the hook point wraps around towards the hook shank. These hooks are most often used for live bait presentations.

Clevis: A small metal or plastic device that accepts a spinner blade and allows the blade to spin around a metal shaft or monofilament line.

Colorado Blade: A spinner blade shape that's nearly round.

Continuous Anti-Reverse: A feature on a fishing reel that insures no slop or play is found in the reel handle. When the handle is turned the gears are instantly engaged and the spool turns.

Co-Polymer Lines: Fishing lines made from a special nylon material that provides a better compromise of properties such as low stretch, strength, good knot strength and thin diameter.

Crankbait: The collective term for hard-bodied fishing lures often called plugs. Crankbaits normally are equipped with at least two treble hooks and are made from either plastic or wood.

Cranking Battery: The battery used to start the main outboard motor.

Culling: (Also known as high-grading.)The process of replacing smaller fish in the livewell with larger fish as they are caught. Tournament anglers frequently use culling to achieve the largest possible stringer of fish. In some areas it is not legal for anglers return fish to the water once they have been placed in the livewell.

Deep-Cycle Battery: The battery(s) used to operate electric trolling motors.

Digital Scale: A type of weight measuring device that prints out the weight of fish on a digital screen.

Dual Frequency Transducer: A sonar unit that can provide information from two different frequency transducers.

Electric Motor: A boat control tool normally mounted on the bow of the bow and used to position the boat for various fishing presentations. Also called an electric trolling motor.

Flasher: A type of sonar equipment often used as a navigation aid when running a bass boat at high speed. A flasher can also be used to locate bottom structure and fish.

Flippin': A technique of underhand casting a jig or other lure so the bait is positioned precisely and with very little splash upon hitting the water.

Fluorocarbon Lines: A special type of fishing line that matches the reflex index of water closely, making the line invisible in water.

Four-Stroke Motor: An outboard motor that burns straight gasoline, as opposed to two-stroke motors that burn a mixture of gasoline and oil.

Fused Fishing Lines: Fishing lines that are made by fusing fibers together to form an ultra thin, supple and tough fishing line.

Gore-Tex: A type of waterproof and breathable material that is used to line foul weather gear.

GPS: An electronic navigation aid. GPS stands for Global Positioning System which uses satellites to guide navigation on land and water.

Grayline: A feature of a sonar unit that indicates the hardness of the bottom. A thin grayline is an indication of a soft or muddy bottom while a wide grayline is an indication of a sand, gravel or rock bottom.

Hot Foot: A floor-mounted throttle control that is worked with the foot similar to the gas pedal of an automobile.

Hydraulic Steering: A steering system that eliminates torque in the steering wheel when traveling at high speed.

Icon: A term used to describe a temporary marker on the screen of a GPS unit. Icons are often used to show the location of fish that have been caught or to designate navigation hazards, etc.

Indiana Blade: A spinner blade shape that's oblong.

In-Line Spinner: A spinner built on a straight shaft of wire that features a spinner blade, treble hook and weighted body.

Insert Weights: Small weights designed to be inserted into a soft plastic lure to make the bait sink faster or make them easier to cast greater distances.

Interline Rods: Rods that the line threads through the rod blank instead of using traditional rod guides.

Jerkbait: A minnow shaped crankbait that sfished using a sharp jerking motion of the rod tip.

Jig Spinner: A jighead with a small clip-on style spinner blade attached.

Jigging Spoon: A heavy plated spoon used for fishing in deep water situations.

Keel: The center line of the fishing boat that runs along the running surface from the transom to the nose of the boat.

Laydown: A log or other object that is positioned partly in the water and partly out of the water.

LCR Graph: A type of sonar with a liquid crystal Readout screen. LCR type sonar units are the most common type used by bass anglers.

Lipless Crankbait: A style of fishing plug that features a thin body without a diving lip. Normally these baits are weighted and fished using a count down method.

Livewell Timers: Many livewells are equipped with a timing device that turns the livewell on and off automatically to insure the fish always have a fresh supply of oxygenated water.

Monofilament: A nylon based fishing line that features a controlled amount of stretch and acceptable levels of strength, diameter and abrasion resistance.

Offset Hook: A hook style often used when fishing soft plastic lures so the hook can be aligned with the bait to produce a lure that is straight in the water.

Padded Hull Boats: High performance bass boats are most often designed with a padded style hull that gives the boat more bow lift and speed when under power.

Pistol Grip: A term given to baitcasting rods with a short curved grip.

Pixel: A small dot or matrix on the screen of a LCR style fishing sonar. The more pixels per inch the screen has the more detailed the viewing screen will become. The best sonar units feature 200-300 vertical pixels while entry level machines normally feature 100-160 vertical pixels.

Pork: A term used to describe a jig trailer made from a piece of pork rind.

Power Pedestals: Hydraulic seat posts that adjust at the touch of a lever for height adjustment.

Setback or Jack Plate: An after market item often added to a bass boat that's designed to mount between the transom of the boat and the outboard. A jack plate gives the motor more trim travel and increases the overall performance of the boat at all speed levels.

Skirted Grub: A soft plastic lure that incorporates a traditional grub body with a soft plastic skirt for more action. These baits are most often used on a jighead and fished on bottom to imitate crayfish.

Soft Plastic: A term often given to a wide variety of soft plastic lures such as worms, grubs, spinnerbait trailers, etc.

Soft Tackle Storage: A type of tackle box that incorporates a soft bag that s used to house a number of small plastic boxes for better tackle organization.

Spinnerbait: A wire bass fishing lure that features a spinner blade positioned above a weighted hook that s normally dressed in a rubber skirt.

Spinning Reel: An open faced style fishing reel most often used for finesse tactics such as casting light lures and light line.

Split Screen: A feature on a LCR fishing sonar that enables the angler to view two different screens of information at the same time.

Stainless Prop: A propeller made from stainless steel. Steel props flex less under power and provide a better bite and performance than aluminum props.

Star Drag: A drag adjustment system most often used on baitcasting style reels.

Strake: A molded in rib or feature of the hull of a bass boat that insures the boat will turn in a controlled manner.

Stretch-Forming: A manufacturing process for aluminum boats that bends sheets of the metal into curves previously impossible to form with traditional metal fabricating methods.

Swing-Away Tongue: A detachable trailer tongue feature that allows the trailer and boat to be stored in a smaller space.

Tennessee Grip: A term given to a spinning rod handle that doesn't feature a mechanical reel seat. Instead the reel is taped into position on the handle.

Titanium: A strong and very light alloy often used to make spinnerbait frames or used on fishing reels to reduce weight and strategic wear spots such as line guides and bails.

Trailer: A term given to describe a wide variety of soft plastic and pork products that are used on jigs and spinnerbaits to add color, action and to slow down the sinking speed of these lures.

Transducer: A device that emits sound into the water at a controlled speed so that a sonar unit can measure water depth and mark the location of fish, weeds, cover and other important targets.

Transom Saver: A bracket used to support the weight of the outboard motor against the trailer while traveling. This device helps to reduce strain on the boat's transom.

Triggerstick: A term given to baitcasting rods with straight grip style handles.

Trim Switch: A switch normally mounted on the throttle handle of the outboard that controls the trim level of the motor. When the motor is trimmed in, the boat enjoys the best holeshot. As the boat planes out, trimming up the motor increases top end speed.

Tube Bait: A type of soft plastic lure that's tube shaped and designed to accept a special type of leadhead jig.

Two Bank Charger: A battery charging system that charges a bank of two batteries at the same time, often used to charge deep-cycle batteries.

Waypoint: A term used to describe a specific location saved on a Global Positioning System unit.

Weedless Jig: A leadhead with some sort of weed guard molded into the lure to help the lure fish among heavy cover without snagging.

Wide Gap Hook: A hook style that increases the distance from the hook point and eye tie, making the hook ideal for use with soft plastic lures.

Willow Blade: A spinner blade shape that's similar to a willow leaf.

Zoom Feature: A feature of many sonar units that allows the angler to zoom in and achieve a more detailed picture of the underwater environment.

INDEX

Rock piles 36, 172
Rock River 31
Rocks 47
Rod locker 74
RPM 81
Rubber skirt 56

S

Saginaw Bay 27-28
Salt 87, 125
Salty Fat Albert 58
San Antonio River 18
Savannah River 18
Scent 84
Scent-impregnated 125
Scents 87
Scott, Ray 215
SeaArk 78
Sensitivity 35, 45, 64
Setback plates 81
Sexual maturity 24
Shad baits 52
Shad 87, 101, 110, 182
Shadows 86
Shallow draft 72
Shallow water 20, 101, 114, 140, 147-148, 152
Shiner minow 84
Shipping channel 28
Shoals 172
Shoreline 133
Sight fishing 119
Sight 84
Silt 21
Silver Buddy 173
Sinker 160
Sinking 126
Skeeter 72
Skip casting 186
Skirt types 57
Slack line 142, 171
Slip bobbers 198
Slop 36, 39, 55, 146
Sloping contours 65
Slo-Poke GrubMaster 56
Slug-O 59
Smallmouth bass 18
Smell 86

Smelt 27
Smithwick 55
Snagged 107
Snag-proof 55
Snakes 24
Snap 107
Snyder, Jeff 168
Soft plastic baits 39, 55, 58, 87
Soft plastic jerkbaits 120
Soft plastic lures 195
Sonar 62
Sound energy 62
Sound waves 62
Sound 84
South Carolina 30
South Dakota 19, 29
South Fox Islands 28
Spawining 134
Spawn 22, 29
Spawning 190
Special knots 45
Spectra 45
Spinnerbaits 186
Spinning combinations 33, 37, 57, 86, 94
Spinning line 44
Spinning reels 36
Spinning rods 32
Split ring 183
Split shot rigging 166
Split-shot 36
Sponsors 210
Spoons 47, 168
Spot fishing 123
Spottail shiners 27
Spotted bass 18, 186
Sprague, Jim 132, 186
St. Clair River 29, 158
St. Mary River 29
Stacey's Choice 141
Stained water 86, 96
Stainless steel props 80
Standard features 76
Stanley flat eye 56
Stanley Jigs 141
Stimuli 89
Stock Dams 32
Stockton Lake 30
Storm Lures 53, 181
Straits of Mackinaw 28

Stretch 42
Strike King 54
Strike zone 116
Structures 20
Stumps 124
Sturgeon Bay 28
Submerged brush 56
Submerged timber 20
Submerged weeds 133, 147
Subspecies 21
Sunfish 18, 53, 100
Sunken Islands 102, 141
Sunken logs 36
Super Glue 155
Suppression system 65
Surface fishing 176-177
Suspended fish 161, 165
Suspending 117
Suwanne bass 18
Swamp Frog 55
Swimming 137, 153

T

Table Rock 30
Tackle box 50, 60
Tackle Logic 60
Tackle Storage 60
Tandem blades 99
Target fishing 101
Taxonomists 21
Technology 74
Television commercials 51
Television programming 16
Tennessee 30
Tennessee River 18
Tennessee Valley Authority 30, 215
Texas rigged 120
Texas 30, 36, 39, 122, 128, 148, 132
Thin wire hooks 141
Thunder Bay 28
Timber Tiger 54, 109
Timber 20, 133
Titanium 58, 100, 159
Toledo Bend 140
Toledo 27
Top Brass 57
Top-end speed 81